Organization and

the Human Services

at Case Western Reserve, is currently on leave and serving as Senior Advisor to the Executive Director, United Nations Children's Fund. He is the author, editor, or co-editor of *The Crisis in Welfare in Cleveland*, *Planning for Children in Developing Countries*, and *Social Perspectives on Behavior*.

Organization and the Human Services

Cross-Disciplinary Reflections

Edited by Herman D. Stein

Temple University Press   Philadelphia

Temple University Press, Philadelphia 19122

© 1981 by Temple University. All rights reserved

Published 1981

Printed in the United States of America

Library of Congress Cataloging in Publication Data
Main entry under title:

Organization and the human services.

    Papers from a conference which was held at the Center
for Advanced Studies in the Behavioral Sciences at
Stanford, Calif., March 1979.
    Includes bibliographies and index.
    1. Social service—Addresses, essays, lectures.
I. Stein, Herman David.
HV37.0′73   361   80-29303
ISBN 0-87722-209-6

Contents

3 61
S4 819

114289

Foreword

In March of 1979, a two-day conference was held at the Center for Advanced Studies in the Behavioral Sciences at Stanford, California, to share some of the recent developments in organizational theory and research that may affect organizations in the human services, and to examine what new ideas and departures might bear further research. The conference focused on major scenarios for such organizations, and on what social science research might pursue in order to anticipate future needs. It drew upon concepts in research economics, business, law, psychology, sociology, and social work to develop perspectives for examining current and future trends. Papers were prepared by a number of the participants and distributed in advance. Introduced briefly by the writers and commented on by two participants, the papers led to discussions stemming from, but not confined to, the subjects of the papers.

The writers were not requested to cover specific subjects laid out in advance. Rather, they were to provide cross-disciplinary reflections that could deepen understanding, identify conflicts and confusions, and possibly shake up conventional models of thinking about social service organizations in both the public and the private sectors. It was hoped that they would also shed light on possible answers to "so what?" questions, the rare illumination of implications for policy and practice of research and theory.

There was no way of telling in advance what the outcome of the conference would be. That would depend mainly on the mix of people, most of whom knew personally only two or three of those present. The chemistry apparently worked, for the debate was sharp, providing an intellectually significant experience for all present. Ideas introduced from the various fields of inquiry were examined critically from as many different perspectives.

There was no attempt to come to agreement about any issue, let alone to arrive at recommendations. Rather, the meeting was an open-ended exploration. One conclusion, however, was quite firm. The participants felt that the papers should become a book.

The meeting was funded by the Lois and Samuel Silberman Fund, which has contributed greatly to raising the level of management of the social services. I am grateful to the Fund as well for support during this year at the Center. As always, Mr. Silberman was a constant source of encouragement and helpful counsel.

To the Center itself goes my lasting gratitude for the rare privilege of a second year in its unique ambiance, so hospitable to the needs and the vagaries of its exceptional yearly flock of Fellows, and for providing the setting for the meeting that resulted in this book.

A number of people helped make the conference and the book possible, and I am happy to acknowledge their help. Gretta Rathjen, my administrative assistant to prepare for the meeting and its aftermath, was responsible for making all the arrangements that go into such an enterprise. Her performance was superb in helping to create an orderly, snag-free, and relaxed operation.

Krista Page was most helpful in restoring coherence to sections of the discussion transcript.

Cleo Berkun, as a research assistant on a companion project, worked with me in combing through ten years of publications in social welfare dealing with organizational theory and administrative practice.

Teresa Westbrook, my gifted secretary at Case Western Reserve University, picked up the threads once I returned from the Center, and has patiently, diligently, and expertly managed all the secretarial work necessary, arranging her time generously to fit the uncertainties of mine.

To Jacqueline Slater, who happens to be in the field of banking, goes my gratitude for allowing me to tap her sharp and versatile intellect while working on the organization and themes of the Introduction.

My deep thanks and appreciation go to the conference participants. It would be hard to imagine a more congenial, intellectually spirited, cooperative group. The introduction only occasionally refers to points raised in discussion. It cannot possibly do justice to the content and quality of the actual exchange.

Herman D. Stein

Organization and

the Human Services

Introduction

Herman D. Stein
with Jacqueline Slater

In a 1978 essay on organization theory, Dwight Waldo used the fable of the blind men examining an elephant to portray how various disciplines have perceived organizations during the last fifteen years. He found no standard definition of organization theory, and noted that the modern period has been particularly plagued by diversity, competition, and changing fashions. Since the mid-sixties, the most prominent sources of what passes for theory have been schools of business or management, which focus on "management science," and graduate departments of sociology, which are concerned with bureaucratic theory, organizational structure, and the relationship between organization and society. Well behind these sources in popularity were the schools of social psychology, economics, and political science.

A decade ago, our conference on organizations and organization theory—held at the Center for Advanced Studies in Behavorial Sciences in Stanford in March 1979—would likely have been preoccupied with a human relations approach, and with analyses of bureaucratic functions, processes, and variations, particularly in considering nonprofit organizations in the human services. By contrast, the themes covered in these essays are the impact of differing control systems, the relationship between level of technology and degree of public acceptance, the response of organizational systems to different societal requirements, the preconditions for organizational survival, and the influence of chronic misperception in organization-environment relationships. The control theme dominates the organizational literature on the human services. When a "management science" approach is called for, control mechanisms are implicit; in order to defend good service,

3

practitioners are called upon to attack the threat of over-zealous control.

Defining Human Service Organizations

The essay by Stein and the initial discussion at the conference revealed that *human service organization* (HSO) was a loose umbrella term with a variety of connotations. The term, as used, generally signified those not-for-profit organizations in the public and private sectors that fall under the rubrics of health, education, and welfare, roughly equivalent to the British term *social services*. Employed in this loose way, the term HSO has merit. But when it is forced into the elegant status of an analytic construct, signifying organizations with common features of structure, dynamics, environment or management behavior, and requirements, it becomes confusing and misleading. If it suggests unified theory and practice, sophisticated clarity and order, it is deceptive.

A number of chapters in this volume illustrate the gross contrasts that exist not only between organizations in different service sectors, but between organizations within the same fields. These include differences in environment, in latent and manifest goals, in structure, and in management methods and controls. There is no unified theory to encompass all of these variations, and a taxonomy does not yet exist. We are still at the threshold of disaggregating the variety of organizations in the human services.

Austin approaches this problem by suggesting, along with Stein, several variables for classifying organizations, including size, auspice, governmental level, care specialization, degree of professionalization, degree of bureaucratization, and character of inter-organizational relationship. Taking off from Herzlinger's four models of government administration of HSO, Myra Strober at the conference suggested* dividing the human services along such industry variables as degree of capital intensity, financial viability, and competitive position.

*When individuals at the conference are cited, the present tense is used when the reference is to their papers, and the past tense when to the conference discussion.

The development of a typology of organizations in the non-profit sector, categorized by structural, functional, behavioral, and legal variables, is a major emphasis of the Program of Non-Profit Organizations at the Institution for Social and Policy Studies at Yale University. John Simon explained that the program stemmed from a need to understand the nonprofit sector better during a period of increased delegation of tasks by government to nonprofit organizations, and increased responsibility for tracking "where the money goes." Research in progress there centers on the function, accountability, and financial survival of nonprofit organizations, which include not only those in the human services, but mutual aid groups, veterans' organizations, and others.

Control Systems: Process and Structure

Although Herzlinger and Young both identify the lack of efficient control systems as their major concern in human service organizations, each offers a different solution. Herzlinger asserts that improvement in the control *process* is unlikely due to the absence of organizational competition for survival. She argues that improvement in the control system must come from changing the organizational *structure*.

Stein granted that better transfer pricing mechanisms may make organizations more accountable or more businesslike, but asked, "What are the consequences to the people who are supposed to be getting the service?" Young responded that the delivery of hospital services, for example, can be improved through a reimbursement scheme that eliminates incentives to do things that are not in the patient's best interest, such as extending the length of stay. At the very least, the financial control system could be structured to neutralize those incentives, although Herzlinger has doubts about the practical implementation of such schemes.

Herzlinger asserts that, although the size of governmental human service programs has increased enormously, the three critical tasks required to execute income transfer programs—marketing, production, and control—have remained the same. Since the tasks are stable in nature, requiring specialized and standardized procedures, she advocates "incremental reorganizations" to approach an organizational structure where units are responsible for executing these critical functions.

In connection with Herzlinger's emphasis on accountability and control as the most urgent administrative needs, Stein observed that accountability is more than fiscal and bears on the values undergirding an agency's work. The reluctance on the part of many staff in the social services to support control measures is based on the apprehension that the responsibility for directing such efforts would be put in the wrong hands, that is, hands overly preoccupied with cost-efficiency measures at the expense of other values.

Herzlinger also finds a pressing need for integration among the numerous agencies involved in the current income transfer system. In short, she maintains that human service organizations need a more standardized, functional structure. Salancik believes that this may be possible in health and education, but not for the welfare services in the near future.

The Technological Core: Standard Operating Procedures, Structures, and Myths

Salancik argues that the degree to which the "technological core" is developed influences organizational structures within the human services. Hospital services organize many of their activities around "standard operating procedures," while school services are regulated by "standard operating structures." But the technological base of social services related to welfare and social problem treatment is diffuse. The latter organizations, Salancik suggests, coalesce around "standard operating myths." Stable forms of social service organization probably cannot develop until their technological core develops. Thus, "organizational forms lacking a verifiable technological core must survive for sufficient length of time and in sufficient numbers to be able to develop the technology they currently lack." As such technology emerges, Salancik argues, the organizational forms from which it developed will be discarded.

He then examines how social service agencies might be structured and operated to promote and survive the development of the technological base. The organizational form that Salancik proposes for welfare services is founded on the creation and maintenance of self-serving and self-motivating myths. He advocates political responsiveness (greater than that of schools or medical organizations) to the prevailing myths of those organizations that provide or control resources. Salancik also suggests frequent changing of treatment and program labels to avoid association with programs under criticism, and to cultivate the latest funding interests. Although this approach was initially criticized during the discussion for conveying cynicism and condescension to social welfare programs, Salancik used "myth" not pejoratively, but supportively, for myth (which he defines as an unverifiable belief) is a necessary phenomenon at this state, particularly with programs aimed at social action.

Scott observed, at this juncture, that whether or not a myth is verifiable is less important than whether it is widely believed. Stein noted that many social welfare agencies are not sustained by sheer faith. Their concern is to meet the public demand. Despite the absence of compelling evidence of effectiveness, there is a pragmatic sense that "it works."

One further issue Salancik pursues is that of retention, a concept that Weick develops, for it is the recording and transmitting of innovations that form the technological base.

In discussion, Weick asked if Salancik arranges myths, structures, and procedures in any historical or evolutionary sequence, so that one could assert that medical institutions are complex and social welfare agencies are rudimentary because of their relative ages. But Salancik is more interested in the historical problem of how organizations can survive long enough to develop the knowledge that they currently lack. He concludes that it is thanks to myths that sell in the social and political world that organizations exist, get funding, and motivate individuals to work in the social service field.

Young also found such myths essential. Those who do the "hard, dirty business of working in social welfare" must believe that they are doing the right thing, for otherwise "none of this would get done." It is better to retain the myth, in his view, than to rely too much on cost-efficiency data.

The Institutional Model

Meyer, Scott, and Deal are also interested in how HSOs develop their technological base and whether or not they survive and stay healthy as organizations. The authors sketch two theoretical models of organizations. One emphasizes organizational structures built around the coordination of technical production processes, while the other is an institutional model that defines certain roles and programs as rational and legitimate. The latter has come into being largely because the state has defined a production function and created organizations to fulfill it. Such organizations must conform to prescribed ways of doing things, for example, organizing a school around standard grades and pupil classifications, in order to obtain legitimacy and funding. The intent of the first model is to "decouple technical work from environmental conditions so that it can be more tightly managed," while the intent of the second model is to decouple technical work from the organizational structure to enable maximum conformity to the institutional environment.

In both models, buffers are necessary to the decoupling of technical work. Under the first model, the organizational structure buffers institutions from external forces and thus "seals off their technical cores" so that they can be more tightly managed, as in factory production. Under the second model, organizations are structured to conform to their institutional environments, rather than their technical activities, so that the latter may be diverse and loosely managed.

Meyer, Scott, and Deal suggest that the institutional model is best applied to organizations in the human services, because such organizations lack a technological core and must conform to elaborate institutional structures within society for survival.

(Salancik, too, notes that the lack of a technological base characterizes HSOs, especially in the welfare services and least so in the health services.) They state that "in many respects conformity to wider institutional rules is incompatible with detailed control over technical work activity," for such controls would raise questions about the effectiveness of the programs and make explicit problems of implementation. This conceptual framework argues that Young's sophisticated transfer pricing mechanisms would not improve the efficiency of human service organizations, because such organizations, to survive, must be tightly coupled with external institutional frameworks and decoupled from specific internal activity. Meyer, Scott, and Deal concur with Weick that "loose coupling, which permits the simultaneous operation of inconsistent programs, permits schools to be responsive to contradictory environmental pressures." This responsiveness, Salancik argues, must be preserved at all costs.

Enacted Environments

Weick focuses on the relationship between theories of natural selection and properties of organizations in order to identify four major phases of organizational evolution: ecological change, enactment, selection, and retention. Ecological changes are changes or differences in the stream of experience that draw the attention of organizational members. These ecological changes provide the "enactable environment," or raw materials, used in the organization's evolution. Enactment occurs when managers isolate and constrain changes for closer attention and interpretation. This moves managers into the selection phase, when schemes of interpretation are selected and those "cause maps" that prove helpful are retained, while others are eliminated. The retention phase, which completes the cycle, occurs when interpretation schemes that have been accepted as "successful sense-making" products are retained for possible imposition on future situations.

Weick calls these retained products "enacted environments," and he emphasizes that meaningful environments are outputs of, not inputs to, organizing. He presumes that administrators know much less about their environments and organizations than they think they do, and that this "stunted enactment" is the reason why talk, socializing, and consensus building among administrators "often results in pluralistic ignorance of the environment." He concludes that when organizations or people wish to change their environments, they must begin by changing themselves and their actions. "Enactment is to organizing as variation is to natural selection."

The ideas and interpretations of managers exert as much selective force in organizations as do actual events. Enacted environments act as artificial selection mechanisms—surrogates for the natural environment. This portrait of selection, where managers often discard or misread changes that do not agree with their previous expectations, suggests why organizations show inertia and resist change. This is why newcomers, entrepreneurs, outsiders, "hot shots," and the like are crucial sources of innovation (Richards and Freedman, 1978).

Weick asserts that administrative orderliness is overestimated and erroneously credited for organizations' adaptive success; indeed, structural loose coupling within an organization is critical to adaptive success and must be preserved. Weick asks, "Is there too much reliance on past wisdom and too little doubt within the organization?" He points out that one major cause of failure in organizations is an absence of variability or different images of the organization's goals and processes. Meyer cited a study made by Alan Keith-Lucas a generation ago of public welfare in North Carolina. Public welfare caseworkers, after almost no testing, defined community attitudes as primitive. They thereupon found themselves stabilizing a very restrictive administration, rather than performing on the basis of their own client-centered values.

Scott suggested that Weick's approach seemed to favor behaviorial prescriptions for questioning and discrediting existing systems and operating procedures, rather than building better ones. Meyer also noted the value Weick implicitly gave to disorder, and argued for the need to maintain coherence, if only to highlight variability. Weick conceded that he may have come down too heavily on the need for variation and mutations.

Young, arguing from the history of successfully innovating industries, maintained that they did not change their environments so much as obtain a better fit with them, and that this process is consistent with an evolutionary model. Weick, at a later point, noted that one of the functions of R and D within industry is to raise doubts, note errors, and propose changes. Scott put Weick's contribution in perspective as an approach to a social psychology of individual organizations, helping to explain variations among organizations of the same type through the way they enact and see different environments. This is in contrast to the traditional ecological question of explaining differences between different types of organizations, such as welfare agencies compared to hospitals, or hospitals compared to banks.

Social Science and Decision-making

In her paper, Weiss argues that by offering new frames of reference, information can effect organizational evolution. It can provoke critical thinking about the organization and may stimulate internal reexamination, which is often the best route to organizational renewal. She concludes that, although information has little direct impact on decision-making, it makes a significant contribution through "a diffuse accretion of understanding on issues of policy importance."

She advances a number of reasons why research has little direct impact. First, the nonrational nature of decision-making in bureaucracies (businesses as well as HSOs) must be taken into account. Second, the view of organizations as bundles of standardized routines—the "constrained repertoire" image—may be overdrawn, but it is true enough to explain partially organizations' limited ability to utilize information. Thirdly, few organizational decisions depend mainly on information, and research rarely answers vital factual questions unambiguously and authoritatively. Moreover, organizations are not simply concerned with the logically "best" solution to a problem, but must balance it with such other considerations as survival, credibility, and convenience. All these factors help explain why we see few direct results from evaluative studies (which tend to reduce uncertainty about what the organization is going to do anyway), policy related research (which can provide signals that the organization is not meeting its goals and other warning mechanisms), and technology assessment.

Nevertheless, research does make a major contribution through "diffuse accretion of understanding." This process is reminiscent of Weick's evolutionary process of enacted environments and Salancik's comments on the transmission of standard operating myths among social service organizations. Weiss agrees with Weick that adaptations made today limit potential future adaptations. Research information offers "a new way of thinking about issues, new models for making sense of organizational activities and outcomes." This may be one way for managers to overcome Weick's "stunted enactment." But the provision of alternative perspectives for understanding and interpreting events (Weick's "enacted environments") is only one of three distinct functions that research information can perform for organizations. Weiss emphasizes that it also provides a warning mechanism and can guide improvements.

Sometimes social science research is also used to legitimize, clarify, and document. Such research provides a framework of ideas that is used by executives as a way to think about issues and raise questions. It therefore "serves as continuing education to keep office holders up to date on issues in their field," and gives them assurance that they are in touch with the relevant intellectual issues. Social science research provides a language of discourse, a vocabulary that has become essential for communication and persuasion, and that thus has pervaded public debate on decisions. However, many social science generalizations that officials "absorb into their stock of knowledge are partial, biased, obsolete, or just plain wrong." No quality control exists for screening the true from the false. The process by which these understandings "percolate through" is also inefficient and can lead to eventual over-simplification and distortion of original findings. Finally, enlightenment does not necessarily lead to appropriate action. But these cautions do not detract from the good that can result from the enlightenment process.

In discussion, Fuchs endorsed Weiss's analysis on the basis of his own experience. The impact of research on policymaking or administrative decisions is seldom direct and immediate, for there seldom exists a definitive experiment that will settle a question. Instead, an accretion of evidence builds over time, leading to a change in the language of the discussion and finally a change in ideas and behavior. Fuchs noted, however, the importance of the market for research ideas, the demand for and timing of research, which help explain research projects' impact, along with the quality of the research.

Scott, drawing on Austin, suggested that evaluation research can be seen as a merit good, in the sense that it is usually done to somebody else, ostensibly for their own good, when in fact there is a social control component.

Public Goods and Merit Goods

Unlike Weick, whose focus is the organization enacting its own environment, Austin centers on the organization as defined and molded by environmental forces. He defines human service organizations as formal organizations under government or philanthropic auspices that produce public services or public goods. Such public goods have a collective or public benefit, in addition to an individual user or consumer benefit. Austin argues that it is not the absence of profit as a goal, but rather the nature and assessment of their ouput that distinguishes HSOs from other organizations.

Austin proposes that an organization's type of public good output determines its relationship to its societal environment. He also finds such type responsible for differences in organizational performances. He argues that the societal function of public goods is defined through the historical development of a nation's political economy. This function may not be reflected accurately in formal statements of organizational these often reflect ambiguous compromises among various political groups. Austin therefore examines products and services, rather than goals, to understand the dynamics that determine organizational performance.

Austin identifies four categories of public goods defined in terms of *consumption characteristics*: (1) Indivisible, collectively consumed public goods, such as national defense. (2) Divisible, universally available public goods, such as public library circulation services. (3) Categorically targeted divisible public goods that are individually consumed by a group of individuals not defined by income level, such as hot lunches for the elderly. (4) Redistributional divisible public goods that are individually consumed by those whose income level is below the general norm of society, such as welfare. Austin then asserts that a more meaningful analysis is possible if these distinctions are combined into functional categories of public goods and services, which include: (1) Protection services. (2) Standard of living enhancement services. (3) Development enhancing services. (4) Redistributional services/basic necessities. (5) Redistributive, remedial, rehabilitative, curative, social care, and deviance treatment services.

Austin pursues the implications of the "merit good aspect" of providing redistributive goods and services through a set of organizations that he designates as social benefit organizations. He defines merit goods as goods that reflect the preferences of the provider as well as those of the consumer, for example, a parent giving a child scientific equipment in the hope that the gift will both please the child and also stimulate career interest and encourage greater academic effort. Therefore, merit goods provide a direct benefit for the user and a control objective for the provider that may or may not be realized. Austin asserts that when the secondary benefits—the performance of desired behavior or the reduction of undesired behavior—accrue to the general public, merit goods become a form of public goods.

In tracing the history of twentieth-century social benefit organizations, Austin isolates the absence of consumer choice in the selection of service professionals, and the shift of control from lay people to professionals, as major characteristics that differentiate these organizations from others. He marks the 1930s as a time when the responsibility for basic necessity redistribution programs shifted from philanthropic to predominantly governmental auspices. By the end of the 1930s, the financial responsibility for a high proportion of all types of social benefit programs shifted from the wealthy elite to a much broader base of middle-income households. However, policy control of these programs remained in the hands of the philanthropic sector's civic elite, who acted as trustees for the public interest until well into the 1950s. The 1960s produced the belief that beneficiaries had both a formal entitlement to benefits and a right to control policies governing the provision of benefits. During the 1970s, the courts reinforced the concept that beneficiaries had a right to treatment services, a right to evaluate the outcome of such services, and a right to demand compliance with quality standards.

Interaction among constituency groups has included (1) a clash of interests between professional service staff and groups representing funding sources, (2) conflict between professionals and managers over program priorities and objectives, and (3) alliances of professionals and user constituencies. Austin identifies a variety of environmental inputs at all levels of the organization. He describes the implementation structure of these organizations as marked by the loose coupling of multiple private and public constituent groups. Like Weick and Meyer, Austin finds this loose coupling essential for responding to contradictory environmental pressures.

Austin concludes that the combination of social control objectives and redistributional objectives has a direct effect on the pattern of operational problems in social benefit organizations. First, there is no way of showing cause and effect relationships between the output of social benefit organizations and the attainment of social control objectives. Therefore, the mere effort to achieve social control objectives is sufficient to justify continuing programs. Second, there is no clearly defined proper mix of social control and direct benefit objectives. This makes it difficult to specify worker activities. In order to resolve this ambiguity, organizational objectives would have to be classified—which is impossible, because they are the subject of continuing contests among various constituencies.

Austin suggests that the political economy surrounding social benefit organizations *causes* the existence of a loosely coupled form of program implementation structures. The politics of maintaining social service programs requires that administrators devote more energy to responding to inputs from the political economy at the institutional level than they devote to maintaining tight control linkages over the activities of service personnel. For example, modest shifts of power in the general environment can result in such sharp swings in organizational policy as the demand for a crash fraud-control campaign. Therefore, because the organization must be resilient and responsive to major changes in demand from its surrounding political economy, it must have only the loosest connections between legal mandates, organizational goals, official objectives statements, and the ongoing operations of the service staff.

Too tight a linkage among any of the above would be dysfunctional. For example, an efficient management information system might indicate that social objectives of funding sources are not being met, although users are finding services useful. Effective information and control systems could provide data that would force implementation of procedures to attain social control objectives, causing strong opposition from user constituencies and external groups. Thus Austin opposes the better control systems advocated by Young and Herzlinger. He agrees with Weick and Meyer that operating equilibrium and survival of social benefit organizations is best maintained "under conditions of loose coupling between policy levels, administrative levels, and staff levels."

Increased centralization versus decentralization has become a major issue as human service organizations have increased in size and scope. Funding and policymaking sources support centralization for maintaining and monitoring consistency of programs with social control objectives. However, this will make the programs' multiple goals and objectives increasingly obvious. It may also result in a "decision logjam" at the top administrative level, which will generate pressures for decentralization. A high degree of centralization will also establish a fixed relationship between social control and redistributive aspects of service on an institutional basis, ignoring a wide variety of local conditions and relative strengths of constituencies at the community level. However, decentralization of policy and administration has shortcomings as well. Particular segments of a program may be captured by local constituencies that either impose severe social control criteria (leading to legal attacks) or move the program too far in the direction of redistributional aims (leading to attacks from funding and legitimating groups).

Austin therefore asserts that the problems of organizational structure in social benefit organizations cannot be comprehended by traditional concepts of organizational theory and do not lend themselves to simple solutions through the application of standard management procedures. He argues that standard management concepts ignore the central issue: the dilemmas and contradictions that stem from the combination of multiple social control and redistributional/individual benefit objectives within a single service program. He suggests that administrative theory should therefore focus on "program management" and contingency planning.

Tensions between redistributional objectives and social control objectives are not easily resolved. If large-scale programs are to be organized around a predominantly redistributional principle, there must be broad ideological support for the principles of social justice and persuasive arguments that there are indirect collective benefits to be had. It is difficult to conceive of this type of social ethic serving as an overriding motivation in a society characterized by diverse ethnic, national, and language groups, and an economy that gives its highest recognition to individual economic achievement.

Since a purely redistributional principle is not likely, a social control justification may also be required to maintain majority support. This means administrators must either enforce the social control objectives set by the larger society, or accept the stresses inherent in a loosely coupled organizational structure. The second solution entails role ambiguity, chronic conflict, and an endless search for a type of reorganization that will be simultaneously committed to consumer interests and social control objectives established by funding and legitimating sources.

Austin closes by suggesting an alternative direction of development—a shift of organizational sponsorship. "Various forms of consumer control, prepaid group practice, or cooperative organizations might provide a framework through which consumer benefits are maximized and merit good, social control purposes are minimized." Prepaid legal services, health maintenance organizations, and cooperative day-care centers may be relevant models. Income redistribution to enable access to such services by all households could take the form of increased levels of income maintenance programs or voucher or in-kind provisions whereby payment of membership costs for low-income households would be subsidized by the government.

Among the themes considered in Austin's comprehensive treatment of the human services were social control and the concept of public good. Herzlinger maintained that many human service activities do not follow the economic definition of public good—indivisibility—for example, lighthouses. Austin maintained that one indivisible social benefit of public goods is social control, and that a public good exists if most people define it as such. Weiss observed that justifying a service on the basis of its social control functions can lead to accepting the ineffectiveness of the service.

Social Control of the Welfare Industry

While Austin considers the social control function of public goods produced by the human services, Zald examines the ways in which social welfare itself is being controlled. In an effort to predict likely future directions of the welfare state, Zald centers on (1) changes in the control and administration of welfare policies, and (2) changes in the structure of policymaking that affect the performance of the welfare state. Before discussing these trends, he offers a conceptual framework for examining systems of social control in both profit and nonprofit industries.

Social control by definition entails expectations of behavior or performance, surveillance (evaluation), and sanction of deviation. "Control agents" (such as professional groups, government agencies, and more recently, courts and client advocacy groups) establish norms of behavior or performance and apply sanctions and incentives to gain compliance. Organizational performance within an industry vis-à-vis established norms can be tracked along a "performance curve." Several control agents may have overlapping jurisdictions, so that competitive or contradictory norms can be enforced simultaneously. This "structural context," or organization of control agents, shapes and limits the range of organizational performance.

Austin stresses the structural context of varying constituency groups for the same reason. Zald refers to them as "control agents" to emphasize their critical role in determining federal policies. In addition to establishing and interpreting operational norms, control agents survey for malperformance and apply sanctions and incentives. Their effectiveness depends upon the strength and authority of the norms. However, Zald also notes that different segments of an industry have varying ideological, organizational, or economic capabilities to comply with or resist imposed control standards. He calls this capacity "compliance readiness."

Zald makes three further refinements. First, he draws no sharp distinction between policymaking and implementation, because "new policy problems emerge from old policy implementation." Second, his emphasis on social control and norms does not assume a societal consensus about norms and the legitimacy of power holders. Third, he states that the idea of a performance curve can refer to compliance with a policy by organizational officials or the actual social impact of a policy.

In applying his theoretical framework, Zald first examines how changes in control agents of control policies have influenced the performance of the welfare state. He isolates the growing "federalization of welfare policy" as one of the clearest trends in the last fifty years. In terms of gross expenditure, public welfare items increased 485 percent in constant dollars between 1950 and 1975. But more importantly, the composition of expenditures has shifted. In 1950, for example, 43 percent of social insurance was provided through federal funds; by 1975 the figure was 80 percent. Dramatic growths and similar shifts in composition would be found in expenditures for education and medical care as well. The organs of society that set norms for welfare policies have shifted from the local and state levels to the federal level.

Through subsidies and the establishment of minimum standards and operating criteria, federalization has reduced variance in monies and quality of services among states. However, it has not had as great an effect in reducing the variance in poverty among states. This is because many federal social welfare programs are not sharply targeted on the poor (whereas previous state programs were), and welfare programs in general may have little impact upon regional and state variations in unemployment and poverty.

Federalization has various administrative forms. Takeover, the transfer of state functions to federal agencies, has abolished state administrative apparatus in many instances. Federal subsidies of specific programs have led to federal guidelines, technical assistance, and programmatic control. General revenue sharing has involved the loosest control mechanism.

Whatever the form, federalization has had a profound effect. The existence of welfare payment policies has given rise to such new agencies as nursing homes and community health centers. Such providers find that the price of government grants or third-party payments is conformity to reporting requirements, access criteria, professional standards, accreditation, licensing, and the like.

Zald points out that "as agencies become more dependent upon public monies or upon third-party payments, they increasingly dance to the tune of the public piper." This may lead to increased emphasis on what Austin refers to as "social control objectives." In addition, the growth of collective fundraising agencies and community health and welfare councils begin to bring organizations under increased external scrutiny. But the alternative is "federal subsidy without federal accountability."

A second major trend is the intervention of courts and legislatures into welfare agency operations through protection of minority rights, due process, and substantive standards. Legal norms prohibiting the use of sex, race, and age as criteria for the allocation of benefits and positions have led to major modifications of institutional functioning. Due process norms have been imposed, leading organizations to develop formal procedures of representation and appeal. Court-imposed substantive changes in the functioning of institutions may require massive changes in operating procedures and in budgets. Substantive change involves both the quality and quantity of personnel and facilities allocated to a function. Through all of these interventions, priorities developed by elected officials of administrative agents may be superceded by court-imposed requirements. As Zald summarizes, "the growth of a politics of rights leads to a decline in the power of local officials, just as did the federalization of welfare policy."

A third major force is the increasing influence of the dispossessed through the growth of advocacy groups, which use the courts, the media, and legislatures to raise the quality and quantity of goods and services allocated to their client populations. Client groups have historically been weak largely because of their dispossessed condition, but a politics of advocacy might keep some programs and institutions under more continuous scrutiny.

These trends suggest a decline in the influence of state and local legislators and an increase in the power of the courts and federal legislators and administrators. Moreover, organizations delivering services are subject to a wider variety of interventions and their procedures are more visible. Nevertheless, there is considerable variation among agencies in both their ideological and capability readiness to comply with the changing norms resulting from these and other forces.

Zald concludes with two scenarios. On the positive side, the service sector may be expected to continue to grow, with a larger percentage of GNP allocated to the population's welfare and dependency needs. Within this scenario, today's concerns with accountability and effectiveness will be seen as transient pennypinching in a long-range process of public beneficence.

But with higher proportions of people over 65 necessitating increased social security and medical care expenses, with reduced economic growth and continuing inflation, welfare's priority may decline further, to be replaced with a demand for financial solvency in our cities and states. Welfare needs of dependent populations may take a back seat to more central issues of maintaining the well-being of the whole population. Even the politics of advocacy depends upon the ability of advocate groups to raise funds.

Zald takes a middle ground between these two scenarios, although he favors the second. He concludes that "the welfare state is here and well established." Its central programs will remain in place and some will continue to grow. The slowdown in economic growth and the rise in inflation will, however, curb ambitious programs. They will also affect the spread of federalization, and if federalization continues unabated, the least expensive solutions will be sought.

Changes in the control, administration, and structure of the welfare state will be set in the larger context of national and international politics and economics. He argues that selective growth will occur, but offers no forecasts as to what will drop away, what will expand, and what new HSOs might adapt to the new environment.

Concluding Reflections

The thinking expressed in these papers, as in the conference in which they were discussed, is not discipline-bound. It is indeed often characterized by skepticism about conventional thinking regarding organizational concepts in the human services. The spurious mystique of "management science" is given little heed, and the term is not once used. Instead, in addition to the substantive themes, there is an undercurrent of attention to unsystematic and non-rational elements, not only in decision making, but in organizational judgments of external forces, and in the public criteria for assessment of organizational performance.

Social scientists concerned with the nature of organization may be encouraged, not so much with their impact on great or small executive decisions, but as Weiss demonstrates, by their influence on the context of decision-making vocabulary and thought in a subtle, complex and continuing process. Somehow, the public debate is similarly penetrated, and this is no small achievement. It is possible that a measured skepticism about conventional management wisdom may also enter the dialogue.

Of the three central administrative functions described by Herzlinger, the control function currently gives health, education and welfare systems the greatest problem. Health organizations and schools suffer conflicting accounting systems and competing external demands, but welfare agencies often have the additional problem of defining just what it is they do, with respect to which effectiveness and efficiency are to be measured. Agencies must be fiscally prudent, and it is clearly important to improve information systems, but not necessarily to demand rigorous control measures, particularly where the essential production function is not routinized.

While fiscal control and cost effectiveness measures are essential, agencies may be hyper-responsive to such pressures, by conjuring up menacing environments of imaginary publics watching ratios to judge performance and decide on support. As Austin and others suggest, decisions on resource allocation, in both the public and private sectors in the human services, are not likely to be based primarily on cost-benefit studies, but on the demand factor and forces not subject to agency control in the larger political and economic environment. Moreover, not everything has to be quantitatively proven, even if it could be, to justify services. The prevailing myths to which Salancik refers are still necessary, whether or not they are potent. They may even be true.

Zald's analysis indicates that with a long-range slowdown in the economies of the US and other industrial nations, and continuing inflation, the share of national revenue to meet the needs of the worst off in the population is not likely to continue to rise. The control pressures may be expected to grow more intense in the human services, especially in welfare, partly to enhance effectiveness, but principally to keep expenditures down. Under such conditions, the wisdom needed for the management of human services truly in the principal interest of those to be served will have to be great indeed.

Chapter 1.

The Concept of Human Service

Organization: A Critique

Herman D. Stein

Each of the words in the expression *human service organization* is so pleasant and straightforward, that together they shine with good will. The term has caught on rapidly since about 1968, and has substantially replaced the more traditional categorical names, such as *social service agency* or *health and welfare organization*. A review of social work journal articles and books from the 1970s reveals that HSO is commonly used without definition, as if it were so readily understandable and obvious that no explanation is necessary. In the serious efforts to define the term, the variations, ambiguities, and contradictions have been considerable.

The interpretations and definitions can be grouped in the following categories: societal function; movement; special attributes; workplace of "human service professional"; governmental designation.

Societal Function

Sarri's interpretation of the societal function of HSO (1971) has been widely used and adapted. She states in a footnote that "the distinguishing features of human service organizations" were elaborated on by Vinter (1963). However, Vinter's incisive analysis of "treatment organizations" does not refer to HSOs at all. Sarri goes far beyond Vinter, referring to HSOs as "community agencies for welfare, education, social control, and the preservation of social values [that] are mandated by society to contribute to the fulfillment of essential societal functions." As illustrations she cites juvenile courts, mental health and correctional agencies, family service and children's agencies, general and special hospitals, and agencies for the physically handicapped, retarded, and aged, "as well as a large number of specific health and welfare organizations." She states further that "the substantive goals of the organization are to process and change people as a means toward social rather than nonsocial ends. Furthermore, the clients who are served are both the major input and output of the organization."

In their book of readings on HSOs, Hasenfeld and English (1974) also make a dubious reference to Vinter as their source:

> A key derivative of the technological problems encountered by human service organizations is their difficulty in developing reliable and valid measures of effectiveness (Vinter, 1963).

Vinter refers to two major types of "people-changing organizations," socialization and treatment agencies. The first type includes schools and youth-serving agencies that prepare individuals for their social roles. The second type seeks to resolve problems of deviants. Since delinquents and criminals, emotionally disturbed persons and the chronically unemployed, are regarded as possessing defective attributes or as improperly motivated and oriented, they therefore are "treated" with means ranging from coercive repression to manipulative persuasion. Vinter's essay is principally a critique of the treatment organization thus defined, where professionals assert the principle of autonomy in the exercise of their skills. He argues that treatment organizations tend to become contexts for professional practice rather than for goal-directed enterprises, and they come to overvalue organizational stability, administrative convenience, and the preservation of order.

Hasenfeld and English define HSO as "the set of organizations, whose primary function is to define or alter the person's behavior, attributes and social status in order to maintain or enhance his well being." Their "input of raw material" consists of human beings, and their "production output" is persons processed or changed in a predetermined manner. Their general mandate is "service," that is, to maintain or improve the general well-being or function of people. As illustrations they cite schools, social and recreation centers, universities, youth-serving agencies, police and similar agencies, hospitals, prisons, and all social service agencies. A similar definition is provided by Brager and Holloway (1978) and other publications. This expanded interpretation blurs Vinter's distinction between socializing and treatment organizations; Vinter at no point refers to hospitals, universities, police departments, and so forth, nor does he use the term HSO.

Drawing on Etzioni, Rosengren and Lefton, Perrow, and Hasenfeld, Hasenfeld and English present two dimensions for human service organizations: how "normal" or "malfunctioning" their clients are, and whether their services are "people-changing" or "people-processing." These two dimensions are combined into one typology of function and domain. A second typology, of "organization-client relations," combined Etzioni's classification of normative, utilitarian, and coercive compliance systems with Rosengren and Lefton's dimension of the nature of the organization's interest in the client.

Hasenfeld and English conclude by noting the difficulties of applying the "new science of management" to such HSOs as hospitals, police departments, and schools. They state that the success of "sophisticated management tools," like operations research and management information systems, has been limited to the more routine and peripheral aspects of the organization. However, "full cognizance and understanding of the unique parameters that shape the service delivery systems of human services organizations may enable the development of a new science of human service management that is applicable to these organizations." The dubious inference is that there is sufficient commonality in "these organizations" including, as earlier specified, schools, law enforcement agencies, hospitals, correctional institutions, as well as all manner of social service agencies, to warrant an applicable "science of human service management."

Other approaches have been taken by those oriented to the status-enhancing, people-processing, or people-changing function of the human services. However, more mundane distinctions for purposes of classification are rare in the social work literature. These would include governmental or private sector funding or auspice, whether the organization is governed by the market, for profit or not for profit, whether custodial or not, whether large or small (although HSOs are frequently assumed to be complex, bureaucratic, and governmental). One result is ambiguity about boundaries. While most definitions include education, health, and social work services, some can lump together a dentist's office, a law firm, a maximum-security prison, a public library, a for-profit marital counseling agency, a state public welfare system, and a barber shop.

Movement

Schulberg, Baker, and Rowen (1973) interpret the human services as a reaction away from the isolated clinic or other agency, toward designing "far-flung human service systems which seek to provide comprehensive and coordinated assistance to clients." The emphasis is on new care-giving systems incorporating the following features: comprehensive services; decentralized facilities located in areas of high population density; and integrated program administration that permits continuity of care from one service element to the next with a minimum of wasted time and duplication. Their underlying premise is that the "increasing tendency to designate a community's variety of health and social welfare services as human service organizations reflects not only the desire to provide services more efficiently but also a growing societal as well as professional recognition of the common denominator inherent in the various problems presented us by clients." Thus, traditional child guidance or adult psychiatric clinics not part of comprehensive systems would fall outside the human services framework. The "involvement and cooperation of the target community" are essential to this premise.

Demone and Harshbarger (1973) state that HSOs are similar to other complex organizations. They share problems of differentiation-integration, resource acquisition, and role strain and role conflict. However, they are supported by public and voluntary resources and do not expect to make a profit (the authors exclude for-profit organizations). At another point, however, Demone and Harshbarger say that "profit making in the human services represents a significant future development" in the health and education industry. "The human services complex is a growth industry of the profit making sector and is moving into this larger arena."

Demone and Schulberg (1975) interpret the concept of human services as a reaction to decades of growth, expansion, and specialization, insufficiently related to comprehensiveness and linkages for client service. "The increasing tendency to designate a community's variety of education, health and social welfare interventions as human services reflects both a discontent with existing practice and a recognition of the common elements underlying the helping actions of diverse professional and nonprofessional care givers."

Bridenbaugh (1975) interprets the movement features of the human services concept as an attack on the traditional helping service (health, welfare, and rehabilitation) for being over-professionalized, over-bureaucratized, and too distant from those they intend to serve. The movement interpretation may be accurate in referring to public and legislative dissatisfaction. But it begs the questions of whether an organization becomes an HSO only when it joins other HSOs in coordination and comprehensiveness or, in the more militant approach, when it engages in social change efforts. In general, the boundary or classification concerns are untouched by this line of interpretation, which has fallen into disuse.

A variant of the movement notion is given by Alexander (1978). He says human services result from pressure by graduates of expanded programs in "psychology, theology, law, sociology, education and social work," and from the creation of such new vocations as urban and health planning and counseling. The graduates of these programs, according to this view, tried to "rationalize" national, state, and local service efforts and to establish new domains in which they were identified as experts. These attempts to move away from the more traditional "social welfare" or "social service" agencies led to the title "human service organizations."

Special Attributes

A recent statement in terms of HSOs' attributes rather than their functions is provided by Sarri and Hasenfeld in their introduction to *The Management of Human Services* (1978). First, they introduce their now familiar theme that "HSO's work on people by processing and/or changing them individually or collectively. The persons directly handled by these organizations are simultaneously their input, raw material and product." This factory analogy, developed also in Hasenfeld and English (1974) and apparently drawn from Hasenfeld's previous work, suggests that in a counseling service, for example, what the professional staff does is not input, nor is any other resource applied for service to the clientele; that in a hospital what the staff does is not input, that research is not a product, but that the hospital "produces" patients. This is awkward and confusing.

Sarri and Hasenfeld have moved from their previous concentration on the social function of HSOs to observations about their characteristics and the ways in which they work. Thus, first "HSO's must adopt ideological systems to justify their activities, yet always face the risk that these ideologies will be contested by various social groups." Second, HSOs are characterized by "a precarious domain consensus . . . . They confront multiple expectations and conflicting demands in a pluralistic society." "Third, human service organizations, particularly in the public sector, acquire very limited autonomy in relation to their task environment . . . . These organizations are highly dependent on resources controlled by other organizations and are often subject to extensive regulation by various legislative and administrative bodies." Fourth, "the lack of determinate and effective technologies" appears. "With few exceptions, particularly in the health field, most human service technologies are based on limited and fragmented knowledge bases while having to deal with complex human behavior . . . . Consequently HSO's develop ideological systems in lieu of technologies which guide and justify the behavior of staff."

Sarri and Hasenfeld then make a plea for an organizational theory that accounts for all of these characteristics. "These four mentioned characteristics indicate that, at the very least, organization and management theories must incorporate them into their explanatory models and prescriptive paradigms in order to be of any relevance to HSO's."

Workplace of "Human Service Professionals"

A number of statements in the literature directly or indirectly suggest that HSOs are places where "human service professionals" work. Who the human service professionals are may be as unclear as what human service organizations are. Thus John Turner (1968) considers "human service professions" broader than social work, mentioning education, health, housing, economics, and the law. Hokenstad (1977) says they include services that promote social and psychological as well as physical and economic, well-being. They include "self-development and self-actualization, hard and soft services, health and social services."

Robert Morris (1974) forthrightly focuses on social workers, stating that "the term human services covers several subsystems of the social welfare system that employs [*sic*] social workers in either a dominant or peripheral position. The subsystems include health and medical care, law and justice, education, income security, and reinforcement of personal growth and family cohesiveness (family services, character building, and the like)." In many states "the human services thus interpreted include as much as 50% of state government employees and account for between 50 and 65% of state government expenditures."

Governmental Designation

Most states have by this time created human service umbrella organizations under such titles as Department of Health and Rehabilitation Services or Department of Human Resources. All of the agencies reporting to the superagency then automatically become identified as human service organizations. In most states these include public welfare, health, mental health, retardation, youth services, aging, child care, medical programs, and vocational rehabilitation. Sometimes corrections agencies are included. Education, however, rarely appears within this comprehensive rubric.

This designation includes not only governmental human service organizations, but also those within the private nonprofit sector. Thus, which organizations are within or without the "human service industry" is administratively defined. Whether grouping these organizations under one state administration provides more comprehensive, less expensive, or easier administration is still under review. The process has, however, been stimulated by the 1977 HEW reorganization, during which the Office of Human Development Services was established, consolidating the former Social and Rehabilitation Services and human development programs.

This is not a conceptual but an administrative approach, for what is and is not an HSO is administratively determined. A program now in may later be out, or vice versa, in a reorganization, but at any one time what is declared a human service organization for these purposes is clear. This is not, however, how social work literature currently prefers to use the term.

Why HSO?

Richan (1969) calls the term social services "a marvel of imprecision." By comparison to human service organization, it is a model of clarity.

But why has the term become so popular with social work? Educators don't call schools HSOs. Doctors and nurses don't call hospitals HSOs. Lawyers don't call their offices HSOs.

Judges don't call courts HSOs. Even wardens don't call prisons HSOs. Yet in the social work literature they are all called HSOs, along with the familiar family agencies, mental health clinics, and child care institutions.

One reason may be the social work perspective, which is sensitive to the commonalities of working with people. An awareness of the interconnections between different fields of service is intrinsic to the very activities of social workers and social agencies. HSO may have these connotations, when no precision is required for usage. Another reason for the expression's popularity is perhaps similar to social work's fondness for the term *helping professions*, which is alien to the older, more prestigious professions. That is, there may be a need to be associated with institutions and professions more solidly rooted, and to find social work located more securely within a broader social context.

Why Not HSO?

There can be no great objection to the use of global generic terms that are loose and comfortable, particularly where understanding of their sense is sufficient for general communication. *Social services* is one of these terms. It defies consensus in the United States, but will not cause more confusion unless used for serious analysis without further definition. *Human services* likewise poses no serious problem, and may be preferable, if what is meant is the range of institutional provisions known in Western Europe as the *social services*. However uncertain its boundaries are in health, education, and welfare, it signifies direct services to people, implicitly not for profit. By suggesting commonly understood, identifiable professions, *human service professions* is riskier. *Human service organizations*, unless referring to organizations providing health, education, and welfare services in the European sense, begins to fade into a haze.

But no serious problem arises until the term is given analytic teeth, whereupon it turns into a voracious shark, swallowing diverse organizations like so many schools of fish. When HSO is treated as a recognizable entity, and used to analyze organizational structure, function, and process, it causes extensive mischief by suggesting that it is part of an authentic taxonomy of organizations. This is an illusion and blocks more discriminating analytic development. The contrast is striking between Vinter's careful consideration of the treatment agency, which is defined clearly, and the way his precise formulation has been inflated and transmuted into the current diffuseness of the HSO.

The typologies of HSOs, such as those presented by Hasenfeld and English, provide useful perspectives for understanding and researching certain aspects of organizations. However, they reflect conceptual and analytic concerns of interest to particular researchers. They neither derive from a general scheme of organizational classification nor attempt to identify the variables necessary to define boundaries within which organizations can be located, either structurally or functionally, for theory development, aggregation, comparative analysis, or simple systematic description. No one system of classification can satisfy all interests, but having one would help advance organizational research and theory, particularly with respect to nonprofit so-called human service organizations.

The Need for an Organization Taxonomy

Blau and Scott (1962) made a major effort at classification, utilizing their cui bono criterion. There they distinguished among mutual benefit associations, business concerns, service organizations, and commonweal organizations. However insightful and forward-looking their analysis at the time, it no longer suffices for classification, for it concentrates on one dimension of societal function.

An interesting and valuable effort was made by Harshbarger (1974) to outline "dimensions for a taxonomy of complex organizations" by incorporating Blau and Scott's approach with that of Etzioni (1961) and Katz and Kahn (1966). Harshbarger's own use of it, to contrast production and service organizations, is insightful and provocative but replete with

34 • *Herman D. Stein*

questionable assumptions. Although he narrows the field by generalizing only for "public sector human service organizations," it is still too heterogeneous a catch-all, and does no better as an analytic concept than "public social agencies." His position on the need to develop a taxonomy of organizations for purposes of theory and research is, however, unexceptionable.

Conclusion

There can be little objection to the employment of the term HSO as connoting a movement, if that is the way anyone still wishes to define it. This sense of the term is at least clear, and requires no precision as to boundaries or internal arrangements of organizations, for these are virtually irrelevant to the ideological message. Nor is its use for administrative or regulatory purposes troublesome. As an omnibus term to specify certain services falling under a state coordinating umbrella of "human resources agency" or "Human Service Development Office," it poses no conceptual dilemma. The very special human definition of human service organization as an agency wherever social workers practice is awkward and possibly unnecessary, but at least it is not misleading.

All of the intepretations of HSO can live side by side, as long as their particular meaning is made clear in specific usage. Moreover, the term can be used generically to blanket organizations commonly grouped in Europe as the social services. However, the use of the term to connote a defined type of organization with specific behavioral, functional, and management characteristics is confusing because it does not reflect reality. In current usage, it usually lumps together service agencies that differ markedly in function, auspice, relationship to marketplace, size and structure, and other critical variables, and therefore does little, when used as an analytic concept, to help in understanding organizational behavior, management, or implications for service delivery. There is a need for a general taxonomy, to which Austin's chapter in this volume contributes, within which the variety of organizations can be appropriately identified so that analysis and research, and understanding of management implications, can progress.

References

Alexander, Chauncey. "Management of Human Service Organizations." *Encyclopedia of Social Work* 17 (1978): 844–49.

Blau, Peter M., and W. R. Scott. *Formal Organization: A Comparative Approach.* Novato, Cal.: Chandler Publishing, 1962.

Brager, George, and Stephen Holloway. *Changing Human Service Organizations: Politics and Practice.* New York: Free Press, 1978.

Bridenbaugh, W. Duane. "A Descriptive Study of the Development, Organization, and Implications of Human Services: An Interdisciplinary Analysis." St. Louis University: Ph.D. diss., 1975.

Demone, Harold W., Jr., and Dwight A. Harshbarger. *The Planning and Administration of Human Services,* vol. 1, pt. 2. Ed. Hubert C. Schulberg, Frank Baker, and Shelton R. Rowen. New York: Behavioral Publications, 1973.

Demone, Harold W., and Herbert C. Schulberg. "Human Services Trends in the Mid-1970's." *Social Casework,* May 1975.

Etzioni, A., ed. *Complex Organization: A Sociological Reader.* New York: Holt, Rinehart, and Winston, 1961.

Harshbarger, Dwight. "The Human Service Organization." In H. W.

Demone, Jr., and Dwight Harshbarger, eds., *A Handbook of Human Service Organizations.* New York: Behavioral Publications, 1974.

Hasenfeld, Yeheskel, and Richard A. English, eds. *Human Service Organizations: A Book of Readings.* Ann Arbor: University of Michigan Press, 1974.

Hokenstad, Merl. "Higher Education and the Human Service Professions: What Role for Social Work?" *Journal of Education for Social Work* 13, no. 2 (spring 1977).

Katz, Daniel, and Robert L. Kahn. *The Social Psychology of Organizations.* New York: Wiley, 1966.

Morris, Robert. "The Place of Social Work in the Human Services." *Social Work,* July 1974.

Richan, Willard. "The Two Kinds of Social Service in Public Welfare." *Public Welfare* 27, no. 4 (Oct. 1969).

Sarri, Rosemary. "Administration in Social Welfare." *Encyclopedia of Social Work* 16 (1971).

———, and Yeheskel Hasenfeld, eds. *The Management of Human Services.* New York: Columbia University Press, 1978.

Schulberg, Hubert C., Frank Baker, and Shelton R. Rowen, eds. *Developments in Human Services,* vol. 1. New York: Behavioral Publications, 1973.

Turner, John B. "On Response to Change: Social Work at the Crossroads." *Social Work*, July 1968.

Vinter, Robert. "The Analysis of Treatment Organizations." *Social Work*, 8, no. 3 (July 1963): 3–15.

Chapter 2.

The Political Economy of

Social Benefit Organizations:

Redistributive Services

and Merit Goods

David M. Austin

Issues

This paper will focus primarily on the operational problems question: How can theory help to explain the existence of certain widespread problematic situations in human service organizations?[1] Many operational problems have been identified; the following list is intended only to suggest some of the issues that appear frequently.

1. There is general uncertainty about the relationship between the outputs of human service organizations and the outcomes experienced by the individuals' households, and communities that are the consumers and beneficiaries of those outputs.

2. There is uncertainty about the relationship between the administrative and management processes in human service organizations and the content and pattern of service worker activity directed to the production of organizational outputs.

3. There is a similar problem about the relationship between official goals and objectives of the organization (as estab-

lished by legislative mandate or by policymaking units), and the operational objectives of the administrative component.

4. One of the most persistent anomalies is the inconsistency between the widespread evidence of public dissatisfaction with large-scale public service organizations, and the stable functioning of certain public service organizations over extended periods of time.

5. One of the more frequently debated issues is that of the meaning and consequences of the "increased professionalization" of service activities.

6. A related issue involves the linkage between professional education, other forms of specialized occupational training, and the quality of work of service-providing personnel.

7. A recurrent structural problem is the simultaneous push toward centralized administrative control with a high degree of rule prescription, and decentralized responsibility, professional qualifications, and a preference for a high level of worker autonomy. Many human service organizations have gone through endless vacillations between these two patterns, suggesting that each has inherent and perhaps unresolvable difficulties.

8. A final issue is the extent of the impact of the organizational environment on the actual performance of service organizations.

Before analyzing specific aspects of these problems, we must clarify the nature of organizations and organizational phenomena.

Definitions

An initial consideration is the definition of *human service organization*. This term will be used to refer to the large group of formal organizations under government and nonprofit philanthropic auspices that produce public services.[2] (All service production and provision activities in society can be broadly classified into four sectors: primary group, including self and family; marketplace; philanthropic; and governmental. In terms of any one type of service there is much potential substitution among these four sectors.) This definition excludes organizations that provide similar types of service, such as psychological counseling, through the marketplace or private proprietary sector, although my analysis may have implications for such organizations.

Organizational theory literature is full of relatively general definitions that distinguish human service organizations from other organizations. Much previous discussion of organizational and administrative theory is based upon the study of business and industrial organizations. From this perspective, human service organizations have often been treated as a minor subcategory defined by some single characteristic that can be used to distinguish it from the larger set of business organizations. For example, the term *nonprofit* is frequently used to characterize all noncommercial organizations, philanthropic and governmental.[3]

Other writers have also tended to characterize human service organizations by using one or two characteristics, implicitly limiting their concept to those human service organizations that fit their limited definition. These definitional criteria are frequently stated in normative terms, so that the concept of human service organizations comes to imply "good," "people-serving" organizations, in contrast to "people-exploiting" business and industrial organizations.[4]

These approaches to definition have serious deficiencies, particularly because they tend to rely on normative distinctions between business and industrial organizations and human service organizations. There is one definitional framework, however, that does provide an initial base for analysis that is not primarily normative. This uses the distinction between private goods and public goods. Human service organizations have in common the fact that they produce *public goods*, or goods that have a mixed public and private character. That is, the organizational outputs are assumed to have a collective or public benefit in addition to any benefits accruing to individual users or consumers. While the profit/nonprofit distinction primarily points to the absence of profit maximization as a goal in human service organizations, the public good criterion makes a positive characterization. Because they produce outputs with a public good element, human service organizations always involve some type of collective or public assessment of performance, in addition to or in place of individual user assessment. It is not the absence of an organizational performance criterion (profit) that marks all human service organizations, but the existence of a different type of output assessment, using different criteria, that has distinctly different organizational consequences.

However, this paper will focus primarily on variations within the general set of human service organizations, rather than on definitional commonalities. There are a number of variables that can be used to assess the pattern of diversity among the total range of human service organizations. These include: size,[5] auspice,[6] core profession, degree of professionalization,[7] degree of bureaucratization,[8] and character of inter-organizational relationships.[9]

However, this paper proposes to focus on a dimension different from any of the above as a basic point of departure for examining the pattern of diversity among human service organizations, and the relation of this diversity to the nature of operational problems, administrative theory, and organizational theory. This dimension involves the differential public good characteristics of the outputs of human service organizations. Variations in the public good characteristics of the organizational outputs constitute the most significant factor in differences in the relationships between organizations and the societal environment, and differences in the pattern of organizational performances. The nature of the public good output of the organization determines the relationship of the outputs to the service consumers and users, the dominant technology and pattern of activities of the service personnel, the basis for the evaluation carried out by the larger society, and the relationship of the evaluative processes to the legitimation and support functions through which the organization is sustained within the larger society.

The societal function of the public good outputs of an organization is an aspect of the political economy within which the organization functions.[10] It is the historical developmental process within the political economy of the national society that defines the societal function of the outputs, a function that may or may not be accurately reflected in formal statements of organizational goals or objectives. Since one constant in the political economy surrounding human service organizations is the existence of conflicts among various interest elements and constituencies, statements of goals and objectives generally reflect ambiguous compromises that serve to obscure rather than clarify and direct the purposes of administration and production. Therefore, the characteristics of the organizational outputs, rather than organizational goals and objectives, must be examined to understand the dynamics that determine organizational performance.

Characteristics of Human Service Public Goods

This section is a limited analysis of differences in the type of public good output that the human service organization produces or creates. A first set of distinctions can be made in terms of the *consumption characteristics* of the public good involved.[11] Public goods produced or created by human service organizations can be characterized under the following headings:

1. *Indivisible public goods, collectively consumed.* The indivisible public good is the most basic form of public good as generally defined by economists. This is a product or benefit that if produced for one individual will be available to all other members of the community. This would result in a high level of spillover or externalization of benefits if a single individual or small group of persons were to pay for the good. Since there is little incentive for individuals to support such an arrangement, the cost of production of an indivisible benefit is usually assessed across the entire community, with community sanctions used, if necessary, to ensure universal participation in the costs. This is the basic political-economic justification for any system of taxation. The most dramatic example of such an indivisible collectively consumed public good is the provision of national defense through military forces. In principle all residents of a nation benefit and all should contribute to the

cost. Enforcement activities to protect air quality through restrictions on air pollution and enforcement activities to protect
water quality in large bodies of water to which the public has
access are other examples of indivisible collectively consumed
public goods. The maintenance of an orderly society through
the enforcement of basic law and order and through the orderly resolution of civil disputes are still other examples. These
involve the legislative process of defining social norms, the
provision of basic police patrol services, and the maintenance
of the civil courts. In the economic arena, the establishment
and protection of a common currency and the enforcement of
laws against fraud and the violation of contracts are another
indivisible public good.

2. *Divisible public goods, universally available.* These are public
goods, available to all members of a society or community, that
are consumed separately or used on an individual basis. Usually when such services are provided under governmental
auspices, production requires some type of large-scale initial
collective investment, frequently on an exclusive or monopoly
basis, although the benefits are individually consumed. Examples of these benefits include public utility services, emergency
medical services, circulation services of the public library, and
the individual use of sports facilities in public parks and playgrounds. In this instance the governmental unit functions
much like a membership cooperative in which the members
have voluntarily decided to levy a charge on themselves to
provide a service that all of them may use individually. Unlike
the collectively consumed public good, which is evaluated
through a unitary political decision, divisible public good is
evaluated by individual users. These individual judgments in
turn are aggregated in such ways as voter referendums into
collective political decisions affecting the future development
of the service organization.

3. *Categorically targeted divisible public goods.* These are public
goods intended for individual consumption by all members of
particular categories, categories that are not defined by user
income. For example, elementary and secondary education is
targeted at a particular age group. Similarly, hot lunch programs under the Older Americans Act are targeted at and

available only to individuals sixty and over. Agricultural extension homemaker education and 4-H clubs are targeted primarily to rural citizens. Categorically targeted services involve a distinction between the characteristics of the funding/policy-determining constituency, for example all voters in a given political unit, and the target service constituency. In the case of elementary and secondary education, the immediate consumers of service are in fact excluded entirely from membership in the policymaking and funding constituency. Thus categorically targeted divisible public goods may be produced in response to the preferences and perspectives of one set of individuals aggregated through an intermediary governmental body that has the delegated authority to make specific decisions, to be used or consumed by a different set of individuals.[12] This constitutes an element of public merit goods, which are considered in more detail later in this paper.

4. *Redistributional divisible public goods.* These are individually consumed public goods provided with the explicit intent that the public good benefit will go only to particular persons or households whose income level is below the general norm of the society. This means the provision of income or the direct provision of service benefits to individuals and households that lack financial resources to obtain such benefits through marketplace purchase. While this is in fact a form of categorical targeting, it has particular social and political consequences. The decision to provide redistributional goods, and decisions determining the characteristics of these goods, are also made by a policy constituency that is different from the user constituency. It is, of course, possible to have a negative redistributional program providing public goods to persons with above average incomes. Such a policy is more likely to be unstated, rather than explicit, however, and to be unacknowledged in official statements of program purpose.

These differences in consumption characteristics of public goods have a variety of consequences for the nature of organizational performance. However, a more meaningful analysis is possible if these distinctions are combined with an analytic framework dealing with functional variations among human service programs. These functional distinctions parallel, to some degree, the distinctions already made dealing with consumption characteristics. The following is a brief and preliminary outline of functional categories and their characteristics. (see Figure 2-1).

PROTECTION SERVICES

The most basic and widespread form of public good/human service provision involves indivisible public goods that are identified in various ways with the concept of "common protection." This includes national defense, protection of air quality, the maintenance of basic law and order, regulation of currency, and other forms of activity intended to protect the economic, social, and physical environment, which affects everyone. Protection services also include those intended to protect individuals against certain risks that have a significant probability of harming someone but that occur on an unpredictable basis or that individuals cannot effectively protect themselves against on a person-by-person basis. These risks include fire, medical emergencies, communicable disease epidemics, natural catastrophes, and increasingly in our society, the risks of violence occurring within families, between spouses, and between parents and children. Organizations that provide protection service outputs have certain common characteristics:

Auspices. The auspices are largely governmental. The problem of "free riders" is so pervasive, for example in trying to support fire protection services on a fee-for-service basis, that the authority of government is needed to ensure that all potential beneficiaries participate in the cost through a tax system. There are limited exceptions, for example when service providers function on a voluntary basis rather than on a salary basis, as in the case of volunteer fire departments and rescue squads and, in earlier times, volunteer militias.

Outputs. The activity outputs from any protection organization are likely to be highly diverse, because they must be fully responsive to the immediate situation to be effective. Documentary or fictional representations of protection activities tend to emphasize the ability of personnel to perform a wide variety of tasks as situational conditions require. For example,

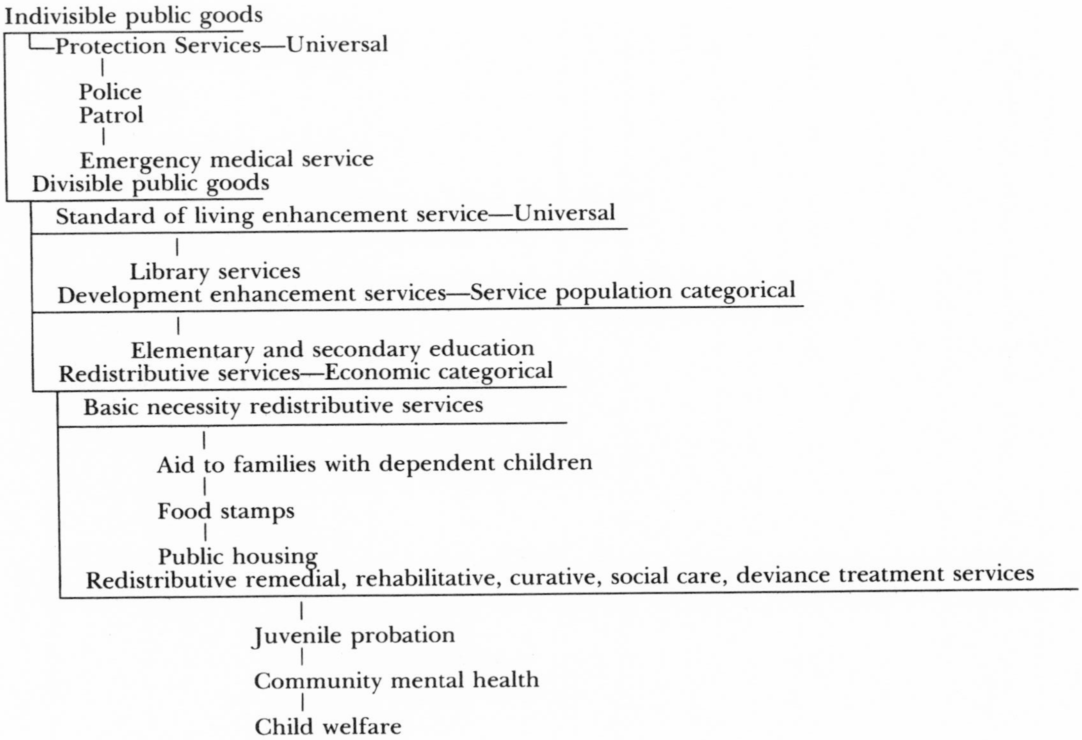

Indivisible public goods
└─Protection Services—Universal
    │─Police
    │─Patrol
    │─Emergency medical service
Divisible public goods
    Standard of living enhancement service—Universal
        │─Library services
        Development enhancement services—Service population categorical
            │─Elementary and secondary education
            Redistributive services—Economic categorical
                │─Basic necessity redistributive services
                    │─Aid to families with dependent children
                    │─Food stamps
                    │─Public housing
                    Redistributive remedial, rehabilitative, curative, social care, deviance treatment services
                        │─Juvenile probation
                        │─Community mental health
                        │─Child welfare

Figure 2-1.
Functional Distinctions among Human Service Programs

various forms of lifesaving activities are often part of the output mix in many different types of protection services.

Relation of outputs to beneficiaries. Many of the protection services involve activities directed at other parties or at the source of risk or hazard, rather than at the ultimate service beneficiary. Thus, national defense activities are directed at the enemy, the maintenance of law and order is directed at potential lawbreakers, epidemic control may involve quarantining sick persons to protect others, protection of air quality may require action against a polluting industry. In child abuse cases most of the actual staff activities involve filing charges against the parents, or providing counseling to them, rather than providing services directly to the child.

Technology. Characteristic of the technology in protection services is maintenance of a high state of response readiness at all times, due to the unpredictable timing and location of risk events. Thus, the existence of a standing army, fully manned fire departments even when there are no fires, police patrols around the clock, an air pollution monitoring process even when there is no air pollution, and emergency call numbers on evenings and weekends for child abuse workers. Also, standardized, rehearsed procedures are emphasized to ensure dependability when services are required. In many instances protection services also require a high degree of internal discipline and an assumption of the readiness of service personnel to risk personal injury.

Evaluation. The basis for evaluation of protection services is the effectiveness of those services at the point at which protection is needed. In some instances, as for example in the case of a national military force, this may occur once in a lifetime. In the instance of emergency medical services, fire services, and police patrol services, assessment deals with performance at time of need, irrespective of other measures that might be used to measure the quality and characteristics of routine, non-emergency activities of the organization. The assessment of performance in emergencies is nearly always open to public observation and in many cases is highly publicized. A similar situation applies to the abuse protection function of child welfare services.

Legitimation. In the instance of protective services, the link between assessment and societal legitimation and support is often not very direct.[13] Many factors can intervene between either positive or negative public assessments and the actual level of funding. For example, armies and police departments may perform a number of other functions, as well as general public protection, that affect patterns of funding. Aggressive child protection programs, or the aggressive development of other protection services, may, under some circumstances, result in a political process leading to less rather than more funding. This is most likely to occur when the objects of protective services (organized crime, polluting factories) have more economic and political power than the beneficiaries of such services.

STANDARD OF LIVING ENHANCEMENT SERVICES

Standard of living enhancement services are divisible, individually consumed, and provided on a universal access basis. They differ from market-produced individual consumable services primarily because of the collective political decisions needed to create the basic capital resources for the provision of such services or benefits, or because of a desire by members of a user constituency to control the quality and distribution of such services through political processes rather than through market processes. Included are such public utility services as sewers, drinking water, and electricity. These services may also be provided through monopoly franchises involving publicly regulated (but privately owned) utilities that have many of the characteristics of governmental providers. Also included are such services as public libraries, exhibits at art museums, and the individual utilization of playgrounds and sports facilities in publicly funded recreational areas. The service organizations have significantly different characteristics from those of protection organizations.

Auspices. Auspices are governmental or philanthropic, depending largely on the extent to which the service is valued broadly by a majority of citizens, or more highly prized by a well-to-do minority, as in the case of many symphonies and museums.[14] Auspices are most likely to be local, and the pattern of auspices will reflect differences in preferences among local communities, the importance attached by local residents to ready access to such services, and local traditions around the assessment of costs for such services against the local property tax base.

Outputs. Service outputs are continuous and regular, rather than episodic or emergency. Outputs from any one type of organization are likely to be highly similar and consistent over time. Output is generally measured by units of consumption or participation.

Relation of outputs to beneficiaries. The service outputs are provided directly to the service consumer. Use of the service requires a positive decision to do so by the consumer, but use is voluntary. Direct payment of part or all of the costs for direct services may be required.

Technology. The technologies in these service organizations are often highly standardized, and the outputs are primarily in a form that can be easily monitored and calculated. The technical skills may be very specialized (playing in an orchestra), or very routine (reading water meters). The organization of the service-providing activities focused primarily on consistency and dependability of services, rather than on the highly intensified emergency services involved under protection. Personal risks for service staff are seldom involved.

Evaluation. Evaluation is made by individual consumers based upon their satisfaction with the regularity, and dependability, and quality of the service. Negative evaluation of services is often fed back in the form of a judgment on organizational administration rather than as judgment on individual workers. Only when users band together to express a negative judgment do the evaluations become a public issue. Then the administrator of a water or sewer system or of a library, rather than individual service personnel, is held responsible for the quality of services. The evaluation framework for these services tends to reflect the general pattern of political activity in the relevant political system. Utilization experience of those individuals or groups most active politically is likely to determine the policies affecting particular service organizations.

Legitimation. Legitimation exists through explicit enabling legislation or ordinance. Because of the consistency and regularity of operations there may be relatively stable relations between the service organization and the political/social environment, with the possibilities of relatively long-range planning, particularly where the development of capital facilities requires a long lead time. Five- to ten-year development plans for public utilities, parks, and playgrounds are frequent. There may be some redistributional efforts within such universal service programs, such as the development of playgrounds in highly congested slum areas even when there is relatively low political participation in such an area. However, the more general pattern is that the best quality services in a community-wide service program are provided in middle- and upper-middle-income areas. These areas include those families who are both politically active and who occupy leadership positions within the administrative and policy units that are responsible for the legitimation of such services.

DEVELOPMENT ENHANCING SERVICES

Development enhancing services categorically targeted divisible services that supplement and support "normal" developmental and socializing patterns. The term people-changing is probably inappropriate for these services, which facilitate development. They include preschool educational services, elementary and secondary education services, colleges and universities, senior citizen centers, special skill training programs, character-building youth programs, physical development services, and so forth.

Auspices. Auspices are both governmental and philanthropic, and primarily local. Philanthropic auspices are particularly likely to be utilized where there is by intent a distinct ideological or religious content to the developmental services, for example, Boy Scouts, CYO, parochial school education, YWCA, and Junior Achievement.

Outputs. Like standard of living enhancing services, these service outputs are characterized by being consistent and regular and involving largely standardized content. Outputs are usually measured in terms of participation units, for example, average daily attendance for elementary and secondary schools or turnstile counts in some youth-serving recreational programs. The specific impact of service outputs is difficult to evaluate. It is difficult to separate the unique contribution made by the developmental service activity from the interests, skills, motivation, and capacities that the service consumer brings to the activity, the positive or negative reinforcement provided within the family or other primary groups, and the impact of the cultural traditions within which the user has grown up.

Relation of outputs to beneficiaries. These services are for the most part targeted to particular age groups and provided directly to the immediate beneficiaries. However, the content and structure of the activity often reflects general societal assumptions about what is needed by and what will be good for this particular group. The service consumers are usually not the only constituency involved in defining the actual content of the service provided. In the instance of early childhood education, the beneficiaries have no part in the definition of the service. However, for the service to be even marginally effective, the developmental or socializing interests of the user must be stimulated, since developmental services require the involvement of the consumer. The outputs of these services are, therefore, coproduced in varying degrees through an interchange process between the service provider and the user.

Technology. In developmental services, the technologies involved are largely person-to-person. The major forces involved in personal development, in fact, emerge from processes within the user rather than from the activities of the service provider.[15] Therefore, the service provider motivates as much as instructs, or, as with socializing services, creates conditions under which normal socializing activities are likely to occur. Role modeling, as much as technology, may be an important function of the service provider. An important part of effective modeling may be the mastery of particular skills or of particular bodies of knowledge.

Evaluation. Evaluating such services involves a mixture of participation rates, assessment of service-user satisfaction, and assessing the satisfaction of funding and legitimating groups that their objectives are being met. The assessment of these services by the larger society often reflects normative expectations for the targeted category as much or more than it reflects explicit evaluation of service outcomes. Thus, as social and political recognition has emerged of the increasing role of senior citizens, there has been a steady expansion of senior citizen centers on the assumption that social participation must be good for their physical and mental health. There is little systematic evaluation, other than through individual testimonials and expressions of political endorsement, of the actual developmental or socializing consequences of such services.

Legitimation. In services targeted to both the young and the elderly that are supported by general community contributions or taxes, the assessment of funders and legitimators, rather than the personal satisfactions of the service consumers, is most often decisive for public endorsement and support. This is particularly so where service participation is not fully voluntary, as with preschool, elementary, and secondary education. But it is also relatively true even where participation is essentially voluntary, as in the case of senior citizen centers.

REDISTRIBUTIONAL SERVICES/BASIC NECESSITIES

Redistributional services are individually consumed services that are also categorically targeted, but in this instance the targeting is based on the economic status of individuals or households. Basic necessity redistributional programs involve essentially three categories of benefits: (1) income, that is, direct cash provision; (2) in-kind benefits, primarily food, housing, and medical services; and (3) access to or direct provision of employment.

Auspices. Administrative auspices for such redistributional services are now largely governmental, and financial auspices have become largely state and federal governments.[16] Historically the auspices were largely local, both governmental and philanthropic. The current pattern reflects the fact that low-income housholds are very unevenly distributed among local communities. As a consequence redistributional basic necessity programs are also redistributional among communities, and in fact among states and regions, taxing wealthy populations wherever they live and providing the greatest pool of benefits to residents in predominantly low-income communities.

Outputs. Outputs in basic necessity redistributional programs consist of discrete dollar units, or units that can in most instances be translated into equivalent dollar amounts, for example the value of housing, the bonus value of food stamps, potential earnings in a CETA public service job, the cost value of medical care. The organizational outputs from the administrative agency responsible for a redistributional basic needs program often consist of authorizations to receive benefits rather than the actual benefits, for example food stamps, a Medicaid eligibility card, an AFDC benefit check, a clinic eligibility card, or an assignment to a public service job.

Relation of outputs to beneficiaries. The outputs of such redistributional programs in nearly all cases are provided directly to consumers who meet the eligibility criteria. (Grocery orders, or two-party checks issued jointly to AFDC recipients and landlords, are instances in which the organizational output goes to the provider rather than the user.) There are two basic policy issues in redistributional programs involving the rules that determine the pattern of outputs for particular consumers. These are the issues of *equity* and *entitlement.* Equity implies the existence of criteria and rules by which the provision to one person or household can be judged to be comparable to the provision to another in similar circumstances (horizontal equity), and is in appropriate proportion to the provision to persons in different circumstances (vertical equity). Entitlement involves the extent to which the recipient is considered to have a morally or legally enforceable right to demand benefits, in comparison to situations in which benefits are partially or wholly discretionary. Entitlement rights are nearly absolute in the instance of social security insurance payments, and are largely nonexistent in the instance of county administered general assistance in states such as Texas, for example. Entitlement rights and equity requirements substantially constrain the degree of discretion allowed to service staff in determining benefits in individual situations. Since the 1930s, when most

current redistributional programs began, both of these constraints have been consistently tightened, step by step.

Technology. The administrative technology involved in determining eligibility and providing direct income is highly standardized. (The provision of highly discretionary "emergency
assistance" financial aid for limited periods of time is more like
a "social service" than "income maintenance" and, therefore, is
more like the services described in the next category.) The
current trend is to move towards substitution of computers for
human workers in many aspects of the work sequence. Administrative structure and procedures are adapted to the routinized aspects of worker activity. Determination of eligibility
for in-kind benefits is also increasingly routinized. Determination of eligibility for CETA jobs may vary more widely. However, in all of these programs there may also be a largely unstruc-
tured, and officially unrecognized, set of ad hoc procedures
that staff use to find additional resources for some households
from other community sources to supplement limited benefits
available under existing rules. Administrative structures may
make little provision for these functions.

Evaluation. The primary basis of evaluation for these programs is a procedural evaluation, that is, an assessment of the
economic characteristics of the user population in relation to
the economic profile of the general population. It is a measure
of the extent to which the "in-need" population is receiving
benefits. This involves comparing actual recipients to official
eligiblity criteria. There is also what may be described as an
adequacy evaluation of outputs. Here there are three sets of
criteria that may be used. The first is a *minimal subsistance*
criterion, which is support at a level expected temporarily to
prevent illness and death, but little more. The second level can
be identified as a *minimal adequacy* criterion. In current usage
this is roughly equivalent to the "poverty line." This level is
expected to meet long-term living costs, but it leaves individuals or households in an economic, and therefore social,
position well below the median of the society. The third level
can be identified as *full participation adequacy*, which is roughly
equivalent to median income. Current debates on the level of
benefits to be provided retired persons under the Social Secur-

ity system reflect the disagreements about which of these standards should be used, and in turn the level of costs to be met through taxation.

Legitimation. The legitimation of basic necessity redistributional programs is complex because the motivation for establishing and maintaining such programs varies among different constituencies within society.[17] For those receiving direct benefits, and among members of some other segments of the society, basic redistribution is a valued objective in and of itself under the general concept of social justice, and as one aspect of the ideal society. For other segments of society, the justification for redistributional programs is instrumental or utilitarian. Some believe that providing benefits will induce individual behavior that will reduce the extent to which that person or household will require future redistributional benefits; or that benefits will prevent such undesirable behaviors as crime and riots. The legitimation of these programs and the provision of funding rest largely in the hands of persons in governmental policy bodies who hold to this latter, "social control" view, so that it is the probability of undesired behavior (riots) or the probability of producing desired behavior that determine the eligibility criteria and the actual level of benefits. This position is also reflected in the consistent refusal of the Supreme Court to accept the concept of entitlement rights as applied to the AFDC program, although insisting on procedural equity under such rules or regulations as are established by the administrative agency.

REDISTRIBUTIVE REMEDIAL, REHABILITATIVE, CURATIVE, SOCIAL CARE, AND DEVIANCE TREATMENT SERVICES

The redistributive remedial services are divisible goods provided to individuals, households, and neighborhoods. Similar services are available to the majority of households in society through the marketplace, using either direct payment or contributory insurance plans. Governmental or philanthropic provision of such services, whether in the form of health care, psychological counseling, foster care, institutional custodial care, or neighborhood community development services, has historically been primarily redistributive in intent. While use of these services is basically voluntary, certain types are mandated for particular individuals, such as juvenile probationers or parolled offenders.

These services and benefits differ from programs dealing with redistributive basic benefits in that the specific form of the benefit provided is under the discretionary control of agency staff persons. The actual pattern of benefits in any individual situation depends upon a diagnostic or assessment process controlled by the staff person who determines the need for a particular type of service on a case-by-case basis. Therefore, these services always require an intermediary, generally designated as a "professional" or a "program specialist," who is accountable for assessment and service prescription. Even when the service user presents a self-assessment in the request for services, the program specialist is responsible for confirming or modifying the self-assessment. This professional intermediary, depending upon the type of service or benefit, may or may not be the actual provider of the services. When one individual both makes the diagnostic assessment and provides the actual service, as is true in most counseling services, there is a high level of control by the professional over the user. This is particularly so if the user has an urgent need or desire for the service and there is only one source for the service.

Auspices. These services involve a wide variety of philanthropic and governmental auspices, and all levels of government. The distinctions between governmental and philanthropic auspices largely reflect the extent of public support for the redistributive aspect of the service. Where there is majority support there is likely to be a governmental auspice.

Outputs. The outputs in these services constitute a series of discrete activities by the service provider that come closest to the term people-changing. However, the most extensive outputs in this class of services involve care and protection in institutional and foster-home types of settings, which are primarily "maintenance of functioning" or "social care" services. These services may also include other types of activities, such as the direct provision of pharmaceutical drugs, direct provision of primary health services, or prosthetic devices and other rehabilitation aids.

Relation of outputs to beneficiaries. In nearly all instances it is characteristic of the outputs that there must be cooperation by the user, first if there is to be any service provision, and more importantly if there is to be a successful outcome. Thus the provision of primary health care requires cooperation from the individual in the diagnostic and assessment process, in taking prescribed medicines or following health regimens. This coproduction of outputs is even more explicit in counseling activities and in work training activities. Social care "maintenance of functioning" services also depend heavily on the initiative and effort put forth by the individual user.

Technology. The rehabilitative, remedial, curative, social care, deviance treatment services are marked by technologies in which there is a high degree of uncertainty as to outcomes. Compared to the technology for determining eligibility for or providing checks to AFDC beneficiaries or the technology used by emergency medical services, the technologies involved in counseling a juvenile delinquent, community care of a schizophrenic ex-hospital patient, treating an abusive parent, or treating depression in an elderly individual are considerably more uncertain. Moreover, since these technologies require coproduction, the technologies require strong user-motivating procedures. Most of the technologies used are not research based, depending rather on cumulative professional wisdom and individual practitioner trial-and-error experience.

Evaluation. Monitoring this type of service provision is even more imprecise than providing it.[18] Efforts to determine directly if high quality services are being provided by a particular worker to a particular user are generally of no avail. The basis of outcome evaluation in individual cases consists primarily of two major elements. The first and by far the most generally used is a determination if the recipient of the service feels after the fact that the service has been of value. This form of evaluation is extremely imprecise, but it is used in the absence of other alternatives. The other basis of evaluation is to determine whether intended outcomes have been achieved across a group of service users. For example, have mentally ill persons been maintained in the community? Many types of programs are marked by a high degree of complexity in even attempting to measure these gross outcomes.

Legitimation. A very important element in understanding the relation of these services to the political economy, including the persistence of such service organizations in the absence of conclusive positive evaluation feedback, is the fact that the benefits these programs provide are simultaneously a type of redistributive benefit and a type of collective merit good provision. The continued legitimation and funding support for such services depends heavily on the assessment by community decisionmakers, or state or federal policymakers, of the continued need for merit good provision, rather than on a direct evaluation of the quality of the benefit provided to the user.[19] Therefore, it is the desire for a collective benefit, rather than redistribution or user satisfaction, that primarily determines the level of support for a particular program and the program characteristics built into the legal authorizations.

Merit Good Provision

The preceding section has illustrated very briefly the diversity of program and organizational characteristics that exist within the broad category of human service programs. The balance of this chapter will focus primarily on the implications of the merit good aspect of the provision of remedial, rehabilitative, curative, social care, and deviance treatment services for organizational performance problems in a set of organizations, which will be designated here as *social benefit organizations*. These are organizations that provide a combination of redistributive and merit good benefits.

This chapter's basic premise is that two sources of operational problems underlie social benefit organizations. One is the general nature of public good provision, a factor common to all human service organizations. Fundamental to all public good provision is the fact that the determination of the amount and form of the public good to be provided, and the assessment of the service outputs and outcomes, is a collective or political process. Any political process has a significant degree of uncertainty and unpredictability in relation to the defining of either demand or need. The policymakers and administrators of any particular program, therefore, have no firm and precise basis upon which to project the future development of the organization, except to assume that need is unlimited and that resources will always be inadequate. In turn, the assessment of the value or adequacy of the services provided is ultimately political. It may or may not be directly related to the stated goals and objectives of the organization. It also may or may not be directly related to the quality of the services provided as assessed by either provider staff or by the users.

Frequently, the public, political decision processes create a high level of uncertainty and unpredictability for administrators and service staff of organizations providing public goods. This is particularly intense for organizations whose goals and objectives are highly ambiguous and whose outputs are difficult to define. It is particularly acute under conditions of political contest or political instability.

A variety of structural and procedural devices have been developed to attempt to buffer social benefit organizations against these uncertainties.[20] One such procedure is the legitimation of professional expertise as the source of policy decisions and administrative authority, as in many health-related organizations. Another is the assignment of policy authority to "nonpartisan" boards and commissions, with long-term member appointments. Another is to emphasize political skills and political connections on the part of the organization executive, or to produce a wide variety of evaluative information, ranging from heartstrings case examples to elaborate statistical reports. Another adaptation is to provide some services under nongovernmental, philanthropic auspices, sponsored by a particular segment of the population that holds a high degree of consensus about goals and objectives.

But each of these structural or procedural devices reduces the political responsiveness of the organization in favor of stabile organizational performance. During periods of rapid social change, which are also likely to be periods of political and

ideological conflict, these devices for buffering the organization against political tides may be relatively ineffective. The
turmoil in the larger society may be expected to appear in the
immediate environment of the organization, and within the
organization itself. In the 1960s, the civil rights movement and
the citizen empowerment movement created a high level of
political instability affecting most, if not all, organizations providing public goods. In the mid-1970s, "Proposition 13 fever"
was the political ideology impacting the operational environment of the public goods organization.

However, this chapter is primarily concerned with the impact of the merit goods aspect of public good provision. The
concept of merit good as used by economists, a concept particularly identified with Richard Musgrave, involves a benefit or
good provided to a user or consumer in which the values and
preferences of the provider, or a third party, rather than the
preferences of the consumer, determine the form and amount
of the good or benefit provided.[21] (In the discussion that follows, the term *initiator* refers to the party that defines the terms
of the merit good provision. This may be the service provider,
or a third party that funds the provision of a particular service.) Thus, the initiator receives a benefit from the provision
of the service, in addition to any benefit received by the consumer.

In the instance of an action by a single individual, the provision of an unsolicited benefit to a consumer or a user may take
the form of an unrestricted or *pure* gift. Such gifts, or *grants* (as
they are designated by Kenneth Boulding and Martin Pfaff),
occur on a widespread basis within families, between friends,
and within population groups that are closely linked through
bonds of mutual obligation and affection.[22] However, such a
gift may also be intended to affect the behavior of the consumer or user in a particular way. Thus the contribution of a
charitable gift to a starving individual may be unrestricted, or it
may be intended in part to induce the individual to foresake
begging on the street and to seek stable employment. The
amount of the gift may therefore be larger than it would be as a
pure gift. A parent may pay for a college that is more expensive
than the academic ability or career interests of a child would

warrant in order to improve the probability that the child's marriage partner will be from a higher-income background. Or a parent buys a child an expensive birthday gift involving scientific equipment in the hope that the gift will not only please the child but will also stimulate his career interests and academic efforts.

These examples illustrate that a merit good by definition includes several elements.[23] First there is a direct benefit for the user or consumer. This benefit must be sufficiently attractive and relevant to the preferences and desires of the consumer that it will be used or consumed. Second, the amount or quality of the good or benefit provided must be greater than that which the consumer can or would purchase, so that there are excess supply costs. Third, there is a control objective on the part of the initiator that is related to some personal behavior of the consumer that is to be either encouraged or inhibited. This potential control benefit to the initiator accounts for the existence of the excess supply costs. Finally, there is a dependent relationship between the user or consumer and the initiator, so that the user does not have the option of substituting a good or benefit that does not have such control aspects. Among the dependent relationships often involved in merit good provision are economic dependency, minority group status, patient status, childhood status, or dependency because of physical or mental handicaps. Finally, there exists a high degree of uncertainty as to whether the control objective of the initiator will in fact be realized, that is, it is uncertain whether the user will exhibit the desired pattern of behavior as a consequence of the utilization of the benefit or good provided.

Merit goods are not just a form of public good, because, as already indicated, merit good characteristics may apply to gifts or grants between individuals. In these instances the perceived benefit from the desired behavior accrues primarily to the initiator. Thus the parents of the college student gain the greatest benefit if there results a marriage connection into a family with higher income or social status. It is when the secondary benefits, flowing from the performance of desired behavior or the reduction of undesired behavior, accrue to the general public that merit goods become a form of public good.

When an alcoholic whose drunken behavior is visible to the public at large changes that behavior, there is a potential benefit to a substantial number of persons, including members of his family, employers, fellow workers, and citizens walking the streets of the city. In a similar way, when an unemployed individual utilizes training and social services to prepare for and obtain self-supporting employment, the benefit from the reduction in dependence accrues to all persons whose taxes may have contributed to providing a public assistance payment.

It is characteristic of the merit good that is is provided before the desired behavior is performed; therefore it is not a reward or payment for the desired behavior. Because of the high degree of uncertainty, it must be recognized that much of the benefit to the initiator of a merit good comes only from the knowledge that an effort has been made to induce desired behavior, whether or not the desired behavior results. It would therefore be logical to assume that the provision of a public merit good, as a form of collectively provided public good, would depend upon an assessment of the probability that desired behaviors would be induced, rather than upon firm evidence that the desired behaviors had in fact appeared in all instances.

MERIT GOODS AND POLICY DILEMMAS

In the development of social benefit organizations, three continuing policy issues are related to many of the ambiguities and uncertainties that have always affected the operation of these organizations. (1) What is to be the mixture of social control objectives and individual benefit objectives in any particular type of service provision? (2) Who should decide the mixture of social control and individual benefits involved in any particular service provision? (3) What technology will be most effective in achieving both the social control and the individual benefit objectives?

In the history of the emergence of social benefit organizations, whether under governmental auspices (almshouses, orphanages, and reformatories), or under philanthropic auspices (charity societies and child welfare agencies), these policy issues are evident.[24] The original motivations involved very substantial merit good or social control objectives, as well as direct benefit or gift objectives. However, since the control or merit good benefits were expected to accrue to society in general, or to particular social classes, rather than to any single person, it was logical that various forms of joint or collective provision of services were developed. The prevention of pauperism through charity organizations was expected to benefit society at large, as well as the particular individuals receiving financial assistance, through the reduction of street begging and through the production of economic goods by those who became employed workers.[25] The institutionalization of the mentally retarded not only assured the protection and care of the retarded, but it removed from the community persons who were viewed as high risks for criminal and immoral behavior.

A major characteristic of American society has been the investment of personal efforts and economic resources in a deliberate effort to "improve the general welfare" or to encourage "social progress." The provision of merit goods through social welfare (or social benefit) organizations became one major element in a broader effort to improve society. This improvement involved not only the elimination of destitution, but the elimination of undesirable behaviors—crime, drunkeness, prostitution, child labor—and the promotion of desired behaviors—hard work, good citizenship, community cooperation, educational initiative. Social welfare programs simultaneously sought to help the needy (charity) and to encourage desired behaviors (social control). This combined concern led to the formation of the National Conference on Charities and Corrections in the 1870s, and was supported, first, by a religious philosophy common in particular forms of Protestant theology and later, by the end of the nineteenth century, by applied science. Both motivations, the religious and the rational or scientific, are still powerful factors in the political economy of social benefit organizations.

The development of social benefit organizations has always required a coalition between two types of individuals. First are

those directly concerned with providing specific and uncon-
ditional benefits to particular individuals or family units who
they view as handicapped or disadvantaged. In the most obvious sense the interests of these persons are immediate and
personal, centering around an individual situation. Examples
include individuals like Dorothea Dix, whose concern about
the plight of individuals in prisons and almshouses led to a
one-woman crusade to promote the creation of state-
supported specialized institutions for medical and social care.
In the nineteenth century, the motivations of these individuals
were frequently stated in terms of religious imperatives. In
contemporary language, their motivations are usually stated in
terms of social justice. Second are those individuals primarily
interested in influencing or controlling particular classes
whose behavior is seen as detrimental to society or to particular
elements in society, or whose behavior might benefit society if
changed in particular ways. In the nineteenth century, the
motivations of these social control initiators were frequently
stated in terms of religious morality. Today, their motivations
are usually stated in terms of economic benefit and social
order.

For many individuals, and within social groups such as religious groups, these motives of personal assistance and social
control were frequently mixed. From the very beginnings of
both tax-supported and community philanthropic organizations, organizers and administrators learned to appeal simultaneously to potential financial supporters' humane senti-
ments, through dramatic case examples, and to their "enlight-
ened self-interest," by stressing the collective social control
benefits of effective service provision. This dual appeal often
succeeded, and social benefit programs, in the form of tax-
supported institutions and philanthropically supported community programs, expanded steadily during the last half of the
nineteenth century.

The social benefit organizations that emerged reflected a
rather substantial consensus around certain basic principles
related to the policy issues stated above.

First, they reflected the premise that the collective social
control benefits achieved by encouraging desired behavior and

limiting undesired behavior should be greater than the direct benefits to individuals. These programs were not intended to be a pure redistributional benefit. The attractiveness of the benefit should be only that minimum necessary to achieve participation in the service activity. If the individual or family was in great need, unemployed, without money, and did not speak English, the attractiveness of the benefit could be reduced to a very low level. If the family was employed and had connections with the ward political organization, the direct benefit had to be more compelling in order to be utilized. Some of the early differences in program content and staff attitudes that emerged between charity organizations and settlement houses reflect this difference in the degree of dependency in their service constituencies.

Second was the premise that those who provided financial support and social legitimation, not the employed staff or those receiving the services, should establish the policies governing the mix of social control and individual benefits. In many early social benefit organizations, the board, not the staff, made detailed decisions about the benefits to be provided in individual cases.

Third was their assumption that households that could obtain such services as medical care, child care, and home nursing in the marketplace should always receive better service and greater benefits than those receiving benefits through collectively supported social benefit programs. In many service sectors, this resulted in the development of a dual pattern of service provision, for example the single room for the well-to-do private patient in the general hospital and the large ward for the charity patients.

In addition to these basic principles, it was assumed that the methods policymakers and administrators chose were in fact effective in achieving the program objectives. That is, legitimation of a method or technology was assumed to signify its satisfactory performance. Even general debates about service methods, for example between foster care and institutional care for dependent children, were seldom viewed as involving specific judgements on the effectiveness of any single service agency.

One important characteristic of many nineteenth-century social benefit programs was that the basic mode of operation involved modifying the social environment, rather than providing highly specialized professional services to particular individuals. For example, most special purpose institutions were established around models that emphasized the importance of the environmental setting (assuming a general pattern of humane and supportive behavior on the part of custodial staff), rather than specifying a highly specialized treatment technology. Prisons were designed around social environmental principles. Similarly, child welfare agencies emphasized placing the child in a supportive family or custodial environment, rather than providing specialized therapeutic services directly to the child. Administrators in these programs were therefore primarily involved with establishing and maintaining an environment, rather than directing a group of treatment specialists.

It is relevant to point out some contrasts between these social benefit organizations, with their combination of merit goods and direct benefits provided under the auspices of the civic or political elite, and the alternative nineteenth-century model, which emerged out of marxist philosophy. The marxist model argued for redistribution of political power within the state, rather than redistribution of goods and services on an individual case basis. The objective was equal status and access to goods and services. This implied that collective provision of goods and services should constitute pure benefits rather than merit goods. The ultimate goal was the reduction of governmental authority and ultimately a social and economic process that would function on the basis of equality of status without collective control. It is ironic that most collective provision by modern marxist governments has been in the form of merit goods; that is, collective benefits have been intended to encourage some behaviors and inhibit others. The underlying dynamics of collective provision of public goods appear to be relatively constant regardless of official social ideology.

At the turn of the century, social benefit organizations took on new characteristics with the emergence of the concepts of scientific philanthropy and, later, the professionalization of social work, elementary education, public health, mental health, and many other types of human service activities.[28] Initially these changes did not modify social benefit principles, except for the promise of more effective technologies that would ensure a higher probability of both achieving social control objectives and improving the quality of the direct benefits to service consumers. This new rationality was first applied to the processes of diagnosis, classification, and assessment, rather than to treatment, under the proposition that more exact classification of problems would lead to more precise treatment and more successes. Since this objective was already being realized in the diagnosis and treatment of acute medical conditions, including contagious diseases, it seemed reasonable to assume that it could be achieved in other areas as well. This emphasis upon systematic rationality brought an increased emphasis on the role of professional specialists in the operation of social benefit programs. As professional specialists took on the expanded role of diagnosticians, their role in directing the provision of specialized treatment services also began to take on more importance.

This emphasis upon assessment and diagnosis provided occupational specialists with a different base for professional status than that of the lawyer or the clergyman. In both of these professions there was, and still is, limited emphasis upon scientific procedures in diagnosis. The professional service provided by these professionals was not a people-changing type of service directly provided on a case-by-case basis. Even medicine did not involve a people-changing philosophy except as a secondary consequence of the treatment of a disease condition. The development of the new human service professions as a social institution involved, therefore, an entirely different set of processes. It was not simply a twentieth-century addition to the roster of traditional professions. One important difference from the traditional professions is the absence of consumer choice in the selection of a service professional in social benefit programs. The provision of professional services primarily through organizations not controlled by professionals is another. Trying to analyze the human service professions on the basis of an "ideal type" model of "profession" based on the historic professions is a waste of time.

Once the process of systematizing an occupational specialization ("professionalization") began to occur within social benefit organizations, a number of consequences followed.

First, the process of diagnosis and assessment was rationalized. Mary Richmond's book on *Social Diagnosis* and the comprehensive analysis of community social conditions incorporated in the Pittsburgh Survey are only two examples that parallel the development of laboratory methods for diagnosing disease conditions. With the rationalization of diagnosis it is the professional, rather than the person seeking assistance, who defines the condition and specifies the treatment.

Second, a variety of service provision activities were developed that required the training, skills, and motivations of employed specialists, rather than the services of untrained volunteers. Administrators became responsible for directing the work of a staff of specialists.

Third, increased emphasis on diagnosis and specialized treatment activities increased the organizational status and income of staff personnel with specialist qualifications.[27] This led to explicit distinctions between the functions of the professional specialists on the staff and the functions of volunteer policymakers, and similar distinctions between the functions of treatment specialists and those of social care personnel such as mental hospital attendants, child care workers in children's institutions, foster parents, and so forth.

Fourth and finally, the emergence of a body of professional specialists in such fields as social work, public health, elementary education, and vocational counseling led to a shift in the control of the instruments of ideology in these fields, including publications, conferences, and the orientation and training of new staff personnel. These ideology-defining functions were controlled in the nineteenth century largely by volunteer lay leadership and community elite. Now they came to be controlled by senior professional specialists and program administrators.

The increased status of professional specialists that resulted from the emphasis on rationality, and the increase in their numbers as programs expanded, led to an important shift toward redistributional objectives in the provision of service benefits. The increased emphasis during the Progressive Era on the importance of providing direct benefits to the poor as a matter of social justice reflected in part the personal social motivations of persons entering the new professional specializations. It also reflected the background of these individuals, who often came from upwardly mobile middle- and lower-middle-income families that resented the power of wealthy elite families who had historically established the policy of social benefit organizations.

However, while conference addresses and professional publications showed more emphasis upon social justice rather than earlier moralistic objectives, the need to obtain financial support from governmental and voluntary philanthropic sources remained. This necessitated continued emphasis on collective social benefits along with benefits to particular individuals or households. The collective benefits were increasingly represented as rehabilitative or curative, substituting a medical model for the earlier morality model. Program objectives were stated in terms of rehabilitation of the dependent household, the delinquent, the slow-achieving child, the physically handicapped individual, rather than in terms of control of laziness, immorality, vagrancy, begging, and other forms of sin.

The 1920s and 1930s brought an important shift in the political economy context. The 1920s saw a shift from financial support by small groups of wealthy individuals to more broadly based middle-income support organized through the Community Chest and other community-wide fund-raising campaigns. This coincided with passage of the income tax amendment to the Constitution. Also in the 1920s, new forms of social benefit programs arose supported by state governments: widows pensions (for widows with young children) and old-age pensions. At the same time the voter constituency involved in establishing these state government programs, as well as in providing increased support to state institutions such as mental hospitals and state schools for the retarded, was substantially broadened through the inclusion of women.

In the 1930s, the responsibility for basic necessity redistributional programs was shifted from philanthropic to predominantly governmental auspices. The new governmental programs included the direct provision of financial support, the beginnings of public housing, and a brief experiment with food stamps. The taxes required for the support of these services came primarily from middle-income and working-class families. Many members of the financial elite, the original supporters of social benefit programs, were increasingly able to utilize tax deduction procedures to limit the impact of these tax-supported services on their own economic status. By the end of the 1930s, the financial responsibility for basic necessity redistributional programs, and indeed for a high proportion of all types of social benefit programs, both governmental and philanthropic, had been shifted from the wealthy elite to a much broader base of middle-income households.

However, the general assumption continued at least through the 1950s that policy control of social benefit programs (and therefore the determination of the merit good characteristics of such programs) should rest with the civic elite leadership. Tax-supported programs were controlled by persons from relatively similar backgrounds in state and federal legislatures, and governmental bodies often turned to civic elite leaders for policy advice. Through the 1950s it was still widely assumed that those receiving benefits from redistributional programs in general, and from rehabilitative, remedial, and social care programs in particular, had neither a legal nor a moral entitlement to such benefits. In particular they had no right to participate in determining the character of the benefits or the mix of social control objectives and direct benefit objectives in any particular program.

The 1960s brought forth in a variety of forms the assertion that beneficiaries or potential beneficiaries of social benefit programs had both a formal entitlement to benefits and a legitimate claim to participate in, or even to control, policies governing the provision of benefits. The principles of "community control" and "maximum feasible participation" were assertions of the right of beneficiaries or beneficiary constituencies to determine both the content and the level of benefits. This challenge to the authority of elite policymakers and professional specialists was made in behalf of low-income populations through the welfare rights movement and in behalf of black and Mexican American citizens through the antipoverty program and through the black power and Chicano movements.

Similarly, parents groups speaking for families of children with developmental disabilities began to assert that such families were entitled to treatment services and had a right to evaluate the services' effectiveness and to demand compliance with quality standards. Later, groups of handicapped adults began to speak for themselves, attacking in particular the uncontrolled use of professional authority to determine institutional commitment. This assertion of an enforceable right of disabled individuals to receive treatment under least restrictive conditions was reinforced in the 1970s by actions of the courts in such areas as mental retardation, mental illness, and developmental disabilities.

MERIT GOODS AND ORGANIZATIONAL DILEMMAS

The political economy of social benefit organizations in the 1970s was marked by a high level of conflict over the three policy issues set out above. A variety of interest-group constituencies sought to affect the definition of the content of service provision, including the balance between social control benefits and benefits to the service consumer and the choice of a service technology. This not only affected formal organizational goals and the level of resource provision, it also penetrated the operation of the organization, since several of the interest-group constituencies involved organizational participants.

The major interest group constituencies include:

1. Traditional "liberal" elite philanthropic leaders, who support merit good social benefit programs for both charitable and social control purposes. This leadership group today exerts its influence through participation in issue-oriented lobbying, rather than through personal participation in philanthropic financing of services, although some foundations under the control of these leaders are significant funding sources.

2. The middle-class majority of voters and philanthropic contributors, who tend to oppose general expansion of social

benefit programs under philanthropic and governmental auspices, and in particular to oppose increases in the general level of taxation. The interests of this majority of the taxpayers are frequently responded to by "populist" antibureaucracy, anti-big-government political candidates, who avoid as much as possible committing themselves to cutting back specific governmental programs.

3. Libertarians and monetarists, who object in principle to the economic costs and social control aspects of merit good provision. These persons often argue for minimal but standardized redistribution of basic necessities and the elimination of government-supported human services. Similar in philosophic orientation are the "new conservatives," who express support for the objectives of social benefit programs but who are consistently skeptical of the effectiveness of individual programs and policies, particularly those that emerged in the 1960s.[28]

4. Beneficiary constituencies, including senior citizen associations, parents of handicapped children, residents of low-income neighborhoods, and so forth, who have a strong commitment to the expansion of particular social benefit programs. The support for these programs involves a mixture of belief in their effectiveness and a concern for equity, that is, that a particular interest constituency receives its "fair share" of financial support, regardless of the efficiency or effectiveness of particular programs. These groups often exercise their influence through individualized linkages with key persons, such as legislative committee chairmen and career administrators in the legislative and administrative system involved in program legitimation and support. This is often coupled with highly intensive special-interest lobbying around particular legislation or around budgetary allocation processes.

5. Human service professionals, who are guided by an official ideological orientation that includes a positive view of professionalism, which emphasizes autonomous decisionmaking for direct service professionals in diagnosis and prescription, a positive view of the redistributional provision of benefits to low-income consumers, and a negative view of the social control aspects of those benefits. While individual profession-

als may not hold to these views, professional associations and publications reflect these perspectives.

6. Human service executives, who have a particular concern for organizational maintenance and protection. These executives are open to pressure from all interest constituencies, but they must be primarily responsive to those that control funding and legitimation, sources that traditionally have emphasized the merit good–social control aspects of social benefit programs.

One additional complexity in the political economy is that many individuals and households have oeplapping participation in several of these constituencies. The schoolteacher who advocates increased funding for education may join a taxpayers' association to oppose a general increase in municipal property taxes. Elite civic leaders may support "Proposition 13" candidates in a party primary while testifying in legislative hearings in support of expanded child abuse services or sheltered workshop programs for the mentally retarded

One consequence of these interest conflicts, particularly those between community elite/political leadership constituencies, service professional constituencies, and consumer constituencies, has been the emergence of a series of organizational dilemmas that have important consequences for program design and the administrative process.

As a result of the perceived ideological orientation of service professionals to the redistributional aspects of social benefit programs, there has emerged a constant clash of interest between professional service staff and those leaders or groups most direcly representing funding sources. This is evident in United Way philanthropic organizations, where there has been an increased assertion of the policymaking role of funders, despite claims that professional service specialists in voluntary philanthropic organizations should have the dominant role in establishing program priorities and specifying program procedures. There are similar conflicts in every legislative session between appropriation committees and professional staff personnel involved in tax-supported programs. In almost every instance professional staff assert that the funding sources do not understand the real objectives of the service programs and are unwilling to provide adequate funding. Professional associations often become major lobbying forces in support of professional staff priorities.

This lobbying may conflict with budget priorities advocated by program administrators, who are more likely to take funder preferences into account. As organizations increase in size, the distinctions between the priorities of service specialists and the priorities of administrators become more explicit. Because administrators reflect the concerns of funders and policymakers, including concerns with eligibility fraud and program abuse, the ideology of the service professionals increasingly tends to emphasize conflict and confrontation between professionals and managers over program priorities and objectives.[29]

Because of service professionals' general ideological preference for the redistributional aspects of service programs, and opposition to the explicit social control aspects, there are often efforts to form alliances between professionals and user constituencies in support of user entitlement to services and financial resources for program personnel. However, consumer constituencies currently are challenging the exclusive control of professional specialists over diagnosis and the prescription of services. There are other disagreements. Consumer constituencies favor immediate and tangible services (direct personal benefits), while professional service personnel favor comprehensive rehabilitative and development counseling and other services that require specialized professional skills, the benefits of which may not be apparent until an extensive treatment program is completed.

As a consequence of their conflicts with consumer interest groups, professional service staff are often driven to seek the support of civic elite groups in an effort to protect traditional professional standards. In turn, to gain the support of such leadership groups, professional service staff find themselves defending and advocating the merit good concept and minimizing the redistributional aspects of service programs.

An increasingly complex issue is that of access to the employment opportunities provided by social benefit organizations. As indicated above (in the discussion of basic necessity redistributional programs), access to employment opportunities is today a major aspect of redistribution. As a consequence there is increasing conflict over the processes by which employment opportunities within labor-intensive human service organizations are allocated. Professional service staff tend to object to elite leadership groups, which emphasize the social control aspects of employment, that is, the benefits to society of enforcing a "protestant work ethic" on presumably reluctant clients. However, the service consumer sees employment as a positive benefit, particularly when it provides access to a variety of economically valuable fringe benefits and to a defined social status in the occupational system. Consumer constituencies, including adults in low-income households and disabled individuals, may therefore view job opportunities in human service organizations as a potential redistributional benefit to which they should have a right of entitlement. These interests of constituencies may be viewed as conflicting with the interests of professional staff, to the extent that redistribution of job opportunities is viewed as an overriding value in comparison to an exclusive emphasis upon job skills or academic achievement. The literature dealing with paraprofessional service personnel contains a complex mix of arguments that indigenous workers are more effective than highly trained professional specialists, and that unemployed community residents have an a priori right to any job opportunities that may be available. However, the replacement of professional criteria for employment of service staff with job redistribution as an objective undercuts the basis for appealing to civic elite and political leadership groups for increased financial support, on the grounds that high-quality professional services will result in a high level of positive rehabilitative results. Thus strong consumer groups that emphasize employment of nonprofessionals could result in decreased financial resources for all staff functions.

Other complexities emerge as the scope of tax-supported human service organizations, including contract services, continues to be enlarged, replacing explicitly "charitable" nongovernmental services.[30] To increase the base of political support there is a strong tendency to define tax-supported human service programs as serving a universal service constituency, rather than a targeted constituency involving a redistributional purpose, and to argue that the particular service is relevant and indeed necessary for a broad cross-section of the population. This is accompanied by a move to redefine eligibility criteria to include at least the median income group. The change from the eligibility criteria for social services available under Title IV A, limited essentially to AFDC recipients, to the criteria for services available under Title XX, which may be made available to households with up to 115 percent of state median income, is a recent example. To gain the support of, and to promote utilization of services by, a middle-income constituency, the social control aspects of the service must be deemphasized.

Day care, which was once primarily intended to provide a protected social development experience for a small number of children from households "diagnosed" as socially and economically inadequate, has become redefined as a service that is expected to be available, as needed, for almost any household. The rehabilitative reeducation emphasis in early day care programs is played down when such programs promote their services to a middle-class constituency in order to justify increased funding. The original social control justification for which funding was sought from civic leaders is no longer valid. Therefore it is necessary to seek popular support for a broader financial base, rather than depending on the support of elite leadership groups. In order to achieve broad popular support, the redistributional aspects of the program must be minimized.[31] Indeed, it is quite possible that the service programs that become universal and that are largely stripped of social control aspects may no longer be readily accessible or relevant to those with the greatest economic and social deprivation. It is also possible that in a financial pinch the middle-class constituency will decide that certain of these services, while viewed as generally useful to them, are not a high priority for funding, particularly if a tax increase would be required.

This suggests that individual human service organizations cannot be viewed as closed systems with a focused input of goals, objectives, and resources, and with the organizational participants then having autonomous control over the administrative and technical processes that lead to the organizational outputs. It is perhaps not even correct to speak of such organizations as open systems, in the sense that they are relatively well integrated structures that receive a variety of inputs from the environment at all levels of the organization. It is perhaps more accurate to view the social benefit organization as embedded in an implementation structure comprised of multiple public and private actors, a structure marked particularly by the "loose coupling" of the constituent organizational elements.[32] These implementation structures are impacted by general environmental forces in the society. Service implementation structures, indeed, may often become essentially political arenas in which specific policy decisions around a program element, for example the provision of family counseling, abortion counseling, or preschool education, become defined as win–lose contests involving a substantial number of different constituencies. With an intense involvement in the programmatic policy issues, there may be little consideration by any of the constituencies for the impact of either the contest or the issue outcome on the ability of any single organization to continue to function effectively.

The Sources of Operational Problems

The preceding material has examined interrelationships between the political economy and the public merit good aspects of social benefit organizations. The thesis is that the combination of redistributive or personal benefit purposes and collective public benefit purposes affects the pattern of operational problems in social benefit organizations. The following section returns to some of the problematic conditions identified at the beginning of this paper.[33]

Most human service programs lack information about the relationship between the characteristics of organizational outputs and the actual outcomes for persons using these outputs. The circulation of books by a public library may have a wide variety of consequences for the reader; measurement of them would be very complex, and there have been few efforts made to trace such a connection. In the instance of social benefit organizations, the complexities are even greater. Given the complexity involved in verifying an explicit relationship between, for example, family counseling and a reduced level of family conflict in the community, it is not surprising that the simple effort to achieve social control objectives is most often accepted as sufficient justification for the continuation of the program. An enumeration of outputs is frequently used as evidence of this effort. Although the absence of systematic outcome evaluation of social benefit programs is frequently cited in legislative oversight reports, this has not led to any substantial increase in the extent to which outcome evaluation is included as a regular part of program operations. There appears to be a general reluctance to pursue the issue of the relation between outputs and outcomes. It may be that professional service staff and administrators are concerned that it will be impossible to demonstrate a systematic relation between the pattern of outputs and the pattern of benefits to the general society, and that this might undercut the existing rationale for financial support for the program. Meanwhile, civic and political policymakers may be concerned that negative information about the relation of outputs to outcomes would result in demands from the staff and from advocacy groups for increased funding and more intensive and sophisticated technologies.

The performance characteristics of worker activity and their relationship to the characteristics of organizational outputs is a largely unexplored issue. In part this may reflect the high degree of ambiguity that exists within the organization about the desired form of outputs. In particular this involves the question of the balance between outputs intended to achieve social control and outputs intended to provide a direct benefit to the service consumer. Given this ambiguity, it is difficult to arrive at a clear specification of the desired pattern of worker activities. The effort to resolve this ambiguity would require clarification of organizational objectives, which as noted above are often the subject of continuing contests among various constituencies. In most instances, therefore, quantitative measures of worker effort are used, rather than systematic analyses of the functional characteristics of worker activities. Indeed, the study of the relationship between activities and outputs may often be oversimplified to the extent that a quantitative measure of effort, for example the number of hours of counseling provided by staff personnel, may be used directly as the measure of organizational output as well.

The normative model of most formal organizations, particularly that set forth in many discussions of human service organizations, assumes a direct and invariable relationship between policy decisions, administrative direction, and the characteristics of worker activity. As described above, analysis of the political economy around social benefit organizations suggests a loosely coupled form of program implementation structures. This is particularly evident in the relation between the process of policy formation and the pattern of worker activity within particular organizations and for the program implementation network as a whole. The dilemma of service professionals forced to deal with the ambiguity involved in the social control–redistributional characteristics of their services may lead to a high degree of self-imposed isolation of the professional from the policy and administrative components of the organization. The political requirements involved in organizational maintenance and program development require administrative personnel to devote more energy to responding to inputs from the political economy at the institutional level, than to maintaining tight control over the activities of direct service personnel. Given particularly unstable political conditions, modest shifts in the general political balance of power can result in sharp swings in the formal policy inputs to the organization, for example, demands for crash fraud-control campaigns. Under these conditions it may be organizationally functional, from the administrator's perspective, to maintain only the loosest of connections between legal mandates, organizational goals, official objective statements, and the ongoing operations of the service staff. Too tight a linkage could be dysfunctional for users, staff, and administrators. For example, a highly efficient land detailed management information system might provide data indicating that the outputs of the organization are not consistent with the social control objectives set by funding sources, although the outputs may be perceived as beneficial and useful by the service users. This could seriously compromise administrators' ability to cope with the political decisionmaking system and to maintain organizational integrity. An effective information and control system could provide information that would force administrators to implement disciplinary procedures to maintain conformity to social control objectives. These disciplinary procedures might be nearly impossible to implement in a merit or buffered personnel system, but they could serve to mobilize informal resistance from staff and formal opposition from external professional associations and service constituencies. Thus the social benefit organization is more likely to maintain an operating equilibrium under conditions of loose coupling between policy levels, administrative levels, and staff levels, than under conditions of tight linkages between these organizational components.

The simultaneous existence of general dissatisfaction with large social benefit organizations and the stable persistence of most of these organizations over extended periods of time reflects several aspects of the analysis set forth previously.[34] The effort to achieve social control objectives may be a more urgent political necessity than any demonstration of the actual achievement of such objectives. In this case, the existence of an organization officially charged with attempting to achieve social control is more important than the actual degree of success realized. This is evident in the long history of state hospitals and state schools. These institutions have been expected to continue to operate, and to accept, almost without limit, all individuals sent for custodial care, while being chronically underfinanced and constantly under critical public attack. A similar situation frequently exists in regard to probation services and to child welfare protective services. Public discontent with a particular social benefit agency seldom, if ever, results in the elimination of that agency. The most frequent response to criticism is some form of administrative or structural reorganization that usually leaves the core functions and activities of the organization relatively untouched. Moreover, the mere existence of particular types of programs is often viewed as symbolic recognition by public bodies of a need for the provision of some type of redistributive benefit to specific constituencies. Thus, the existence of a community service center for senior citizens is viewed as evidence of public recognition of the right of retired citizens to receive some type of publicly supported services, even if the scope of the service is wholly inadequate. Even where there are obvious social control functions primarily benefiting the general society, an effort to eliminate such a program on the grounds of ineffectiveness may be interpreted as an attack upon the rights and prerogatives of the service constituency, potentially leading to a high level of constituency mobilization to protect the service. When attacked by administrative or policy groups, weak and underutilized service in a low-income minority neighborhood that was designed to deflect local protests over community conditions may be fiercely protected on the grounds that the attack is in fact against the rights of low-income and minority citizens in general.

Uncertainty about the consequences of increased professionalization in social benefit organizations reflects in part the uncertain meaning of professionalization within an organization. It may mean that direct service workers are expected to have a clearly demonstrated set of technical and professional skills, consistent with an established professional tradition. It may also mean the use of academic credentials to screen employees for certain levels of positions, or the organization of workers around an occupational specialization in order to advance its status within the organizational framework. It may also involve the commitment of staff to a specific set of ethical guides that define legitimate and illegitimate practices in service provision. Given this vagueness, it is particularly uncertain what the meaning of increased professionalization is, given the merit good–redistributive characteristics of service provision in social benefit organizations. Individuals with formal professional training who actively participate in a professional association may identify strongly with a social justice ideology reflected in the ethical pronouncements of the profession, or they may advocate that consumer choices and preferences should define the nature of service provision, consistent with the traditions of professional private practice. However, it is at least as possible that professionals will strongly identify with the merit good objectives of the service, on the basis that professional service is an expression of the concerns of larger society and should reflect the public interest rather than the individual preferences of the service user. Such a stance may be taken in part to ensure continued funding for and legitimation of professional specializations as an essential element in the service program. Moreover, professional service workers may view service users as weak and dependent, needing supervision and protection, or as deviant and requiring treatment and control. The attitudes of the professional service worker may therefore reinforce or extend the social control objectives reflected in the general social policies underlying the service program.[35] To the extent that increased professionalization means an increase in the importance of a group of organizational staff persons who define their base of expertise and source of legitimation as beyond the boundaries of the service organization itself, the level of conflict within the organization over issues of defining objectives and service procedures may be increased.

The ambiguous meaning of professionalization is also reflected in uncertainty about the significance for social benefit organizations of professional education and inservice training. Both are viewed variously as indoctrination into the formal policy objectives and procedures of a particular type of service organization, as ideological socialization into the normative structure and traditions of an organized profession, and as transmission of cognitive information and training in specific technical skills associated with the performance of specific occupational tasks. Since these three views imply three different frameworks for evaluating outcomes, it is not surprising that a high degree of dissatisfaction is constantly being expressed by various participants, including students, faculty, administrators, and policymakers. Given these ambiguities and the diversity of participants in education and training, it is highly likely that service personnel will select from their educational and training experiences information that will support their particular view of the balance between social control and redistributional benefits involved in a particular type of human service activity. These attitudes, once formulated, are likely to remain relatively unchanged in the work situation. This results in a variety of tensions within work groups, between workers and supervisors, and between supervisors and managers. Given the diversity of constituencies in the political economy surrounding social benefit organizations, and the ambiguities involved in organizational goals and objectives, each person can justify his particular set of assumptions. As most prevalent assumptions within professional education programs differ from those in most operating agencies, the conflict begins to assume institutional characteristics. This is particularly noteworthy in social work education, which places a high premium on the redistributive/social justice/consumer responsiveness characteristics of professional services and gives minor weight to the social control/public good characteristics of the human service programs carried out through public and philanthropic organizations.

The issue of centralization or decentralization of policymaking and administrative control has emerged as a major organizational issue as human service organizations have increased in size and scope. Much of the analysis applied to these two alternatives has been carried over from the study of production organizations in business and industry. These analyses tend to identify situations in which one or the other structural pattern may be clearly the preferred choice. However, neither centralization nor decentralization is likely to resolve many of the internal conflicts of the social benefit organization unless those conflicts are explicitly recognized. A high degree of centralization may be supported by funding and policymaking sources as essential to maintaining consistency of the program with social control purposes and to monitor compliance with those objectives. However, a high degree of centralization with strong control linkages between administration and service components may make the multiple goals and objectives that the program must serve increasingly obvious. This may result in a large number of decision issues rising to the top administrative level, creating a decision logjam and generating pressures for decentralization. This may also make policy choices explicit around issues, causing significant elements within and without the organization to advocate conflicting positions. A high degree of centralization also makes likely the adoption of a single set of operational policies affecting the agencywide balance between social control and redistributive aspects of the service, ignoring such local conditions as the relative circumstances of service users, political alignments, social traditions, and the relative strength of import constituencies at the community level.

To avoid these difficulties, it may be logical to prefer decentralization. This may reduce the amount of pressure on central agency executives for decisions under ambiguous conditions. However, it also involves a number of risks. Particular segments of the program may be captured by local constituencies that effectively impose severe social control criteria on the service programs, sometimes in opposition to the basic legal provisions of the program. This may open the program to legal attacks. In other instances, local pressures may move the program so far in the direction of a redistributional, individual benefit model, for example through the extensive provision of financial and services assistance to a local group of strikers, that there are serious attacks on the program by funding and legitimating groups. Thus, in the issue of organizational structure, as in the other issues discussed above, the combination of social control and redistributional/individual benefit objectives in a single service program creates dilemmas and contradictions that are not comprehended by traditional concepts of organizational theory and that do not lend themselves to simple solutions by the application of standard management procedures.

Conclusion

It is essential to examine the relationship of human service organizations (and networks of organizations) to the political economy of their environment in order to understand their chronic administrative dilemmas. This relationship is primarily affected by the public goods character of their outputs, and in particular the public merit good character. Thus, various subsets of human service organizations have distinctively different relationships with the political economy. In the case of social benefit organizations, the ambiguities and conflicts related to the mixture of social control and redistributive, individual benefit objectives exacerbate the administrative problems that generally characterize service providing organizations. This suggests that administrative theory as applied to social benefit organizations deals heavily with problem management and contingency planning, rather than with the routinized administration characteristic of a closed-system production organization. The administrative difficulties involved in social benefit organizations are, in fact, vastly greater than those involved in most business or industrial organizations.

The dilemmas created by the tension between redistributional and social control objectives in social benefit organizations are not easily resolved. If large-scale programs are to be organized around a redistributional consumer satisfaction principle, there must be broad ideological support for the goal of social justice and persuasive arguments that indirect collective benefits accrue to the individuals or households that are taxed to provide benefits to other individuals or households, often on a long-term basis.[36] While such motivations are consistent with a societal structure exhibiting a high degree of community identity among its members, it is difficult to conceive of this type of social ethic motivating a society marked by ethnic, national, and linguistic diversity and an economy that gives its highest recognition to individual economic achievement.

If a purely redistributional principle is not sufficient for maintaining majority support for social benefit programs, then a social control justification may be required. This forces administrators and professional service personnel either to enforce the social control objectives set by the larger society or to accept the stresses inherent in a loosely coupled organizational situation in which there are continuing discrepancies between organizational goals, administrative policies, the content of service outputs, and the preferences of service consumers. This involves both role ambiguity and chronic conflict among policymakers, administrators, service professionals, and service consumers. One symptom of these ambiguities and conflicts is the staff burnout, on-the-job dropout, and turnover widely commented on in the human services literature. Another symptom is the endless search for an organization of change that will resolve the ambiguities or that will facilitate stability.

An alternative direction of development would be a shift of organizational sponsorship for many of the services now provided by public and philanthropic social benefit organizations. Various forms of consumer control, prepaid group practice, or cooperative organizations might provide a framework through which consumer benefits are maximized and merit good and social control purposes are minimized. Prepaid legal services, health maintenance organizations, cooperative nurseries and day care centers, parent-controlled community mental health programs may be relevant models. The income redistribution required to enable all families in the community to meet the costs of service provided through such auspices could be provided either through increased levels of income maintenance programs or through voucher or in-kind provision involving governmental payment of membership costs for low-income houscholds. It can be argued that straight income or in-kind redistributional programs would receive broader public support than increases in the size and scope of directly operated service programs under public or philanthropic auspices.[37]

To the extent that these issues remain unresolved in the day-to-day operation of social benefit organizations, organizational theory, administrative theory, and the analysis of organizational problems must deal with the fact that unstable organizational conditions are the norm rather than the exception. Therefore, these unstable and problematic conditions must be the focus of investigation and analysis, in contrast to efforts to discover deductively a normative model of organizational functioning in which goals and objectives are harmonized and administrative and technical procedures are consistently rationalized.

Notes

1. For example, Rocco D'Amico and Bill Benton, "Addressing the Problems in Human Service Delivery" (Washington, D.C.: Urban Institute, 1978, unpublished ms.).

2. The discussion of public services that follows draws on the writings of several economists about public goods: Richard A. Musgrave, *The Theory of Public Finance* (New York: McGraw-Hill, 1959); Kenneth E. Boulding, *The Economy of Love and Fear: A Preface to Grants Economy* (Belmont, Cal.: Wadsworth, 1973); Burton A. Weisbrod, *The Voluntary Non-Profit Sector* (Lexington, Mass.: D. C. Heath, 1977); Victor R. Fuchs, *The Service Economy* (New York: National Bureau of Economic Research, 1968); and Julius Margolis, "The Demand for Urban Public Services," in Harvey S. Perloff and Lowden Wingo, Jr., *Issues in Urban Economics* (Baltimore: The Johns Hopkins Press, 1968).

3. Peter Drucker, *Management: Tasks, Responsibilities, Practices* (New York: Harper and Row, 1974).

4. Kurt Reichert, "The Drift toward Entrepreneurialism in Health and Social Welfare: Implications for Social Work Education," *Administration in Social Work* No. 2 (summer 1977), pp. 123–34.

5. P. M. Blau and R. A. Schoenherr, *The Structure of Organizations* (New York: Basic Books, 1971).

6. See David O. Porter, "Responsiveness to Citizen-Consumers in a Federal System," *Publius* 5, no. 4 (fall 1975), pp. 51–77, for an extended discussion of the intermediary role of governmental bodies in defining the quantity of public services provided through governmental organizations.

7. Irwin Epstein and Kayla Conrad, "The Empirical Limits of Social Work Professionalization," in Rosemary C. Sarri and Yeheskel Hasenfeld, eds., *The Management of Human Services* (New York: Columbia University Press, 1978), pp. 163–83.

8. Marshall W. Meyer and M. Craig Brown, "The Process of Bureaucratization," in Marshall W. Meyer and Associates, *Environments and Organizations* (San Francisco: Jossey-Bass, 1978), pp. 51–77.

9. Meyer, "Introduction," in Meyer and Associates, *Environments*, pp. 1–20.

10. Gary L. Walmsley and Mayer N. Zald, *The Political Economy of Public Organizations* (Lexington, Mass.: D. C. Heath, 1973).

11. The following categories involve both public goods and mixed goods (as discussed by Musgrave) and social wants and merit wants. The term *public good* applies here both to pure public goods and to the public good aspect of mixed goods. See Richard A. Musgrave's discussion of Margolis, "Urban

Public Services," in Perloff and Wingo, *Issues*, pp. 567–76.

12. Porter, *Responsiveness*.

13. See David O. Porter and David C. Warner, "How Effective Are Grantor Controls? The Case of Federal Aid to Education," in Kenneth E. Boulding, Martin Pfaff, and Anita Pfaff, *Transfers in an Urbanized Economy* (Belmont, Cal.: Wadsworth, 1973), pp. 276–302, for a more general discussion of this issue.

14. Weisbrod, *Voluntary Non-Profit Sector*, pp. 1–25.

15. See Fuchs, *Service Economy*, ch. 8, "Some Implications of the Growth of a Service Economy," pp. 183–99, for discussion of co-production as an aspect of service provision.

16. Dick Netzer, "Federal, State, and Local Finance in a Metropolitan Context," in Perloff and Wingo, *Issues*, pp. 430–76.

17. See Boulding, *Economy of Love and Fear*, pp. 1–13, for a discussion of gifts and tributes as two ends of a spectrum of motivations for one-way transfers or grants.

18. James D. Thompson, *Organizations in Action* (New York: McGraw-Hill, 1967). Ch. 7, "The Assessment of Organizations," pp. 83–100, deals with assessment when standards are ambiguous and cause-and-effect knowledge is incomplete.

19. See Porter, *Responsiveness*.

20. See Thompson, *Organizations*, pp. 25–38, for a discussion of processes through which organizations attempt to control unpredictable aspects of the environment.

21. The concept of merit want is primarily identified with Musgrave, *Theory of Public Finance*. It is also discussed in both Margolis and Musgrave in Perloff and Wingo, *Issues*. The term merit good is used in this chapter to refer to services provided in response to a merit want. The term mixed good, representing a combined private and public benefit, is frequently used in this sense. The term merit good emphasizes that public benefit is intended and represents an effort to affect the behavior of the consumer.

22. Boulding, Pfaff, and Pfaff, *Transfers in an Urbanized Economy*, pp. 1–7.

23. See Boulding, *Economy of Love and Fear*, Ch. 2, "The Microtheory of Grants and Granting Behavior."

24. For an extended discussion of the origins of social welfare/social benefit programs in the United States, see James Leiby, *A History of Social Welfare and Social Work in the United States* (New York: Columbia University Press, 1978).

25. See William Rinelander Steward, *The Philanthropic Work of Josephine Shaw Lowell* (New York: Macmillan, 1911), for a number of papers and speeches setting forth the moral purposes of the charity organization societies and other early social welfare services.

26. See Roy Lubove, *The Professional Altruist: The Emergence of Social Work as a Career, 1880–1930* (Cambridge, Mass.: Harvard University Press, 1964).

27. Ibid., ch. 5, "In-Group and Out-Group: The Molding of a Professional Subculture."

28. For example, Daniel P. Moynihan, *Maximum Feasible Misunderstanding* (New York: Free Press, 1969); Edward Banfield, *The Unheavenly City* (Boston: Little,

Brown, 1968); and any issue of *The Public Interest*.

29. For example, "The Manager vs. the Social Worker," *Public Welfare* 36, no. 3 (Summer 1978) pp. 5–10, and a description of the course "The Good Bureaucrat" (School of Social Work, University of California at Berkeley): "How can the professional manage the bureaucratic environment rather than be managed by it?"

30. David W. Young, "Contracting Out for Services: A Researcher's Perspective," in Michael J. Murphy and Thomas Glynn, eds., *Human Services Management: Priorities for Research* (Washington, D.C.: International City Managers Association, 1978), pp. 67–77.

31. Morgan Reynolds and Eugene Smolensky, "The Fading Effect of Government on Inequality," *Challenge* 21, no. 3 (July/Aug. 1978), pp. 32–37.

32. The concept of implementation structures is developed in David O. Porter and David C. Warner, "Organizational Rationality and Program Rationality" (Austin: University of Texas, School of Social Work, 1979; unpublished ms.).

33. Many of the problematic issues discussed in this chapter are similar to those discussed in Thompson, *Organizations*, with specific application here to social benefit organizations.

34. The persistence of community action agencies during a decade of frequent attacks and systematic administrative efforts to eliminate them is one classic example.

35. Janet Rosenberg, "Discovering Natural Types of Role Orientation: An Application of Cluster Analysis," *Social Service Review*, March 1978, pp. 85–106.

36. Mark F. Plattner, "The Welfare State vs. the Redistributive State," *The Public Interest* no. 55 (spring 1979). This argues against redistribution and for a more traditional view of welfare on a case-by-case basis, related to the merits of the individual situation.

37. See Regina E. Herzlinger and Nancy M. Kane, *The Government as Factory, Insurance Company, and Savings Bank: A Managerial Analysis of Federal Income Redistribution Mechanisms* (Cambridge, Mass.: Ballinger, 1979), for a discussion of alternative approaches to the funding and management of public goods. Also Herbert S. Rabinowitz, Bruce R. Simmeth, and Jeanette R. Spero, "The Future of the United Way," *Social Service Review* no. 3 (June 1979), pp. 275–84, for a discussion of the economic and political limitations on the growth of community-based philanthropic financing.

Chapter 3.

Trends in Policy Making

and Implementation in the

Welfare State

Mayer N. Zald

A central accompaniment of industrialization and modernization has been the growth of the welfare state. Governmental provision of care for the dependent and neglected, for the unemployed, and for the aged increases as the economic capacity of nations grows. Although the United States is widely perceived as a welfare state "laggard," it too has clearly developed many of the programs for support and service that we identify with the modern welfare state (Wilensky, 1975). The adoption of the programs and policies of the welfare state varies between nations in timing, administrative mechanisms, and the decision structures and processes. Moreover, these processes change over time, so that actors or groups that were once quite important in formulating welfare policy may be displaced or eliminated.

It is very clear that the 1960s led to the enactment of several policies and programs that provided greater income and services to the poor and elderly. Such programs as Medicare and Medicaid, the expansion of the food stamps program, and the increased federal component of AFDC, were part of an expanded commitment to the welfare state. What has been less clear and less commented upon has been the changes in the modes of making decisions and administering the welfare state. The purpose of this chapter is to begin to address two questions: Have there been important changes in the way we control and administer welfare policies? Have there been important changes in the structure of policymaking such that the performance of the welfare state is affected?

Answering these questions is part of my ongoing attempt to understand likely directions for the future of the welfare state (Zald, 1977). Obviously they are difficult questions, and we need some guidance before even beginning to think about them.

Independent of my efforts to understand the future of the welfare state, I have been developing a theoretical framework and a program of research for understanding the social control of industries. Drawing upon concepts and research from several disciplines (economics, law, political science, psychology, and sociology), the framework guides our thinking about how "society" sets norms for and attempts to control the performance of industries and groups of organizations, whether for profit or nonprofit, offering similar services and products to the society. The framework will be used here to guide our thinking about trends in the control and administration of welfare policy and output. After briefly sketching the framework, I will offer a number of interrelated propositions about those trends.

On the Social Control of Industries

One aspect of modern society relatively ignored by sociologists has been its use of administrative and organizational mechanisms to cope with the negative effects of technological change and the social problems of industry and organization. Sociologists have documented the rate of change and the fallout for individuals and communities, but we have left to political scientists and economists the study of the public and private governance of industry. Thus we have largely ignored the successful implementation of what Marx called "a modest magna carta," the whole achievement of the rights of workers at the workplace (but see Friedman and Ladinsky, 1967; and more recently Ratner, 1977). We have ignored the smooth operation of our regulatory mechanisms, which, for example, have led to a virtual absence of explosions of pressure boilers in commercial and group establishments, or, miracle of miracles, the regulatory process by which radio stations are allocated channels in a way to serve the public's interest in having clear reception. In recent years, my collaborators and I have conducted a number of studies designed to explore this process. The framework has been spelled out elsewhere in some detail (Zald, 1978); here, only a paragraph can be given to each of the major elements.

The components of analysis follow directly from a conception of social control and of industry and from a sociological perspective on the interaction of units in a social system. By definition, social control involves expectations of behavior or performance (for example, standards of behavior, rules of conduct, expectations of output) and the surveillance (evaluation) and sanction of deviation. Because in the first instance we are interested in the social control of industries, not individual organizations, we need a concept that describes industry performance; this is provided by the performance curve. Surveillance and sanction are conducted and imposed by differentiated units of the society, control agents. How control agents are mandated and operate and how they are controlled by other elements of the social system is treated in the sociology of control agents. If there were only one control agent for all of an industry's standards of behavior, we could eliminate analysis of the structural context of control (the organization of the control environment), but since there may be several control agents with overlapping jurisdictions, the organization of the control environment must be considered.

Finally, since a social system view implies interaction and feedback loops, we introduce the concept of compliance readiness and capacity. The target elements of the industry may have varying degrees of readiness to comply with or resist normative standards, and varying capabilities to comply with or resist the imposition of standards. They are not inert recipients of control attempts.

The core of the analysis consists of an explication of five interrelated conceptual clusters:

Structural context refers to the organization of the control agents. Some institutions exist in hierarchical contexts, others in polyarchic ones, and still others in market contexts, with coercive law at the boundary. The structural context shapes and limits the range of performance. Contexts can be described in terms of the number of control agents, the degree of their coordination and consensus, and their sanctions. In the welfare arena, as in many policy areas, a major issue is the balance between federal, state, and local agents in the determination of policy. Moreover, "societies" may choose to change contexts, for example by choosing to utilize market or hierarchical mechanisms.

Norms and performance curves. The organizations that comprise an institution, an industry, vary in their performance. The underlying norms vary in their clarity, their technical visibility, and the consensus about their importance among audiences and control agents. The shape of the performance curve is dependent upon both the clarity and precision of norms, and the strength of demand and sanctions for different levels of performance. Different control processes take place at upper and lower segments of the performance curve. In the welfare area, a concern with norms and performance curves leads us to ask: How has the amount and variance of welfare provision changed? How are the leaders and laggards in the provision of service rewarded or punished?

Control agents must interpret mandates from *their* controller and set operational norms, survey institutions for malperformance, and apply sanctions (incentives) to gain compliance. The multiple functions and limited resources of control agents mean they may have to come to terms with their organizational limits. Moreover, there may be competitive and indeed contradictory norms enforced by different control agents. Further, the division of labor amongst control agents may make one agent dependent upon another whose goals and imperatives are not supportive.

The surveillance capacity of control agents is partly based upon the extent to which performance can be measured and is permanent in its effect. *Sanctions* and *incentives* depend upon the intensity of the norms and the legitimacy and channels for gaining an authoritative position in the control process. Here we are concerned with identifying new control agents in the welfare arena, such as courts and client advocacy groups.

Compliance readiness (or capability) is an important dimension in social control studies because compliance is easily gained where the difference between the control agent and the target object is small. Compliance readiness, a term adapted from studies of the impact of judicial decisions, varies along two dimensions—ideological capability and organizational or economic capability. Compliance readiness deals with organizational resistance to and capabilities for implementing policies and programs. It should be apparent that welfare organizations, such as mental hospitals, correctional systems, or public assistance programs, may vary greatly in their capacity or readiness to change. The basic elements of the framework are diagrammed in Figure 3-1.

Before we proceed, several prefatory comments are in order. First, in this social system framework, a sharp distinction is not made between policymaking and policy implementation. New policy problems emerge from old policy implementation. Many of the same actors are involved, although to different degrees. Implementors have to interpret mandates, and the industries being controlled attempt to shape the policies that the implementors interpret. Second, the emphasis on social control and on norms does not assume a societal consensus about norms and the legitimacy of power holders. First, I would argue that norms are emergent and that total consensus between controllers and controlled over what the standards are or should be is rarely achieved. Second, I would argue that some of the major problematics in the relation between control agents and target elements are found in conflicts over what should be the norms and over the legitimacy of control agents attempting to enforce norms. Third, the idea of a performance curve can be used to cover compliance with a policy by bureaucratic agents or the actual impact of a policy upon social reality. In discussions of performance, it is important to be specific about what is being assessed. Finally, unlike a conventional analysis, which focuses on the logical sequence of policy-implementation-feedback as managed by designated organizational actors, this approach focuses on broader sys-

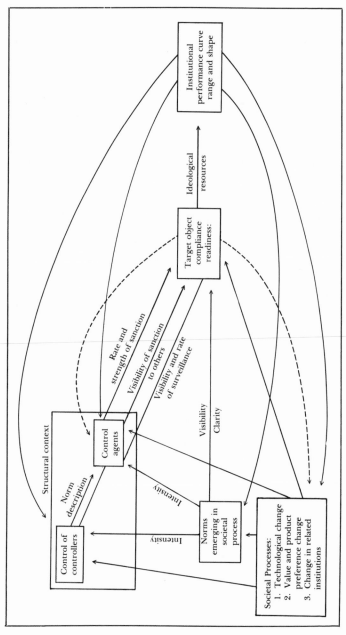

Figure 3-1. A Schematic Overview of the Framework

temic processes that cut across the conventional units used in policy analysis and organizational assessment.

Basic Trends and Their Implications

The basic trends I discuss concern how organs of society set norms for welfare policies, how new control agents have established their jurisdictions over areas of industry behavior that were previously immune to them, how formerly powerless groups have aggregated resources to become control agents, and how all these changes may have influenced the performance of the welfare state. In particular, I am concerned with the federalization of welfare policy, the growing intrusion of the courts into substantive issues in the state delivery of welfare, the rise of a politics of advocacy, and changing dilemmas in the administration of welfare.

THE FEDERALIZATION OF WELFARE POLICY

Over the last half century, the federalization of welfare policy has led to a decline in the variance between states in the access and provision of services and money to needy populations. Less clearly, it has also led to a decline in the variance of impoverishment and utilization rates between states. Skolnik and Dales (1976) present data on both the increasing size of the welfare state and on the composition of state, local, and federal expenditures for welfare. Between 1950 and 1975, total federal, state, and local expenditures for public welfare items increased 485 percent in constant dollars. Education expenditures increased 299 percent, while the core welfare areas of social insurance and public aid increased 744 percent and 451 percent respectively. More important here is the change in the composition of expenditures. In 1950, 43 percent of social insurance was provided through the federal fisc; by 1975, the figure was 80 percent. In 1950, 44 percent of public assistance came through the federal government; by 1975, 66 percent came through this source. Similar dramatic growths and shifts can be found for education and medical care. Even though education remains largely a state and local function in the American scheme of things, the growth of federal funding has had an enormous impact upon American schools. Indeed, as Orfield (1969) shows, the availability of federal funds for secondary and elementary schools accomplished what court orders alone could not: the desegregation of southern schools.

The federalization of social welfare policy reduces the variance between states in the provision of services to the poor and dependent through two different mechanisms. First, where federal law subsidizes specific programs that continue to be administered by the states, the federal government also establishes standards and criteria for the operation of specific programs. Thus, for instance, although unemployment compensation programs are administered by state agencies, they are webbed by federal law. Similar funding-administration arrangements hold for Medicaid and AFDC, though not for OASDI. In most cases the establishment of minimum criteria decreases the variance between states. Where programs are completely administered by the federal government, no state variance may remain.

Although federalization reduces the variance in the provision of services and money between the states, it may have less effect in reducing the variance in amounts of poverty between states. First, many federal social welfare programs are not sharply targeted on the poor. For instance, AFDC is more sharply targeted than is OASDI or unemployment compensation (see Appendix A in Plotnick and Skidmore, 1975, for a detailed comparison of programs). Thus programs with low focus may not affect poverty very much. Second, and more important here, the welfare programs in toto may have little impact upon regional and state variations in unemployment and poverty. If, for instance, one state has very little structural unemployment and has a high wage level, and another state has very high structural unemployment and a low wage level, the latter will obviously have a higher level of poverty. Only if welfare programs had very wide coverage over the range of impoverishment conditions, or were designed to impact heavily on high poverty–high unemployment areas, would they significantly reduce the variance in poverty caused by regional differences in economic opportunity.

The claims made for the consequences of federalization rest upon two underlying processes. First, because groups that are minorities in their own communities are able to have a greater impact at the national level, federal policy is more oriented towards the poor and minorities than are state and local policy. This has become the common sense of political wisdom. Thus, minimum standards are more likely to be raised by federal authorities than by state authorities.[1] Second, bureaucratic and legislative imperatives lead the federal government to develop more procedural consistency, requiring people in similar situations around the country to be treated in similar ways. Without eliminating all of the variance between states, the press is to the homogenization of benefits. Where complete federalization takes place, there is great pressure to treat people in similar situations alike. Where partial federalization takes place, through the use of federal subsidies and regulations, some state variation is allowed, even encouraged (since the federal government does not wish to substitute for state effort in these cases), yet the overall effect will be toward uniform standards among states.

FEDERALIZATION AND THE PRIVATE SECTOR

The growing presence of the state in the provision of welfare support has also had a large impact upon the provision of service by organizations not owned or controlled by government, profit-making and nonprofit alike. First, the existence of welfare payment policies provides opportunities for new agencies to come into existence. For instance, the growth of nursing homes and community mental health centers are largely a response to new sources of federal funding. Second, nursing homes, hospitals, family and children's services, and other providers find that they rely upon their direct grants from government agencies or upon third-party payments that are state-like in their imposition of reporting requirements and the criteria that are imposed for access, professional standards, accreditation and licensing of personnel, and the like. As agencies become more dependent upon public monies or upon third-party payments, they increasingly dance to the tune of the public piper. On the one hand, public monies represent opportunities for agencies existing in starved and insecure niches. Thus the existence of monies for new programs that an agency sees as fitting in with its broad mandate presents a siren call. On the other hand, becoming enmeshed in that web requires that agency accept the reporting criteria and the planning and evaluation requirements of the funding agencies.

This process may be just the latest step in the external rationalization of welfare agencies. Where in the early part of the century, community benefactors and groups might have casually supported and guided an agency or hospital, the growth of collective fund-raising agencies and community health and welfare councils began to bring organizations under external scrutiny. But I would hypothesize that the reporting and accountability criteria of these local councils did not require extensive reporting, evaluation, or planning. Although the growth of federal and third-party reporting and evaluation mechanisms may be artificial and relatively unrelated to quality of service and performance outcomes, agency staff and executives must nevertheless dance to its tune.

The term *federalization* covers a multitude of administrative arrangements. It may mean take-over, the transfer of state functions to federal agencies and the abolition of the state administrative apparatus. It may mean federal subsidization of specific programs, with federal guidelines, technical assistance, and programmatic control. It may mean general revenue sharing, with only the loosest control. In recent years, there has been little impetus to expand the federal government's role in *directly* providing services. Where organizations must provide services to clients, the tendency is to establish agencies under state, local or even private auspices, and to find a federal reimbursement formula for funding them. Nevertheless, a dilemma of control remains. In a loose sense, it can be characterized as a choice between central determination of policy and a tangle of bureaucracy to ensure compliance, or local control of policy and local definitions of need and choice. The more federal programs define categories of recipients and purposes of programs and funds, the larger the federal presence. But the alternative is federal subsidy without federal accountability.

The operation of welfare programs has also been affected in recent years by the politics of rights, the process by which legislatures and federal courts interpret constitutional mandates.

DUE PROCESS, THE POLITICS OF RIGHTS, AND WELFARE

There are three major aspects of the intervention of courts and legislatures into the operations of welfare agencies. Although they are not completely separable, they can be discussed under the headings of nondiscrimination or the protection of minority rights, due process, and substantive standards. All three involve interpreting the bearing of constitutional and juridical norms on public and private agencies; all three involve the penetration of legality deep into the operation of bureaucracies.

Legal norms aimed at eliminating the use of sex, race, and age as criteria for the allocation of benefits and positions have led to major modifications of institutional functioning. In some areas, these norms have thrown out long-established policies related to social welfare. For instance, the automatic assignment of children to their mothers when parents divorce is under attack, as is the assumption that fathers pay for the support of children and that mothers who leave them do not. The use of sex and fixed age provisions in the making of retirement decisions and the assignment of pension benefits is widely under attack. Discrimination against minorities in the allocation of welfare benefits has been effectively eliminated under the Fourteenth Amendment.

Due process norms have been imposed upon the operation of public educational, welfare, and health organizations. The maintenance of order within schools, the application of discipline, and the removal of students from schools have been subject to legislative and judicial mandates. Some states now require consultation with parents before students can be removed from classrooms or disciplined.

Appeal procedures are also mandated wherever welfare agencies control significant entitlements. As a general principle, whenever an organization's decision would deny significant entitlements, due process requirements lead organizations to develop formal procedures of representation and appeal. Moreover, agencies cannot without strong justification provide different types of service for different kinds of clients. For instance, federal law now mandates the mixing of handicapped with non-handicapped students, unless mixing would impose too great a hardship or educational disadvantage on the disabled student.

Due process and substantive issues may become intertwined. Thus the federal courts have imposed procedural constraints upon the use of involuntary admissions procedures to institutions for the retarded or mentally ill. They have also required public facilities offering services to these groups to meet minimal standards of humane care and professional treatment.

Changes in due process procedures may cause problems of morale and administrative confusion in the agencies upon which they are imposed, but I believe they rarely lead to large expenditure shifts. On the other hand, court-imposed substantive changes in the functioning of institutions may require massive changes in operating procedures and in budgets. Substantive change involves both the quality and quantity of personnel and facilities allocated to a function. In such cases the ability of state and local governments to allocate funds may be challenged; the priorities developed by elected officials or administrative agents are superseded by court-imposed requirements. Two examples: busing orders lead to an enlarged expenditure of funds for buses and drivers; and substantial changes in mental hospitals require larger numbers of professional and nonprofessional staff. In this sense, the growth of a politics of rights leads to a decline in the power of local officials, just as did the federalization of welfare policy.

Although the recent trends lead one to expect a continuation of the imposition of legal standards on administrative action, there are counter trends. Where the courts have become overwhelmed by the problem of deep intervention in agencies, they may retreat to less draconian sanctions. Similarly, where class-action suits were used to carry out the politics of rights, the courts may also overturn the court action. Politics intersects with caseloads, and the courts have been backing away from their easy access policy of a decade ago. But recent retrenchments in the use of courts should not be seen as the end of the story. In our society, the courts and the constitution are a major source of control and allocation of the rights of the poor and dispossessed. Given our constitutional structure, they are venues for strategies of change.

REPRESENTATION OF THE DISPOSSESSED

To be used as venues for change, courts must have plaintiffs. Judges, as control agents, are activated by claimants of wrongs. The dependent and dispossessed typically do not have the resources or capacities to press their own claims. The politics of rights is made possible or facilitated by the growth of organizations and groups devoted to the advocacy of the rights of the dispossessed. The 1960s and 1970s saw a marked upsurge in the number of such groups. Sometimes drawing upon people closely linked to the group at risk (for example, parents of retarded children, divorced fathers, homosexuals), at other times drawing upon individuals and organizations with less clear "interests" (such as public interest law firms, professional social welfare workers), these organizations take as their mandate the use of the courts, the media, and legislatures to raise the quality and quantity of goods and services allocated to their client populations.[2]

Even if the courts back off from allowing class-action intervention in the delivery of welfare services, there is no way that legislative and administrative bodies can avoid the attention and demands made by such groups. Indeed, recent trends opening up government to public input at both the legislative and administrative levels guarantee some access to interested parties. The democratization of access turns out to be a guarantee of pressure group access. Of course, groups will vary in their effectiveness and viability. They key ingredient becomes the ability of groups to sustain themselves in the hard schlog of winning concessions with few visible and dramatic rewards.

Because the clients of social welfare programs have typically been weak, dispossessed, and invisible, welfare politics in

America have had an ambivalent and cyclical character. Between periods of great reform, institutions and programs become invisible—out of sight, out of mind. At the same time, altruistic reformers and philanthropists might attempt to keep the light burning with little support. The growth of a politics of advocacy, if it is sustained, might keep some programs and institutions under more continuous scrutiny.

CONTROL AND COMPLIANCE

The trends discussed to this point suggest a decline in the influence of state and local legislative actors and an increase in the power of the courts and of federal legislators and administrators. Moreover, the line organizations delivering services and money are subject to a wider variety of interventions, and their practices and procedures are more visible to the outside. Nevertheless, substantial problems of compliance remain. Visibility and subsidization do not guarantee bureaucratic readiness or capability of compliance with the spirit and intent of client-serving norms. We can conceptualize two somewhat different dimensions of compliance readiness: ideological agreement or disagreement, and organizational capability or incapability. The former refers to the agreement of organizational elites and staff with the goals of welfare policy. The second refers to their capacity to implement the policy, regardless of their agreement with them. As a general proposition, the more a policy depends upon depth penetration of bureaucratic procedures, the less likely it is to be easily implemented. It is easy to change the amount of a welfare check (assuming that the money is in the bank); only the computer formula must be changed. It is difficult to change the attitudes and styles of classroom teachers, of case workers, or of ward attendants. To the extent that welfare organizations have multiple goals, have imprecise technologies, are dependent upon staff attitudes and values, and have decoupled procedures, we would expect changes in welfare programs and policies to be slow to be implemented, and distorted when they are.[3]

Moreover, where there is variance between agencies in their ideological and capability readiness, the introduction of new policies subsidizing or encouraging change may increase the variance in performance between agencies and the states in which they exist. Thus, for instance, an offer to subsidize some aspects of welfare programs may be quickly taken up by those agencies or states that already agree with the program or that have the capacity to respond to the offer, while those opposed to the policy or without capacity to respond lag even further behind.

A small school system or inadequately staffed mental health department may not have the personnel to respond to federal government program guidelines for requesting support; or they may not be prepared to meet the reporting requirements that accompany funding. Similarly, if elites are opposed to the intent of a program subsidy, they will not apply for funds where their more agreeable compeers will apply, thus increasing the variance between programs.

The Nation State and the Welfare State

The welfare state is one part of the modernization of the nation state throughout the world. The last two hundred years have seen a great interconnected revolution—the industrial revolution, which has massively increased the economic well-being of the populace, the power of the state to collect taxes and to control and allocate benefits, and the interdependence of nations in the world economy. On the long view, we would expect the state to continue to grow, the economy to expand, and interdependence to lead to new mechanisms of smoothing and interconnecting the flows of resources between nations. If that Panglossian projection is made, then the malaise of the seventies will turn out to be but a minor setback in a worldwide expansion of the welfare state. The service sector will continue to grow, a larger percent of GNP will be allocated to the welfare and dependency needs of the population, and concerns with accountability and effectiveness, which dominated the welfare scene in the late 1970s, will be seen as momentary penny-pinching in a long-range process of public beneficence.

But there are other scenarios. The percentage of our population over 65 will continue to grow for the next fifty years, and a greater percentage of our income will be devoted to social security and medical care. It is not clear that economic growth in the United States will return to the levels of the 1950s and 1960s. It is not clear that inflation can be effectively managed in our polyarchic, neither-market-nor-command economy.

These politico-economic trends intersect with trends in the control and administration of the welfare state. Revenue sharing is an optimistic policy; it depends upon growth and largesse. Judges will hesitate to intervene in city budget decisions to help the downtrodden, if cities and states are going bankrupt. Welfare needs of dependent populations will take a back seat to more central issues of maintaining the welfare of the whole population, if maintaining the welfare of the whole population seems to be problematic. Even the functioning of the politics of advocacy depends upon the ability of advocate groups to raise funds. Under a really bad scenario, that ability might be squashed, and the invisible clients would become invisible once more.

Politicians are allowed false promises and catchy campaign slogans; scholars have to content themselves with statements of contingent relations. The welfare state is here and well established. Its central programs will continue in place and some will continue to grow. Yet the slowdown in economic growth and continuing inflation curb the most ambitious proponents. They also curb the spread of federalization. And when federalization occurs, the lowest cost solutions will be sought.

Trends in the administration and transformation of the welfare state must ultimately be set in the larger context of national and international politics and economics. For now, we only claim to have raised the issues.[4]

Notes

1. But as Leon Epstein (1978) notes, states may lead the nation on issues where minorities or advocates are strong in a state but weak nationally. Indeed, as we enter a period in which the welfare state is being consolidated and retrenched at the national level, variance may be increased by the establishment of new programs at the state level.

2. See Joel Handler (1978) for a discussion of the public interest law firms' resource needs in conducting legal battles. See Olson (1975), Salisbury (1969), and McCarthy and Zald (1977, 1973) for the problems of mobilizing groups.

3. See Handler (1978) for a discussion of bureaucratic contingencies that impede or facilitate organizational response to normative demands for change.

4. I am indebted to Daniel Steinmetz for criticism of an earlier version.

References

Epstein, Leon. "The Old State in a New System." In Anthony King, ed., *The New American Political System*, pp. 325–70. Washington, D.C.: American Enterprises Institute, 1978.

Friedman, Lawrence M., and Jack Ladinsky. "Social Change and the Law of Industrial Accidents." *Columbia Law Review* 67 (1967).

Handler, Joel. *Social Movements and the Legal System*. New York: Academic Press, 1978.

McCarthy, John D., and Mayer N. Zald. *The Trend of Social Movements in America: Resource Mobilization and Professionalization*. Morristown, N.J.: General Learning Press, 1973.

———. "Resource Mobilization and Social Movements: A Partial Theory." *American Journal of Sociology* 82 (May 1977): 1212–41.

Olson, Mancur. *The Logic of Collective Action*. Cambridge, Mass.: Harvard University Press, 1965.

Orfield, Gary. *The Reconstruction of Southern Education: The Schools and the 1964 Civil Rights Act*. New York: Wiley, 1969.

Plotnick, Robert D., and Felicity

Skidmore. *Progress against Poverty: A Review of the 1964–74 Decade*. New York: Academic Press, 1975.

Ratner, Ronnie Steinberg. *A Modest Magna Charta: The Rise and Growth of Wage and Hour Standards Laws in the United States, 1900–1973; an Indicators Approach*. New York University: Ph.D. diss., 1977.

Salisbury, Robert A. "An Exchange Theory of Interest Groups." *Midwest Journal of Political Science* 13 (Feb. 1969): 1–32.

Skolnick, Alfred M., and Sophia Dales. "Social Welfare Expenditures, 1950–75." *Social Security Bulletin* 39 (Jan. 1976): 3–20.

Wilensky, Harold L. *The Welfare State and Equality: Structural Roots of Public Expenditures*. Berkeley, Cal.: University of California Press, 1975.

Zald, Mayer N. "Demographic Politics and the Future of the Welfare State." *Social Service Review* 51 (March 1977): 110–24.

———"On the Social Control of Industries." *Social Forces* 57 (Sept. 1978): 79–102.

Chapter 4.

Evolutionary Theory as a Backdrop

For Administrative Practice

Karl E. Weick

Many theories of organization are modeled after biological versions of evolutionary theory (e.g., Kaufman, 1975; Jantsch and Waddington, 1976; Ruse, 1974; Freeman, 1974; Bennett, 1976; Alexander, 1975; Aldrich and Pfeffer, 1976; Dunn, 1971; Stebbins, 1965; Bigelow, 1978). Evolutionary thinking does engage some realities of organizations, but the insights provided so far by this form of thinking have been limited because investigators have been concerned with only the most obvious parallels. This chapter proposes to fine-tune the fit between theories of natural selection and properties of organizations, so that more nuances can be derived from the parallelism and so that a greater range of implications for policy and practice can be deduced. It will be argued that discussions of evolution in organizations have been unnecessarily handicapped by four assumptions: (1) Preexisting environments rather than enacted environments exert selective pressure. (2) Natural selection rather than artificial selection is the appropriate metaphor. (3) Variation is abundant rather than problematic in organizations. (4) The pace of evolution is slow, constant, and incommensurate in scale with the pace of organizational activities. Before discussing these assumptions, we will

Preparation of this chapter was supported in part by the National Science Foundation through Grant BNS75-09864. Portions of the argument are adapted from Karl E. Weick, *The Social Psychology of Organizing*, 2nd ed. (Reading, Mass.: Addison-Wesley, 1979).

review briefly the basic features of evolutionary epistemology as applied to organizations.

The Essentials of Evolution

Donald T. Campbell is one of the most vigorous contemporary exponents of an evolutionary model adapted to social behavior, and this section relies heavily on his thinking. The essential ideas are these: (1) three processes—variation, selection, and retention—are responsible for evolution; (2) variations in behaviors and genetic mutations are haphazard, and those variations are selected and retained that enhance, momentarily, adaptation; (3) the processes of variation and retention are opposed; (4) it is unnecessary to resort to such concepts as "plan" or "external guidance" to explain the course of evolution; (5) moderate rates of mutation are necessary for survival and for evolutionary advantage; (6) in complex systems, the majority of the mechanisms activated at any time tend to curb rather than promote variations; (7) any order that appears is due to the hindsight of a selection system and not to foresighted variations; (8) evolution is essentially opportunistic—current advantages outweigh long-run disadvantages in determining survival; (9) characteristics are judged adaptive, in biological evolution, if they increase the reproductive chances of the possessor; and (10) evolution can be thought of as a winnowing model.

EVOLUTION AMENDED FOR ORGANIZATIONS

The four elements associated with organizational evolution are ecological change, enactment, selection, and retention.

Ecological change. Within the flows of experience that engage people and activities, changes frequently occur. These changes may provide the occasion for attempts to remove equivocality and to determine the significance of the changes. Ecological changes provide the *enactable environment*, the raw materials for organizational sense-making. Ecological changes normally would be said to provide raw materials, except that previously enacted environments often provide sufficient materials for sense-making. This initial phase is called ecological change to emphasize that people normally are not aware of things that run smoothly. It is only the occasion of change that draws attention.

Enactment. Enactment is to organizing as variation is to natural selection. The term enactment is preferred over variation because it captures the more active role that we presume members of organizations play in creating their environments. Enactment is intimately bound up with ecological change. When changes occur in the stream of experience, the actor may take some action to isolate them for inspection. That action of bracketing is one form of enactment. The other form occurs when the actor produces an ecological change that then constrains his subsequent actions. For example, farmers with heavy tractors enact the packed earth (ecological change) that requires heavier tractors, more fuel, deeper plows, and wider tires to work. The presence of elaborate multi-track mixers in recording studios has compelled engineers to produce increasingly elaborate effects in recordings, which leads to demands for even more elaborate mixing equipment. Many listeners, however, have become fed up with this meddling and are now purchasing direct-to-disc music that bypasses the engineer with his busy hands, his passion for remixing, his elaborate technology, and his precious output (McDonough, 1978). Nevertheless, engineers have enacted the environment of contrived music that now organizes and threatens to disorganize their jobs. Physicians, through unsubtle diagnostic procedures ("Hmmm, when did you start holding your head at that angle?"), often create maladies that weren't there when the examination began. Their procedures consolidate numerous free-floating symptoms into the felt presence of a single, specific, serious problem. Physician-induced disease is a perfect example of people creating the environment that confronts them (Scheff, 1965). The activity of enactment parallels variation, because it produces strange actions that are often unlike anything that the individual or the organization have seen before.

Selection. Selection involves imposing various structures of equivocal actions in an attempt to reduce their equivocality. These imposed structures often take the form of cause maps (Bougon, Weick, and Binkhorst, 1977) that are built up out of past experience and that contain interconnected variables. When these maps, which have proven sensible on previous occasions, are superimposed on current puzzling displays, they may provide a reasonable interpretation of what has occurred.

Any equivocal enactment is a potential figure-ground arrangement. The act of selection involves both differentiating alternative figures from the ground (equivocal enactments by definition can be read in a variety of ways) and stabilizing a figure-ground arrangement or limited set of arrangements that is reasonably clear and that allows continued living. In organization, selection processes involve schemes of interpretation, in that some cause maps help reduce equivocality, while others add to it. Helpful maps tend to be selected, the rest tend to be eliminated. In addition, interpretations of the equivocal display also are selected and are retained for possible imposition on similar, future situations.

Retention. Retention involves storage of the products of successful sense-making, to create *enacted environments.* An enacted environment is a punctuated and connected summary of a previously equivocal enactment. It is a sensible version of what was previously equivocal, although other versions could have been constructed.

The terms enacted environment and cause map refer to retained content. Each phrase captures a slightly different nuance of what is retained. Enacted environments are outputs of, not inputs to, organizing. The enactment process itself segregates possible environments that the organization could clarify and take seriously, but whether it actually does so is determined in the selection processes. Boundaries between organizations and the environment are never quite as clear or stable as many organizational theorists think. These boundaries shift, disappear, and are arbitrarily drawn. Organizations create environments out of puzzling surroundings; these meaningful environments emerge quite late in organizing processes.

The label *cause map*, which characterizes retained content, emphasizes that retained content is organized and stored in the form of variables connected by causal relationships. These maps summarize covariations between labeled portions of the formerly equivocal display. These maps resemble Schutz's (1964) recipes because they allow people to interpret a situation and to express themselves in that situation and be understood by others.

THE ARRANGEMENT OF EVOLUTIONARY PROCESSES

The four evolutionary processes are presumed to be arranged in the following manner:

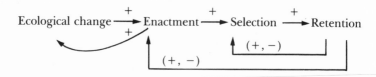

(1) Ecological change and enactment are linked causally in a deviation amplifying circuit; (2) enactment is linked to selection by a direct causal relationship, indicating that the volume of enactment will have a direct effect on the volume of selection activity; (3) likewise, selection has a direct effect on retention—an increase in selection activity will trigger a corresponding increase in retention activity; (4) retention affects both selection and enactment, and these effects can be either direct or inverse, depending on whether the person decides to trust (+) or disbelieve (−) his past experience.

This sequence can be illustrated by a recipe for sense-making and a visual device. The sense-making recipe reads: How can I know what I think until I see what I say? Organizations talk to themselves over and over to find out what they're thinking. The basic recipe coordinates with organizing in the following manner:

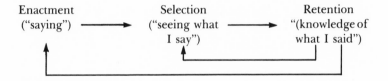

The organization enacts equivocal raw talk, the talk is viewed retrospectively and sense is made of it, and this sense is then stored as knowledge in the retention process. The aim of each process has been to reduce equivocality and to get some idea of what has occurred.

Depicting these processes as linear and sequential may be misleading. The image of a field may be more appropriate (Lana, 1969, ch. 5). Perhaps the best way to loosen this rigid sequential image is to adapt a clever graphic device that William James used (1950, vol. 1, p. 283). If we make a wooden frame with the organizing processes written on the front and a time scale on one side, then spread a sheet of India rubber on which rectangular coordinates are painted over its top, and slide a smooth ball under the rubber from 0 to the word "retention," the bulging of the membrane along this diagonal at successive moments will symbolize the changing content of the organizing process.

This visualization shows a progression from enactment through selection to retention, but also that one process shades into another. More than one process is active at any time. The illustration is even richer when we vary the size of the ball (signifying greater and lesser equivocality), the speed at which the ball moves (swift passage is associated with routine, unequivocal inputs), the pliability of the rubber sheet (very stiff rubber is equivalent to thick sets of assembly rules that allow inputs to have minimal impacts), the spacing of the three words on the front board, and so forth. A stack of these frames, each one having different dimensions, different pliability of rubber, and different sized balls, each with a ball located at a different point on the diagonal, would represent a frozen moment in an organizational structure.

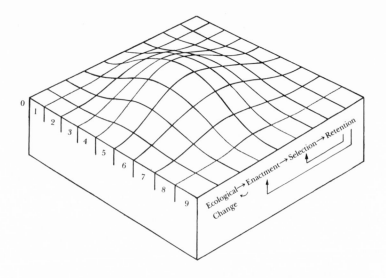

The Assumption of Environmental Creation

Organisms often create their niche or environment (Lewontin, 1978, p. 215). Because very few discussions of evolution in organizations incorporate this, evolutionary arguments addressed to policy issues have been limited. If the enacted quality of environments is given more attention, it will become evident that administrators impose much that imposes on them. Administrators are not docile recipients of environmental inputs; rather, they actively implant much that they have to contend with.

To appreciate this conception of natural selection, we must first view the environment as an output rather than as an input. On the basis of enactments and interpretations, people construct a picture of an environment that could have produced those actions. However, the environment chosen did not necessarily determine the actions and the sense-making, because it appears after the fact as an explanation for what has occurred. Once the enacted environment exists, it guides subsequent actions and interpretations. An enacted environment is a historical document, stored in the retention process, usually in the form of a cause map, that can be superimposed on subsequent activities. Thus in one sense the product, outcome, or goal of any organization is to produce stable interpretations of equivocal displays.

Most of what is contained in retention consists of enacted environments stored in the form of labeled, causally connected variables. These enacted environments act as surrogates for the external world by guiding actors' selections of interpretations. When the enacted environment constrains selection, it *is* an environment into which events being processed and labeled exhibit a better or worse fit. Here the analogy of individuals and species fitting into particular physical environments is instructive. During selection, organizational members select those labels, explanations, interpretations, and meanings that allow new enactments to be fitted into old (enacted) environments. The enacted environment, in other words, acts as stand-in for and editor of the physical environment. The physical environment could be said to delegate its selective function to the selection process and to the enacted environments stored in retention.

In this line of argument, the phrase "survival of the fittest" means that what survives from any confrontation with ecological change are people, events, and actions that, when labeled, find a place in existing cause maps. Survival takes this form only if retention is *credited* in selection. If retention is discredited, then people, events, and actions that differ from previously enacted environments will be given greater attention, fresher labels, and newer connections, and have more likelihood of being stored where they will then assimilate and accommodate to whatever content remains in retention.

Thus the enacted environment, not the physical environment, is the selector.

ENVIRONMENT AS INFERENCE

Not only are environments outputs of sense-making and retrospective constructions, they often do not even involve direct experience. Consider one of Piet Hein's Grooks:

Our so-called limitations, I believe,
Apply to faculties we don't apply.
We don't discover what we can't achieve
Until we make an effort not to try. (Hein, 1968, p. 33.)

Perceptions of personal limitations amount to failing to act, rather than failing while acting. Limitations are deceptive conclusions based on presumption rather than on action. On the basis of avoided tests, people conclude that constraints exist in the environment and that limits exist in their repertoire of responses, and thus justify inaction. These constraints become self-imposed restrictions on the options that managers will consider and exercise. When constraints are breached by someone who is doubting, naive, or uninformed, they often generate sizeable advantages for the breacher.

As a laboratory exercise, Harold Garfinkel had some of his students offer a small fraction of the list price for some item in a department store. The students were apprehensive about doing this, since a rule presumed to exist in most American stores is that things must be bought for the list price. Much to their surprise, the students discovered that once they began to bargain they were able to get rather substantial reductions. The list price "rule" seems to exist only because everyone expects to follow it and no one challenges it. Garfinkel expands this observation to a more general statement about knowledge based on avoided tests.

> If upon the arousal of troubled feelings persons avoid tinkering with these "standardized" expectancies [such as the rule that things must be bought for the list price] the standardization could consist of an *attributed* standardization that is supported by the fact that persons avoid the very situations in which they might learn about them. Lay as well as professional knowledge of the nature of the rule governed actions and the consequences of breaching the rules is prominently based on just such procedure. Indeed, the more important the rule, the greater is the likelihood that knowledge is based on avoided tests. Strange findings must certainly await anyone who examines the expectancies that make

up routine backgrounds of common place activities for
they have rarely been exposed by investigators even to
as much revision as an imaginative rehearsal of their
breach would produce. (1967, p. 70.)

Much of the substance of organizations may consist of spurious knowledge based on avoided tests. Administrators often
know much less about their environments and organizations
than they think. One reason for this is that they unwittingly
collude among themselves to avoid tests. They build elaborate
explanations of why tests should be avoided, why one should
not or could not act in settings presumed to be dangerous. The
disbeliever, the unindoctrinated, and the newcomer will all
wade in where avoiders fear to tread. If they find that the
avoiders' fear is valid, their demise provides vicarious learning
for the avoiders.

The point is that the enormous amount of talk, socializing,
consensus-building, and vicarious learning that goes on
among administrators often results in pluralistic ignorance
about the environment (Shaw and Blum, 1965). Stunted enactment is the reason. Each person watches someone else avoid
certain procedures, goals, and activities, and concludes that
this avoidance is motivated by real noxiants in the environment. The observer profits by avoiding the same acts. As this
sequence is repeated, managers believe that they know more
and more about something that none of them has ever experienced first-hand. This belief is strengthened because everyone
seems to be seeing and avoiding the same things.

To change their environments, people must change themselves and their actions, not someone else. Repeated failures of
organizations to solve their problems are partially explained by
their failure to understand their own prominence in their own
environments. Problems never get solved because managers
tinker with everything but what they do.

ENVIRONMENT AS CONSTRUCTION

The way in which State Department administrators enacted an
environment of incompetence among Foreign Service officers
demonstrates how selective pressure in organizations comes

from constructed rather than preexisting environments (War-wick, 1975).

In July 1965, Deputy Undersecretary of State for Administration William Crockett launched an attempt to reorganize the State Department by reducing the number of hierarchical layers, increasing the autonomous decisionmaking, and decentralizing key functions. One group within the State Department, the Foreign Service officers, did much to undermine this change. Their actions were not intentionally malicious, but they illustrate the inevitable result of linking events together as self-fulfilling prophecies.

The Foreign Service officers are an elite corps within the State Department. Members hold many key policymaking positions in Washington and they also serve as the chiefs and deputy chiefs of the embassies. They pride themselves on being substantive generalists, astute political reporters, and adept negotiators. Their norms are traditional and elitist; they rely heavily on a diplomatic approach to problems, which means that they value subtlety, skill in negotiation, cultural sophistication, and good manners. The pinnacle of this career hierarchy is to be an ambassador.

Given the self-contained, almost guild-like nature of this unit, it should not be surprising to learn that new political appointees to the State Department see the officers as insular, aloof, and uncooperative. The officers, in turn, worry about the newcomers being uninformed, unappreciative of subtleties in diplomacy, and likely to underestimate the importance of Foreign Service officers. In short, the Foreign Service officers enact a hostile environment. Newcomers conclude that they produce little that is creative or progressive, and so avoid involving the Foreign Service in any plans or programs for change. The officers, in turn, become offended when they are excluded from planning and become more suspicious of ideas or suggestions that impinge on their areas of expertise. As a result, members of the service cling even more tightly to the key element in their self-definition within the agency, namely, the traditional concept of diplomacy. When the Foreign Service officers behave defensively, they confirm the newcomers' initial impressions, leading them to pay even less attention to the ideas of the officers.

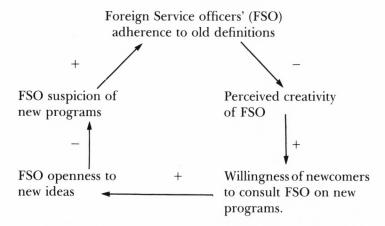

Each subgroup enacts its own hostile environment, then finds itself constrained by the very naiveté and bungling that it projected in the first place. Each subgroup enacts the incompetent environment that it faces. Each subgroup can argue self-righteously that it would be more effective were it not for the incompetent people through whom its intentions have to be mediated. What is not noticed is that this incompetence was enacted by those who so perceived it.

The Assumption of Artificial Selection

To appreciate the form that selection takes in organizations, we must reexamine the nature of selection in biological evolution. Domestic animals exist in bewildering variety; some of this variety is produced by people who select and breed stock. Through the breeder's interventions, groups develop that are characterized by novel properties. If an intelligent agent making choices were not present, could the same shaping process occur? Darwin demonstrated that differential reproductive success is a natural selection device that acts much like the breeder who methodically intervenes (in DeBeer, 1958). Darwin argued that "organisms differ from one another. They produce more young than the available resources can sustain. Those best suited to survive pass on the expedient properties to their offspring, while inferior forms are eliminated. Subsequent generations therefore are most like the better adapted ancestors and the result is a gradual modification, or evolution" (Ghiselin, 1969, p. 46). In natural selection, the environment favors the reproduction of some mutations and the destruction of others. The fitting, failing, mutating, and reproducing is unguided or random.

In organizations, selection is guided less by caprice than by the intention of people to be methodical, deliberate, and plausible; to act, in short, like breeders rather than crapshooters. Intentions commonly fail (Salancik, 1977), so that organizational selection often exhibits the same haphazard quality associated with natural selection. But haphazard moments in organizations are byproducts of bounded rationality applied by fallible rationalizers. Ideas and interpretations, as much as things, exert selective force in organizations. If perceptions are important in the functioning of organization, then there must be a mechanism whereby perceptual environments confer differential advantages on people, positions, or pluralities. The enacted environment, imposed on action and interpretation by selection and enactment, supplies this mechanism. The enacted environment is artificial in the sense that it is laced with preferences, purposes, idiosyncratic punctuations, desires, selective perceptions, and designs. It is the environment of the breeder.

ENACTED ENVIRONMENTS AS ARTIFICIAL SELECTION MECHANISMS

When people in organizations select actions and interpretations, they try to select reasonably, even if they have only modest success doing so. In their attempts to be reasonable, people impose previous interpretations of causal sequences that have worked, that is, cause maps of previously enacted environments. When current equivocalities are filtered through these prior enactments, some things go unnoticed while others are labeled familiar, strange, relevant, and so forth. In all cases the enacted environment is a surrogate for the natural environment. These enacted versions of reality supply the rocks, pools, edges, nutrients, shade, and enemies among which people with equivocal power and equivocal positions fit with varying degrees of success.

The enacted environment acts as the natural environment only when it is unequivocal and credited, only when people who are trying to understand a current equivocal input compose a selection process using many rules and few cycles and treat the incoming input as a known rather than an unknown commodity. Or, in the case of the enactment process, a person who credits an unequivocal enacted environment does what he has done before, regardless of current ecological changes. Credited enactment will appear to be stereotypic and routinized, and will resemble a standard operating procedure. Crediting of past enacted environments can readily undo, reverse, or modify ecological changes. Thus, in organizing, enacted environments can dominate objective environments.

This conservative portrait of selection suggests why organizations show inertia. Actions and interpretations are conformed to enacted environments, not to current natural environments. People try to fit novel interpretations and actions into what they've known all along; when something doesn't fit with the past, it's often discarded or misread. That suggests why newcomers, entrepreneurs, marginal men, outsiders, hatchet men, and other anomalies are crucial sources of innovation (Rickards and Freedman, 1978).

John Child (1972) has similarly argued that environmental influences may not exert an overwhelming constraint on organizations, because decisionmakers are often loosely coupled with environments. Just like animal breeders, decisionmakers can select among several structures, all of which are appropriate in their present environmental niche; choose the type of environment in which they exist; reshape their environment; and improve the accuracy of their perceptions of the environment, thereby enhancing their capacity to control it. Here the unmediated environment is not the major source of selection criteria, or if it is, its influence can be softened.

If decisionmakers intervene between the environment and its effects inside the organization, then selection criteria become lodged more in the actors than in the environment. What the actors attend to and enact, the cues they use, their reasons for using those cues, their patterns of inattention, and their processes for scanning and monitoring all become selection criteria. Administrators act in ways similar to artificial selection.

The Assumption of Variability

There is no shortage of variation in biological systems, but the same does not hold true for organizations. Despite the apparent abundance of individual differences, pressures for innovation, and mavericks, organizations' thin pool of positive mutations is limited. This is because people see things as being more orderly than they actually are, and because people are unwilling to discredit past experience as a prescription for the future. In both cases, current adaptation precludes future adaptability. Administrators must deal with this somewhat novel problem in evolution as it intrudes into human organizations. We will examine, in turn, the misperception of disorder and the hesitance to doubt.

THE MISPERCEPTION OF DISORDER

In the formula, "How can I know what I think till I see what I say?" saying (enactment) can itself be clear or vague. Interpretations can vary dramatically. Because enactment can produce variable raw materials for selection to process, some material can already be sensible by the time it is intercepted by a selection process.

Enactments often consist of trial-and-error behavior. The ecological changes present when trial and error is undertaken seem to favor certain forms of action, forms that have been variously described as structural looseness (Bidwell, 1965), loose coupling (March and Olsen, 1976; Weick, 1976), plasticity (Gould, 1975), and defenses in depth (Bateson, 1972). McAdams describes ecological changes that dominate in social environments, noting in particular that there is a high premium "on the capacity of a social system to make rapid, large-scale adaptive shifts in order to cope with unanticipated conditions. There would also appear to be a premium on structural fluidity and ambiguity that would permit alternative, even opposed, adaptive strategies to coexist. From this point of view there are selective advantages accruing to human social systems that foster and protect innovation, pluralistic differentiation, tolerance of divergence, skepticism toward received wisdom and tradition, dissidence with respect to institutionalized leadership, and even alienation" (1976, p. 351).

Whatever people do during enactment—whether it be operating without goals, misplacing personnel, operating a technology that no one understands, improvising instead of forecasting, dwelling on opportunities, inventing rather than borrowing solutions, cultivating impermanence, arguing, or doubting—if those "strange" actions promote rapid adaptation to shifting conditions, they're likely to become frequent inputs to the selection process.

By their very nature, these contradictory, hypocritical, disorganized, casual actions epitomize equivocality even as they epitomize adaptability. This creates problems, because when selection processes try to make sense of these underorganized enactments they may remove the very adaptability that makes them valuable.

Our concern about the difficulty of preserving loosely coupled enactments is not idle, because one of the most common perceptual errors is the overestimation of an input's unity, orderliness, and clarity. This tendency has been known for a long time. It is preserved in Bacon's "Idols of the Tribe," the first of which reads: "The human understanding, from its peculiar nature, easily supposes a greater degree of order and equality in things than it really finds" (cited in Campbell, 1959, p. 5).

The problem for adapting organizations is that structurally loose enactment is apt to be misread and "tightened" during the reflection that accompanies selection. The perceiver will imagine that a more orderly action was responsible for adaptive success than in fact was the case. Perceptually, the problem for organizations is not entropy but its opposite. Orderliness is overestimated and erroneously credited for adaptive success. Having been credited, orderly actions are implemented again in the future, perhaps tightened even more, and suddenly the organization finds itself out of touch with changes and saddled with an antiquated, tight structure.

THE RELUCTANCE TO DOUBT

Has any organization ever failed to survive because it forgot something important? More likely organizations fail because they remember too much too long and persist too often doing things the way they've always done them. Organizations seldom fail because their memories fail them.

A good example of this is Albert Speer's theory of organizational change. Speer, Adolf Hitler's Minister of Armaments and War, wrote about organizations in his book *Inside the Third Reich*. Speer made strong efforts to debureaucratize his ministry and to create loosely coupled temporary organizational structures that could be swiftly assembled and disassembled. He continually tried to simplify administrative procedures, to do away with the chain of command, and to cut down on requirements for record keeping by allowing his people to make informal verbal agreements.

The strategy that seemed most helpful in accomplishing these changes was to take advantage of Allied bombing raids. "These raids were 'helpful,' according to Speer, because they destroyed the filing facilities, those containers of paper which enable organizations to establish traditions, procedures, and so on, which are mainstays of bureaucracy. Speer was so enamored with the results of these bombing raids that, upon learning of the destruction of his ministry in the Allied air raid of November 22, 1943, he commented: 'Although we have been fortunate in that large parts of the current files of the Ministry have been burned and so relieved us for a time of useless ballast, we cannot really expect that such events will continually introduce the necessary fresh air into our work' " (Singer and Wooton, 1976, pp. 86–87).

Retained information is sacred in most organizations. This means that routines, standard operating procedures, and grooved thinking work against the organization's ability to discredit its past knowledge (Steinbruner, 1974). During the

Cuban missile crisis, the Kennedy Administration tried to persuade the Navy to conduct a custom-made blockade unlike any it had done before. Repeatedly Kennedy people ran into the response that the Navy knew how to conduct blockades and that civilians shouldn't tamper with the routine.

"At one point MacNamara asked Anderson [Chief of Naval Operations] what he would do if a Soviet ship's captain refused to answer questions about his cargo [if naval officers intercepted a vessel and boarded it]. At that point the Navy man picked up the *Manual of Naval Regulations* and, waving it in MacNamara's face, shouted, 'It's all in there.' To which MacNamara replied, 'I don't give a damn what John Paul Jones would have done. I want to know what you're going to do, now.' The encounter ended on Anderson's remark: 'Now, Mr. Secretary, if you and your deputy will go back to your offices, the Navy will run the blockade' " (Allison, 1971, pp. 131–32).

The thick layering of routines coupled with the fact that departures from routine increase vulnerability mean that in most organizations discrediting is rare. Consider that organizations are said to be accountable and that, at least in the eyes of their stockholders, banks, and security analysts, they must give the impression that everything is going fine and that the organization knows what it's doing. Constituencies pressure organizations to give evidence that their past definitions are accurate, that they know what is up, and they know how to cope with it. Outsiders treated doubt, hesitation, and reevaluation of past enactments as evidence that an organization is unsure of itself, rather than as evidence that it is reflecting, preserving adaptability, or preparing for an even more diverse set of circumstances. The moral seems to be that if you're going to discredit, keep quiet about it.

Anything that heightens commitment to an organization should decrease the likelihood of discrediting (Kiesler, 1971, Salancik, 1977). Since most managers continually have to justify the existence of their own subgroups when arguing for personnel and money, the commitment that develops as a byproduct of these arguments works against discrediting, doubting, or suspecting one's view of the world. Furthermore, most organizations favor "the school of hard knocks" over vicarious learning. M.B.A. students, for example, are not taken seriously until they are seasoned and learn what the "real world" is like. Any organization that values hands-on or first-hand experience finds it very difficult to say that that very same direct experience may be fallible, unreliable, or misleading.

Another thing that works against discrediting is the gradual buildup of confidence over time. For example, policemen are in the most danger of being killed during their fifth year on the police force. This appears to be the point where confidence peaks, where they believe that they have already encountered most problems in one form or another. This tempts them to relax enough to become more vulnerable. Dailey (1971) has demonstrated that performance suddenly drops about two-thirds of the way through judgment exercises, even if it had been improving steadily. The explanation for this is that as confidence increases a person pays less attention to details, so that crucial items eventually go unnoticed. In both cases discrediting seems to be at a minimum.

Having described reasons why doubt is difficult, we should balance the picture by describing why it is also desirable. Discrediting makes sense partly because lessons from experience are usually dated. They can't really escape this fate because the world in which they were learned changes discontinuously. Discrediting simply means that every retained experience can be thrown into different figure ground patterns because it has surplus meaning. A single reading of selected enactments does not exhaust their possibilities. Discrediting is also a crucial internal source of novelty when novelty cannot be borrowed from outsiders (Jacob, 1977).

Another argument for discrediting is that the relationships between many variables in a cause map are curvilinear rather than linear. A curvilinear world is the reality to which discrediting makes sense.

Suppose we take the relationship between criticisms received and quality of performance and store this connection in a cause map as a direct relationship: as criticisms increase, the quality of performance also increases. That summary conceals the operation of at least two contradictory processes. As criticisms increase, a person expends more energy to improve

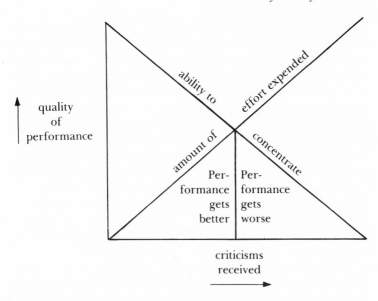

performance. The greater the number of criticisms, the greater the effort. However, as criticisms increase it also becomes harder to concentrate because the criticisms are distracting. Thus, as criticisms increase there is a decrease in concentration. When combined, these two relationships begin to cancel one another. As criticisms first start to increase, the person exerts more effort; concentration is already quite high, and quality improves. As the criticisms continue to increase there comes a point where the additional increments of effort are canceled because the person can't concentrate. Beyond this point, the greater the number of criticisms, the lower the quality of performance.

Part of the time criticisms raise quality, part of the time they lower quality. That's a curvilinear relationship. If it is stored in a cause map as linear and if it is discredited, then a person will act partly as if criticisms help performance and partly as if they hinder it. That split evaluation, applied to an oversimplified summary, captures the entire range of variation for criticism and quality. That is how discrediting linear causal sequences promotes adaptation to non-linear contingencies.

Because curvilinear relationships are complicated to process, remember, and act upon, it is probable that when people build cause maps they build them using linear rather than curvilinear relationships. The act of discrediting linear relationships reintroduces complexity and undoes the simplification, thereby facilitating adaptation.

Discrediting also makes sense because most retained experience contains surplus meaning. Cause maps simplify the fine grain of experience, so that any experience can withstand considerable discrediting because initial interpretations don't exhaust meanings. Retained experience retains surplus meaning; this is how both crediting and discrediting are warranted and reasonable. Surplus meaning justifies discrediting, a typified meaning justifies crediting, and both are true at the same time.

A final virtue of discrediting is that it serves to complicate people. Any person who has a view of the world and also discredits part of that view winds up with two ways to examine a situation. Discrediting is a way to enhance requisite variety and to register more of the variety present in the world. Consider a common situation discussed by dissonance theorists (Wicklund and Brehm, 1976). Many people believe that the greater the amount of smoking, the greater the likelihood of lung cancer. Those two variables are related strongly in a positive direction. That enacted environment, however, is often discredited when people who believe in it continue to smoke. Such people are more complicated than the individual who smokes and disbelieves in the linkage or who doesn't smoke and believes in the linkage.

The complication is this. The smoker-believer simultaneously acts as if smoking causes lung cancer and as if it does not. Both assertions are true. Smoking does cause lung cancer in that high volumes of tobacco intake increase the likelihood of lung cancer. Smoking does not cause cancer in that its effects may be overridden by other factors in the environment surrounding smokers. The stream of experience to which are attached the labels smoking and cancer is equivocal. If smoking is both credited and discredited as a cancer cause, then more of the equivocal world is registered.

It is this sense in which inconsistency promotes adaptability. An environment filled with pollution, chemicals, and additives is not a world in which smoking always produces cancer. A person who believes that it does will see those portions of the world that are consistent with that idea but will overlook those portions that are not.

The Assumption of Timing

Evolution is a slow process that spans hundreds of generations. Since time is reckoned in much shorter stretches in organizations (for example, the fiscal year), there appears to be a serious mismatch in scale between organizations and biology. Given this difference, evolution is viewed as basically unhelpful. But this rejection is premature, because many properties unique to organizations either accelerate time or produce effects analogous to the acceleration of time. Similarly, certain processes within organizations magnify the importance of very small changes, giving them very large effects very swiftly.

This section examines a common property of organizations that both accelerates time and allows for the swift magnification of very minor deviations. This property is deviation amplifying causal loops, which are defined as closed causal loops that have an even number of negative or inverse relationships between the variables that are connected in the closed loop. The one stipulation in defining a closed loop is that the observer be alert to the directions the causal arrows point, and that a loop be defined as a directed pathway in which a person starts with a variable and is able to trace a path that will terminate at that same variable. Once such a pathway is located, the number of negative signs in that pathway are counted; an even number signifies a deviation amplifying loop.

Deviation amplifying loops can be either vicious or virtuous. Any chance event, such as a small crack in a rock that gathers water or a farmer who builds his home on a homogeneous agricultural plain, can become amplified into a tree that grows out of rock or people congregating around the farmer to form a city. The process, not the initial crack or building site, generated the complex outcome (Maruyama, 1963).

What is striking are the disproportions involved. A small initial deviation that is highly probable, such as a wagon breaking down, may develop into a deviation that is very improbable, a city. This final outcome is improbable if one believes in unidirectional causality rather than causal loops. With sufficient cycling, small deviations can be amplified into complex homogeneous events, a sequence that can be quite misleading to analysts (see Waddington, 1977, pp. 145–60).

To return to the city in an agricultural plain. Once the farmer starts to farm at a chance spot, other farmers follow his example, and soon one of them opens a tool shop where they congregate. Later a food store opens next to the tool shop, and a village grows. The village makes it easier to market crops, which attracts still more farmers, and eventually a city develops. Now, if an analyst looks for a geographical cause as to why this particular spot and not some other became a city, he won't find it, because there's no "it" there. The amplifying processes generated the complexity. And because the final outcome is so complex, there are that many more false than true leads or single variables that could have caused the city to form in this place. All of these clues are misleading because none of them caused the city's location. This will be lost on analysts, especially those who view reality as consisting solely of things and structures, rather than as relations and processes.

The analytic problem can be illustrated by a different example, one discussed by Wender (1968). Suppose we observe that an adult experiences social rejection in response to social ineptitude, and that this sequence also is associated with lowered self-esteem and withdrawal. That's what the person now faces and that's what sustains that person's misery. But that isn't how it started.

As an adolescent the person was fat and pimply, withdrew in embarrassment, and failed to acquire social skills. Thus the first diagram should be extended. The acne and obesity disappeared, but the withdrawal and ineptitude persisted thanks to their amplifying linkage. This means that what started the problem no longer exists to sustain it. Insight into the origins

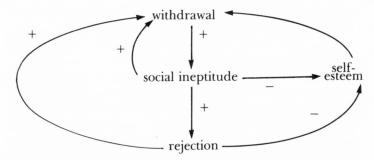

won't help, because they're not responsible for what holds the misery in place. If the original event has disappeared and left no traces, then it may even be undiscoverable.

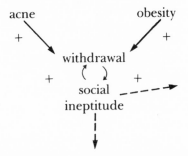

Deviation amplifying circuits mock searches for single original causes proportional to the observed effect (a tiny little stream could never have carved out that huge Grand Canyon). Amplification may cause an outcome produced for one reason to continue for other reasons. When it is argued that organizations enact their environments, some readers may assume that these enactments have always been present on about the scale they now exhibit. That implication is not intended. The modest origins of consequential enactments are illustrated by efforts to desegregate the schools in San Francisco.

In trying to figure out how to implement desegregation in San Francisco, a 67-member Citizen's Advisory Committee was appointed by the board of education. Over time, this committee became increasingly influential in deciding how the desegregation order would be implemented. The committee began its deliberations on February 16, 1971, and concluded them on June 2, 1971. During this time they held seventy meetings, or approximately one meeting every two days. This implies, obviously, that all members could not attend all meetings. This minor difference in participation rates soon became amplified. "Deadlines led to a domination of the decision-making process by middle and upper class white women, who had available time during the day because they were not employed and could arrange care for their children, and by other participants whose employers permitted them to devote daytime hours to the decision making process" (Weiner, 1976, pp. 234–35).

As a result, black committee members did not participate actively in developing the desegregation plan. But the issue here is not just one of time. There is the further issue of differential competence produced by differential attendance. "As high participation rates continue the most active members become a relatively small group possessing a near monopoly position concerning the competencies required in decision making. The joint operation of these factors constitutes a positive feedback loop where activity causes greater competence and greater competence leads to increased activity. . . . Thus, one effect associated with a sharply increased participation rate by some participants in the choice is that most active participants gain a much higher share of the competence and experience necessary to deal with the remaining problems. As they become substantially more competent it becomes more difficult for other potential participants to gain access to the decision making process" (Weiner, 1976, p. 247).

Weiner labels this phenomenon the competence multiplier. The participants who showed up repeatedly produced an environment of sophisticated analysis, which required more participation from them, which made them even more informed to deal with the issues. A vicious circle was created in which regular participants enacted those sophisticated and subtle issues that their new-found competence enabled them to deal with. People who attended less felt less informed, increasingly unable to catch up, and more reluctant to enter the conversation given the level of sophistication voiced by the other participants. The relatively less informed people selected themselves out of the decisionmaking process. This elevated the desegregation planning to an even more detailed and complicated level that even fewer people could comprehend. A minor deviation in participation rates in the beginning over time changed the issues, plans, and environment of the Citizen's Advisory Committee. This is a clear example of a deviation amplifying loop. People with time to spend on a problem transformed that problem into something that only people with time to spend on the problem could manage. The resulting discussion was one from which infrequent attendees became more and more alienated because they understand fewer of its intricacies. Thus the mundane activity of simply showing up at meetings generated an environment which only those who show up at meetings are able to manage and control. Several iterations through the cycle are necessary for this consequence to occur, but again, its plausibility is evident and its relevance to evolutionary timing should be apparent.

Implications

Students of human service organizations should take evolutionary models more seriously. Once a useful evolutionary theory has been fashioned, then it will be possible for investigators to concentrate on policy and practice issues. Until that time, however, such extensions and derivations will be shaky and may look silly.

I feel, however, that we should begin to think deliberately about what some of those issues might be. The administrator-on-the-street has an intuitive feel for evolutionary models, and such models are probably more a part of his background understanding than almost any other pattern of thinking about organized activity. Administrators talk about survival of the fittest, competition, a competitive advantage, an unoccupied niche, trial and error, deviants that solve unsolvable problems, being pragmatic or realistic, going by the book, and so forth. The abundance of these images indicates administrators' readiness to incorporate and elaborate evolutionary images.

To initiate an evolutionary analysis, administrators can photograph the places, people, and tools they work with. After enlarging the pictures so that small details are clear, small gummed labels with the words "ecological change," "enactment," "selection," and "retention" on them are attached to all of the people and things visible in the picture, denoting their place in the evolutionary sequence. The administrators view the setting as if it were a self-contained evolutionary system, and label which features correspond to which evolutionary processes. They then ask questions like, What is there too much and too little of? Is there retention with no enactments or selection? Do some people now seem more or less important than they did before? and so forth.

Intentional usage of evolutionary images can be carried one step farther. A useful device for solving problems is the relational algorithm (Crovitz, 1967, 1970). This is a miniature evolutionary system, making it a suitable exhibit of how evolution operates inside the organization.

Evolutionary systems are creative systems, and creativity usually means putting old things into new combinations and new things into old combinations. In either case, novel relations between pairs are the essence of creativity. Crovitz saw that the forty-two relational words in Basic English (a list of 850 words) could be used to relate two items that one was puzzling over. The prototype sentence for this is, "Take one thing in relation to another thing," or, more sparsely, "Take one thing ( ) another thing." One at a time, the forty-two relational

Complete Relational Algorithm

about	at	for	of	round	to
across	because	from	off	still	under
after	before	if	on	so	up
against	between	in	opposite	then	when
among	but	near	or	though	where
and	by	not	out	through	while
as	down	now	over	till	with

words (for example, about, across, after, where, while, with) are inserted in the brackets to see if they solve the problem (Crovitz, 1970, p. 100).

For example, take the problem that the way in which a service is delivered can negate the treatment (Rossi, 1978, pp. 243–44). Group counseling is introduced into prisons to aid adjustment, but prison guards are used as group leaders. To get a different perspective, the evolutionary analyst works through the possible relations to see what they suggest. "Take delivery *not* treatment" is the problem; possible solutions are implied by: "Take delivery *as* treatment," "Take delivery *before* treatment," "Take delivery *for* treatment," and so forth.

The relevance of the relational algorithm to evolution is diagrammed in this way:

Ecological change →	Enactment →	Selection →	Retention
(the statement of a problem)	(writing words and inserting relations)	(interpreting what combinations mean)	(remembering good ideas, domain words, and relations)

The phrases produce the variations, a very small number of which survive as meaningful interpretations to be imposed again in the future.

The epistemology implicit in evolution is made explicit by the relational algorithm. It is just that kind of concretization that I urge when I say that people should visualize organizations as evolutionary systems.

Interpersonal relationships can also be modeled after evolution. A standard interview format that supervisors use when subordinates have problems proceeds as follows: (1) What's the problem? (ecological change). (2) What have you done about it? (enactment). (3) What do those actions mean? (selection). (4) What should we conclude? (retention). Now comes the twist associated with organizing. At the conclusion of this straightforward interview, when people are discussing what to do, the sensitive manager has to say, in effect, "Go ahead and do what we've decided, *but* it may not be the whole story so be open to the possibility that our conclusion right now is incorrect. And if it's too hard to act and simultaneously doubt what you're doing, then have someone else do your doubting for you." The conversation simulates an evolutionary system, right down to using ambivalence as the ultimate compromise. Split decisions are the tough part to execute. That's why certainty drives out ambiguity, routine drives out improvisation, and why organizations lag seriously in their responses to changed environments.

Conventional features of work situations readily find their place in an evolutionary model. Productivity is an interpretation imposed on enactments by the selection process. A task is a linkage between enactment and ecological change, where ecological change consists of the "requireds" in the task, enactment the behaviors of task performance, and the effect of enactment on ecological change represents "task redefinition."

Technology can be viewed either as an ecological change or as an enacted environment (machines "remember" an organization's routines). When people talk about job enrichment, they are talking about the linkages between enactment and ecological change, as well as possible modifications of retention effects on enactment.

The image of an evolutionary system is not just a convenient gimmick for exposition. It coordinates with many aspects of managing and organizing. This is suggested by the following list.

EVOLUTION IS MORBID

Since most variations are eliminated, attrition is high in evolutionary systems. Very little survives. Repeated utterances of "no," repeated failures, and growing skepticism about experiments can all generate much of the gloominess and pathos in organizations that sociologists love to describe.

YOU'LL ALWAYS BE BEHIND

Since administrators can identify and retain practices or people only after they have become visible in some earlier setting, the advantages of advantageous deviations will always be tied to an earlier, vanished environment. Those retained practices will always be ill-fitted to current circumstance, more so as the speed of environmental change increases. There's no way to beat that. A response must occur at least once before it can be available for selection.

There is a further complication. Responses and practices that are selected do not have to be fully fashioned at the time of their selection. Emission of the minimal features can be sufficient for purposes of initial selection, and the response can then be shaped over time into a more adaptive response. While shaping over time may "solve" the problem of cultural lag (the fit of the responses is updated every time the environment changes), it creates a new problem, that the response may become impossible to eliminate. The contingencies in the environment that shape a response are crucial for explaining its origin. The response is under the control of those stimuli responsible for the shaping, rather than the stimuli that now make it appropriate. What this means, then, is that the response is apt to be quite resistant to change. It would die very slowly if the present stimuli that reinforce it were removed. To speed up extinction, it would be essential that all the associations between the response and all stimuli *responsible for its shaping* also be removed (Rohde, 1967).

TRIAL AND ERROR IS THE EPITOME OF COMPLEXITY

An administrator who abides by evolutionary ideas would seem to have it easy, since all he has to do is gloss the practice of trial and error. Trial is variation, error is selection, and as long as the administrator organizes his world so that this sequence occurs frequently he should have little to worry about.

However, there are complications. Trial and error takes a patient as well as a tolerant superior. It is seldom clear where a trial begins and ends. Those boundaries are drawn arbitrarily in everyday life, something that is concealed by the tidiness with which trials commence in the laboratory. Errors can be evaluated on a long-term or short-term basis, but these assessments are quite different and, in the case of long-term errors, quite difficult to make (not to mention the problem of superstitious behavior developing because of the long interval between action and feedback with a host of intervening events). If a response is judged to be in error, the administrator always has the alternative explanation that the error standard is unrealistic and that the response would be "correct" if a different, more realistic standard were invoked. Errors can also vary in their reversibility, which means that a reversible error is less of an error than a non-reversible one. Normally, judgments of trial and error are not sensitive to this difference.

Other complications could be enumerated, but that would serve no purpose. The point is that evolution is a deceptive guide to action, in that its much-touted simplicity isn't there when it is applied to organizations.

"The concept of natural selection seems unsatisfactory simply because it is intelligible by reason. It is no more impressive than the fact that the more fit players—those who in poker, for example, usually fold on a low pair—tend to accumulate money. One wonders how long it will be, if ever, before laws of nature lose their metaphysical pathos, and are looked upon as no more impressive than sound advice on how to win at cards" (Ghiselin, 1969, p. 69).

In organizations, the counsel of Jonathan Swift (" 'Damn your cards,' said he, 'they are the devil's books' ") or Cervantes ("Patience, I say, and shuffle the cards") seems more apt.

EVOLUTIONARY DIAGNOSTICS ARE DIFFERENT

The administrator who is self-conscious about evolution will ask atypical questions of his organization, such as: Has sufficient time elapsed for gradual changes to emerge? Are there dependencies among the variations? Is the environment so unstable that there is nothing consistent toward which adaptation can take place? Is there an imbalanced resolution of the opposed pressures between variation and retention? Are there insufficient variations among elements, or is there insufficient variability within elements? Are we relying too heavily or not enough on past wisdom? Are doubt and belief distributed throughout the organization? What and where is the retention process? Who ties the retention process to enactment and selection, with what frequency, and with respect to what content? If retention can't be discredited, who argues that the current retained content is totally valid, and why should the person be that committed to such a position? Are there a sufficient number of negative causal relationships? (People mostly see variables that move in the same direction, that is, more leads to more or less leads to less. Therefore, they are apt to miss situations in which variables move in opposite directions; but these movements are crucial for control purposes.) How active is the organization when it inspects its environment? (An organization that is simply registering what goes on outside of it can either stand in a stationary position or can move about in that environment. A mobile existence generates more data than does a sedentary one. [Bateson, 1966, p. 415].) Who cleans out the files, when, with what decision rules, and with what amount of zeal? (This person is looking for something like Allied bombing raids.)

STAMP OUT UTILITY

Whenever people adapt to a particular situation, they lose some of the resources that would enable them to adapt to different situations in the future. They sacrifice future adaptability for current good fit. If they try to beat this trap by cultivating future adaptability and sacrificing current adaptation, they are no better off. They live in an eternal state of readiness and loneliness, able to handle everything except the next customer who walks through the door.

Some people argue that this dilemma is not crucial because when adaptation falters, people can always borrow the solutions used by those who are successfully adapting. I think that argument is naive. If responses become standardized when organizations merge, if people generally praise their own groups and downgrade others, and if people fear appearing frivolous, then from whom are they going to borrow all of these elegant solutions?

Most organizations live in a climate of accountability. Within such climates variability is treated as noise (Klingsporn, 1973), mutations are a nuisance, and unjustified variation is prohibited. The unfortunate effects of these practices may be reversed by clumsy, inefficient acts that reintroduce variation and serve to decouple covariation among elements.

One major cause of failure in organizations is a shortage of images concerning what they're up to, a shortage of time devoted to producing these images, and a shortage of diverse actions to deal with changed circumstances. If believing is seeing, then the person who is bound by the maxim "stamp out utility" is doing everything possible to enrich the believing, so that the things that are seen are rich and important clues for survival.

An organization that is narrow in the images it directs towards its own actions will see only bland displays when it examines what it has said or done. This means that the organization won't be able to make much interesting sense of what's going on or where it is. That's not a trivial outcome, because the sense an organization makes of itself affects its ability to deal with change. An organization that continually sees itself in novel images, images permeated with diverse skills and sensitivities, is thereby equipped to deal with altered surroundings when they appear.

References

Aldrich, H. E., and J. Pfeffer. "Environments of Organizations." In A. Inkeles, J. Coleman, and N. Smelser, eds., *Annual Review of Sociology* 2: 79–105. Palo Alto, Cal.: Annual Reviews, 1976.

Alexander, R. D. "The Search for a General Theory of Behavior." *Behavioral Science* 20 (1975): 77–100.

Allison, G. T. *Essence of Decision: Explaining the Cuban Missile Crisis.* Boston: Little, Brown, 1971.

Bateson, G. W. "Information, Codification, and Metacommunication." In A. G. Smith, ed., *Communication and Culture*, pp. 412–26. New York: Holt, Rinehart, and Winston, 1966.

Bateson, Mary C. *Our Own Metaphor.* New York: Knopf, 1971.

Bennett, J. W. "Anticipation, Adaptation, and the Concept of Culture in Anthropology." *Science* 192 (1976): 847–53.

Bidwell, C. E. "The School as a Formal Organization." In J. G. March, ed., *Handbook of Organizations*, pp. 972–1022. Chicago: Rand, 1965.

Bigelow, J. D. *Evolution in Organizations.* Case Western Reserve University: Ph.D. diss., 1978.

Bougon, M., K. E. Weick, and D. Binkhorst. "Cognition in Organizations: An Analysis of the Utrecht Jazz Orchestra." *Administrative Science Quarterly* 22 (1977): 606–39.

Campbell, D. T. "Systematic Errors to Be Expected of the Social Scientist on the Basis of a General Psychology of Cognitive Bias." Paper presented at APA, 1959.

———. "Ethnocentric and Other Altruistic Motives." In D. Levine, ed., *Nebraska Symposium on Motivation, 1965*, pp. 283–311. Lincoln: University of Nebraska Press, 1965.

———. "Evolutionary Epistemology." In P. A. Schilpp, ed., *The Philosophy of Karl R. Popper*, vol. 14–I, pp. 413–63. Lasalle, Ill.: Open Court, 1974.

Child, J. "Organization Structure, Environment, and Performance: The Role of Strategic Choice. *Sociology* 6 (1972): 1–22.

Crovitz, H. F. "The Form of Logical Solutions." *The American Journal of Psychology* 80 (1967): 461–62.

———. *Galton's Walk*. New York: Harper and Row, 1970.

Dailey, C. A. *Assessment of Lives*. San Francisco: Jossey-Bass, 1971.

DeBeer, G. *Evolution by Natural Selection*. Cambridge: Cambridge University Press, 1958.

Dunn, E. S., Jr. *Economic and Social Development*. Baltimore: Johns Hopkins University Press, 1971.

Freeman, D. "The Evolutionary Theories of Charles Darwin and Herbert Spencer." *Current Anthropology* 15 (1974): 211–37.

Garfinkel, H. *Studies in Ethnomethodology*. Englewood Cliffs, N.J.: Prentice-Hall, 1967.

Ghiselin, M. T. *The Triumph of the Darwinian Method*. Berkeley, Cal.: University of California Press, 1969.

Gould, S. J. "A Threat to Darwinism." *Natural History* 84 (Dec. 1975): 4, 9.

Hein, P. *Grooks II*. Cambridge, Mass.: MIT Press, 1968.

Jacob, F. "Evolution and Tinkering." *Science* 196 (1977): 1161–66.

James, W. *The Principles of Psychology*, vols 1, 2. New York: Dover, 1950.

Jantsch, E., and C. H. Waddington, eds. *Evolution and Consciousness*. Reading, Mass.: Addison-Wesley, 1976.

Kaufman, H. "The Natural History of Organizations." *Administration and Society* 7 (1975): 131–49.

Kiesler, C. A. *The Psychology of Commitment*. New York: Academic Press, 1971.

Klingsporn, M. J. "The Significance of Variability." *Behavioral Science* 18 (1973): 441–47.

Lana, R. E. *Assumptions of Social Psychology*. New York: Appleton-Century Crofts, 1969.

Lewontin, R. C. "Adaptation." *Scientific American* 239, no. 3 (1978): 212–30.

March, J. G., and J. P. Olsen. *Ambiguity and Choice in Organizations*. Bergen, Norway: Universitetsforlaget, 1976.

Maruyama, M. "The Second Cybernetics: Deviation Amplifying Mutual Causal Processes." *American Scientist* 51 (1963): 164–79.

McAdams, R. "Letter Concerning Donald Campbell's Presidential Address." *American Psychologist* 31 (1976): 351–52.

McDonough, J. Review of Harry James, *The King James Version*. *Downbeat*, June 15, 1978, pp. 28–29.

Rickards, T., and B. L. Freedman. "Procedures for Managers in Idea-Deficient Situations: An Examination of Brainstorming Approaches." *The Journal of Management Studies* 15 (1978): 43–55.

Rohde, K. J. "Effect of Early Experience on the Child: Possible Solutions to Controversy." *Psychological Reports* 20 (1967): 134.

Rossi, P. H. "Some Issues in the Evaluation of Human Services Delivery." In R. C. Sarri and Y. Hasenfeld, eds., *The Management of Human Services*, pp. 235–61. New York: Columbia University Press, 1978.

Ruse, M. "Cultural Evolution." *Theory and Decision* 5 (1974): 413–40.

Salancik. G. R. "Commitment and the Control of Organizational Behavior and Belief." In B. M. Staw and G. R. Salancik, eds., *New Directions in Organizational Behavior*, pp. 1–54. Chicago: St. Clair Press, 1977.

———, and J. Pfeffer. "An Examination of Need-Satisfaction Models of Job Attitudes." *Administrative Science Quarterly* 22 (1977): 427–56.

Scheff, T. J. "Decision Rules, Types of Error, and Their Consequences in Medical Diagnosis." In F. Massarik and P. Ratoosk, eds., *Mathematical Explorations in Behavioral Science*, pp. 66–83. Homewood, Ill.: Dorsey, 1965.

Schutz, A. "The Problem of Rationality in the Social World." In A. Brodersen, ed., *Alfred Schutz: Collected Papers*, vol. 2, pp. 64–88. The Hague: Martinus Nijhoff, 1964.

Shaw, M. E. , and J. M. Blum. "Group Performance as a Function of Task Difficulty and the Group's Awareness of Member Satisfaction." *Journal of Applied Psychology* 49 (1965): 151–54.

Singer, E. A. , and L. M. Wooton. "The Triumph and Failure of Albert Speer's Administrative Genius: Implications for Current Management Theory and Practice." *The Journal of Applied Behavioral Science* 12 (1976): 79–103.

Stebbins, G. L. "Pitfalls and Guideposts in Comparing Organic and Social Evolution." *Pacific Sociological Review* 8, no. 1 (1965): 3–10.

Steinbruner, J. D. *The Cybernetic Theory of Decision*. Princeton, N.J.: Princeton University Press, 1974.

Waddington, C. H. *Tools for Thought*. New York: Basic Books, 1977.

Warwick, Donald P. *A Theory of Public Bureaucracy: Politics, Personality, and Organization in the State Department*. Cambridge, Mass.: Harvard University Press, 1975.

Weick, K. E. "Educational Organizations as Loosely Coupled Systems." *Administrative Science Quarterly* 21 (1976): 1–19.

Weiner, S. S. "Participation, Deadlines, and Choice." In J. G. March and J. P. Olsen, *Ambiguity and Choice in Organizations*, pp. 225–50. Bergen, Norway: Universitetsforlaget, 1976.

Wender, P. H. "Vicious and Virtuous Circles: The Role of Deviation Amplifying Feedback in the

Origin and Perpetuation of Behavior." *Psychiatry* 31 (1968): 309–24.

Wicklund, R. A., and J. W. Brehm. *Perspectives on Cognitive Dissonance.* Hillsdale, N.J.: Erlbaum, 1976.

Chapter 5.

The Effectiveness of Ineffective

Social Service Systems

Gerald R. Salancik

One would gather few encouraging impressions about social service delivery by reading the reports of social scientists and investigative reporters for the *Washington Post*. According to either source, it appears that schools fail to educate with the same consistency that they fail to socialize and civilize. Likewise, it seems that prisons foster the growth of crime; that hospitals accelerate disease and death for any but the most critically and terminally ill; that social welfare programs breed poverty; that programs to benefit the elderly have hastened their removal from the mainstream of American life; and that the mainstreaming of handicapped children has created a population of ignorant cripples. In short, one can develop a massive depression from reading social science and newspapers. Hardly a favorable statement can be found about the effectiveness of human service delivery.

Two amazing observations consistently accompany the hue and cry over ineffective social service. The first is that, despite the seemingly enormous evidence to the contrary, the failure of one social service program after another does nothing to diminish society's investment of faith and money into the next. When one program is stomped into history with verbal abuse and revelations of scandal, another is waved high overhead as the promise of the future. The second is that, in criticizing the delivery of human services by one program or organization, there is an undiminished assumption that one knows what is needed in the way of social service.

That criticism of these organizations' ineffectiveness does little to diminish their attempts to deliver social service is a fact that must be understood. It is my purpose to attempt to outline some features of the social service organizations that make intelligible the fact that support continues despite the lack of credibility. I do this without any direct experience in social service organizations, which may be an advantage in that my ignorance will prevent my caricature from being cluttered with detail.

In trying to understand the ineffectiveness of social service delivery, it is important to note that the criticisms against social services are not indiscriminately distributed. Some services are more abused than others. Thus the delivery of medical services is probably abused the least, while the educational services, particularly schooling, face what can be considered moderate amounts of criticism. What probably suffer the most are those social services that aim to modify social and economic inequalities or reduce social and economic problems, such as welfare and drug abuse programs.

Similarly, the kind of criticism each type of social service is subject to varies in its application and use as a basis for removing support for an organization or its administration. Thus, for instance, medical services are likely to be the source of a scandal if there is evidence of mismanagement of funds, such as the charges of fraud against several millionaire doctors who were alleged to have luxuriated off Medicare programs. Rarely do medical agencies come under fire because of a general lack of credibility in their clinical effectiveness. If clinical ineffectiveness is charged in medicine it is usually with regard to particular practitioners. By contrast, criticism against schooling effectiveness is unlikely to be leveled against individual practitioners. Rarely does one read an article in a local newspaper suggesting that a teacher was fired because he or she could not teach the community's children. More likely, teachers come under fire as individuals because they fail to look or act "like teachers." Thus in recent years in certain sections of the country, individual teachers are threatened with job loss because they are admitted homosexuals, just as they were in past years when they were admitted communists. In contrast with teachers, schools are criticized for ineffective delivery of educational services. But the criticism is directed against practices of education, such as open classrooms or what some parents call nonsensical arts and crafts. The criticism comes when schools deviate too much from community conceptions of what a school should look or act like. Ineffectiveness is charged when schools fail to conform.

Other kinds of social programs face more general and undifferentiated criticism, usually directed at the entire program or its underlying concept. Thus the War on Poverty was derided as a nonsensical outgrowth of gross misunderstanding about the nature of the economic, moral, and social order. More recent welfare programs are seen as certifying laziness among the impoverished and disadvantaged. Drug abuse programs are criticized for misunderstanding human nature. The particular content of criticism against programs like these varies over time. Many years ago, programs for alcoholism might have been charged with social, moral, and medical malfeasance all at once. More recently, charges will be expressed in medical terms, in that organizations are alleged to be ineffective because of their failure to recognize alcoholism's medical basis. Alternatively, other alcoholism programs will be labeled ineffective because they fail to recognize the social/industrial bases for drinking. But few programs will be criticized on moral grounds.

If we take these distinctions seriously, they suggest that something is very different about different kinds of social services, and that there might also be differences in the kinds of organizations that form and survive in the delivery of those services. What is the difference? The form and level of criticisms of ineffectiveness are related to the character of verification in each type of social service. The technical cores of social services differ. In medicine, there exists a base technology for inferring appropriate treatments, and there is an established methodology for demonstrating the effectiveness of particular treatments. In education, there is a base technology, but it is not developed to the point where inferences concerning appropriate treatments can be made, so it is not possible to establish the effectiveness of particular treatments (teaching methods, materials, educational activities), but it is possible to demonstrate the effect of treatment compared to no treatment. Years in school (sheer treatment, without regard to particular pedagogy) predicts fairly well a person's cognitive, social, and economic achievements, especially for comparisons of the lowest and highest attainments. Other social services, in contrast with both medicine and education, have no base technology, and even gather their knowledge from a wide range of basis disciplines (psychology, anthropology, sociology, economics, medicine, and so forth).

The availability and character of the base technologies of different forms of social services have considerable effects on the organization of the delivery of those services. The basic distinctions are related to the kinds of criticisms leveled against agencies of each service. Thus practitioners and organizations in medical services are regulated according to Standard Operating Procedures (SOP). One asks of a doctor charged with malpractice not if he did something to harm a patient but if he followed proper procedures. Similarly, hospitals organize a good deal of their activities around standard procedure. Over time, such procedures can be verified as effective or not.

One does not ask of a teacher, however, whether he followed correct teaching procedures. The effectiveness of a particular teaching practice is not verifiable; at least there has been no evidence from thousands upon thousands of studies to suggest much difference between particular methods. Instead, one asks of a teacher whether he has the proper credentials, and a school whether it has the proper accreditation, which is partly determined by whether its personnel have the proper credentials. One also asks whether a teacher has the proper personal characteristics (is he a heterosexual?). This form of ascertaining effectiveness is consistent with the technology available in education. Because educational activities and approaches can not be verified as "working," evaluations are not organized around that issue. It is, however, the case that gross aspects of educational practice are necessary for educational effectiveness. Thus, the presence of teachers is important, but not necessarily what they do. And the presence of books is important, but not necessarily what they say.

From the nature of the technological base in education, in contrast with medicine, it appears that educational services are regulated according to Standard Operating Structures (SOS).

As John Meyer and Brian Rowan from Stanford have suggested, it is important that schools look like schools and that teachers look like teachers. Ineffectiveness is charged when schools fail to have the proper look, when flags are not flown and citizenship training is thereby compromised, when books are from "unapproved lists" and threaten the moral training of students.

Many other social service organizations seem to be regulated by neither standard operating procedures nor standard operating structures. Thus one would not expect those social services to be organized around either. What, then, can serve as the operating principle for such organizations? The nature of the technological base of these social services—at least those being used for illustration here, welfare and social problem treatment—is diffuse and indeterminant. There is no present methodology for verifying or demonstrating the effectiveness of either particular or gross practices. There is thus no verification of particular treatments or of any treatment compared to no treatment.

For lack of a better phrase, the conditions facing many social services regarding the assessment of effectiveness suggest that agencies supplying these services will organize around Standard Operating Myths (SOM). This is intended to be not derisive, but descriptive; myths are simply unverifiable beliefs. Depending upon the fervor with which they are held, myths may represent a harmless form of mysticism, cult, or religion.

Many social services organize around myths and develop a good part of their character, including their relative fluidity, from myths. Many social service organizations that survive and manage to maintain resources are like butterflies that flit from political flower to political flower. Procedures shift with the shifting arguments in academic and political circles, and there is a great deal of trying-out of different strategies for solving the same basic problem: How to lift individuals from their society's poverty. One would expect a good deal of intractability in the particular activities of personnel of such social service organizations, or tracking that changes with the changing demands from alternating myths. Such organizations, moreover, would be lambasted frequently for their ineffectiveness, and the basis for the charge can be expected to change. When a standard operating myth is violated, one would expect charges of ineffectiveness to be made; regulation is on a gross societal or community level. Most likely, regulation would be with regard to social class, groups of individuals with more or less favored status in the society or community—handicapped one time, blacks another, labor still another time. One asks of a practitioner whether he is attending and espousing the proper social values.

Organizations operating under standard operating myths will probably seem to the investigative reporter or social scientist who studies them as sheer chaos and madness. But the madness will be discounted as balanced by dedication, sincerity, and purpose. And personnel within such organizations will probably display considerable commitment and dedication to the social services they attempt to provide. The value of this madness is, of course, that if such organizations were not allowed to persist, or did not manage to persist, then the hard work of experimenting with ways of dealing with social ills would go undone. The fact that there is no technological base for organizing treatments for such problems should not be used to justify not working on such problems. For one thing is reasonably clear: If ignorant attempts are not made, the knowledge base for developing or discovering a more stable technological core will never be obtained, and the delivery of such services will never be organized around either standard operating structures or standard operating procedures.

If the form of organizing social services depends on the technological core underlying assessments of the effectiveness of those services, then stable forms of social service organization probably cannot develop until the technological core develops. This poses an interesting historical and ecological issue regarding the evolution of organizations capable of providing stable and valid treatments. Organizational forms lacking a verifiable technological core must survive long enough and in sufficient numbers to be able to develop the technology they currently lack. As the technology develops, of course, it also means that the organizational forms from which they developed will fall to the wayside, the scrap heap of heredity.

How then might social service agencies be organized and operated so that the necessary ignorant attempts can be made and future knowledge generated and retained?

One way to approach this question is to examine how innovation and knowledge are generated and retained in our three prototype service organizations, medical, educational, and welfare. In medicine, where the effectiveness of new treatments and procedures is derived from the current technology and is potentially verifiable through laboratory or clinical testing and practice, innovation is infrequent in practice and takes place primarily through more than one practitioner. Innovation must confront the history of the standard operating procedure it displaces. If it is successful, diffusion is wide. In schools, where the practice of education goes on in private and the opportunity for verifying and catching the invalidities is low, the amount of innovation is frequent but the diffusion of innovations is slow and narrow, among the few teachers in contact with the innovating practitioner. Both the medical and educational innovation systems are conservative, with basic change in core technologies going slowly. The structure of schools thus protects innovators and makes possible numerous changes in teaching procedures, but the isolation of the structure—its loose coupling—protects the overall system from change, which is intelligent because the effectiveness of changes cannot be verified except through a long process of accumulation. In medicine, change is conservative because deviations from standard operating procedures are likely to be rarer, but a verified one will be more easily incorporated into new standards.

The organizational form for our third prototype social service, welfare, must support innovation in the absence of any methodology for verifying effectiveness; it must be based on faith rather than on evidence or personal persuasion. It is essential that the system be founded on the creation and maintenance of self-serving and motivating myths. The myths must be motivating in order to maintain the dirty business of trying to solve problems whose solutions are unknown. For one thing, the delivery of the social service, its practice, should be even more divorced from central administrative eyes than is the case with medicine and education. The often-heard complaint that an agency administrator does not know what is going on with his agency should be taken as praise. While the work of teachers takes place in enclosed spaces, the work of social workers should take place more off the premises of the agency with a considerable amount of discretion allocated to the worker. This would be an essential condition for innovation to occur.

The social service organization should also be much more politically responsive (at a local and federal level) than schools or medical organizations. Such organizations lack any means for verifying their worth and constantly need to trade on prevailing myths of the organizations that provide or control resources. Social service organizations without core technologies must maintain disparate societal interests just to keep some form of activity going—if they cease to exist, if the activities cease to be handled, innovation and growth of new knowledge will cease. Such delivery systems should be characterized by crass politics of the lowest form—Machiavellian manipulation—and the highest form—mystical mesmerizing. Both administrators and governmental or private interest groups can and should use such organizations, and the social problems they represent, as political footballs in scrimmages for needed resources.

The labels of treatment and programs serviced by such organizations should, moreover, change frequently with the changing myths among resource groups and as the ineffectiveness of prior labeled treatments are learned. They should behave like chameleons in order to attract and reattract interests that fund activities loosely organized around the social problem. Social science researchers in such fields should take an exact same proposal and change a label here and there merely to get the opportunity to do the study and find out if it makes any sense at all. This may seem unspeakable as science, but we are discussing an area of research that has no scientific basis because it lacks the means to verify findings. Workers in the social service area characterized by low technology development should maintain very weak ties to their organizations and should be able and willing to move from agency to agency with great ease and comfort. Thus, as a corollary, they should develop strong and fervent attachments to the domain of social service itself, but not the particular organization operating within that service. The rapidity with which social workers and other service deliverers change jobs is thus commendable. As the money shifts from organization to organization, as organizations come and go, the core personnel must go with the money. Otherwise, the built-up knowledge and the opportunity for extending innovations is lost. Social workers have been known to carry their client with them from agency to agency; this is a reasonable practice.

One further issue that will permit more stable service delivery is that of retention. While chaos and isolation and organizational survival foster innovation, all would be of little value if the usable changes and increments to clinical practice were not retained. In medicine, records of procedural changes are kept through formal laboratory procedures and medical records and autopsy records, with reasonable traces on both the administration of a treatment and the observable medical effects. In schools, records of innovation are less likely to enter the public domain, except through a slow process of personal communication and modeling for teaching aides and student interns. Some may reach local, regional, and national meetings, but the transmittal depends heavily on oral history. In other social service systems, the recording and transmitting of innovation is probably even more erratic. First, case demands on practitioners are so great that record keeping is likely to be a chance output. Moreover, the demand for discretion is partially inconsistent with keeping accurate records that are open to supervisors and funding investigators. Thus retention is most dependent on interpersonal transmission, and will build on a piecemeal, case-by-case basis. From this a slow development can be expected, eventually leading to a reasonable science of clinical practice—much like the history of medicine.

Chapter 6.

Institutional and Technical Sources

of Organizational Structure:

Explaining the Structure of

Educational Organizations

John W. Meyer, W. Richard Scott, and

Terrence E. Deal

In this paper, we sketch out two theoretical models of organizations—the currently fashionable model, which emphasizes organizational structures built around the coordination of technical production processes, and a developing institutional model of organization, which appears to be more appropriate for educational organizations and, perhaps, most types of service organizations. We then review some of the features of educational organizations that this alternative model describes and explains. In doing this, we present some empirical data from our research on elementary schools and school districts—

An early version of part of this chapter was presented at the Sociology of Education Conference, San Diego, April 1977. Work was supported by the Institute for Research on Educational Finance and Governance, Stanford University, a National Research and Development Center funded by the National Institute of Education. The paper does not, of course, reflect NIE positions.

data that conform closely to images of educational organizations found in other empirical studies. Finally, we indicate some of the major unresolved problems confronted in applying these models to the analysis of educational as well as other types of organizations.

Institutional and Technical Sources of Organizational Structure

Formal organizational structures arise mainly through two processes. First, complex technologies and social environments with complex exchanges (such as markets) foster the development of rationalized bureaucratic organizational structures to efficiently coordinate technical work (see Thompson, 1967; Galbraith, 1973). Second, institutional structures emerge that define given types of roles and programs as rational and legitimate. These structures in turn encourage the development of specific bureaucratic organizations that incorporate these elements and conform to these rules (Meyer and Rowan, 1977). The emergence of the factory reflects the first process, while the emergence of the school reflects the second (Meyer and Rowan, 1978).

The history of schools has been misinterpreted as the emergence of organizations that coordinate the technical work of education—and schools have been frequently criticized for their failure to manage this work efficiently. From our point of view, this criticism is misplaced: Educational organizations arose to bring the process of education under a socially standardized set of institutional categories, not necessarily to rationalize the "production processes" involved in carrying out this work.

What difference does it make whether the processes creating modern educational organization are technical or institutional? In our view, it makes a crucial difference: Organizations arising in connection with technical flows closely control and manage them. Their structures act to regulate the flows, to buffer them from uncertainty, and thus to insulate them in some measure from external forces. Such organizations, in other words, are under pressure to become relatively closed systems, sealing off their technical cores from environmental factors (Thompson, 1967). Techniques such as coding, stockpiling, leveling, anticipating, and rationing help to buffer the technical processes from external uncertainties. The intent is to decouple technical work from environmental conditions so that it can be more tightly managed by the organization.

By contrast, institutionalized organizations closely integrate their own structural arrangements with the frameworks established by the larger institutional structures. In doing so, they tend to buffer their structures from the actual technical work activities performed within the organizations. Using such techniques as certification, delegation, secrecy, and ritual, these organizations attempt to decouple their technical work from the organizational structure so that it can be more closely aligned with the institutional framework.

Thus the technical organization faces in toward its technical core and turns its back on the environment, while the institutional organization turns its back on its technical core in order to concentrate on conforming to its institutional environment. A factory, to survive, must develop a well understood process that can turn out desired products at a competitive price; then it must ensure an adequate supply of raw materials, trained personnel, and market outlets, a reasonable tax situation, and so on. A school, to survive, must conform to institutional rules—including community understandings—that define teacher categories and credentials, pupil selection and definition, proper topics of instruction, and appropriate facilities. It is less essential that a school's teaching and learning activities are efficiently coordinated or even that they are in close conformity with institutional rules.

Six propositions, depicted graphically in Figure 6-1, summarize the theory:

1. Organizations evolving in environments with complex technologies create structures that coordinate and control technical work.

2. Organizations with complex technologies buffer their technical activities from the environment.

3. Organizations with efficient production and coordination structures tend to succeed in environments with complex technologies.

4. Organizations evolving in environments with elaborated institutional rules create structures that conform to those rules.

5. Organizations in institutional environments buffer their organizational structures from their technical activities.

6. Organizations with structures that conform to institutional rules tend to succeed in environments with elaborated institutional structures.

We will return in the final section to consider some of the difficulties posed by these propositions. First, we will examine their application to schools in order to illustrate and amplify the differences between the institutional and the technical models.

An Institutional Model of Educational Organization

With few exceptions, social researchers have examined schools from the vantage point of the technical theory of organization. This perspective emphasizes the ways in which organizations succeed by developing effective structures that coordinate and control work processes and regulate environmental demands. Much attention is devoted to rationally organizing the work processes within the organization: Developing an appropriate division of labor, specifying work procedures, and managing the resulting system. Although management must be attuned to the environment as the ultimate source of resources, an important part of its responsibility is to prevent short-term environmental fluctuations from disturbing internal work processes. From this perspective, schools are peculiarly ineffective organizations. They do not control their work processes very well, particularly those most closely related to their central educational purpose, instruction. Instruction goes on behind the closed doors of isolated classrooms. Collegially based professional controls are known to be weak, and there

Figure 6-1.
Institutional and Technical Theories of Organization Structure

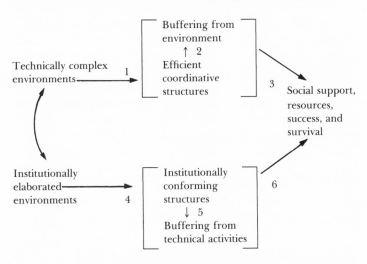

are only minimal efforts to coordinate institutional activities. Further, the ability of school organizations to buffer their activities from their environments is very limited. Schools are highly penetrated organizations.

Thus, the standard social science portrait of the schools depicts weak and ineffective organizations with little internal rationalization of work, little capacity to produce useful effects as measured by student performance, and little ability to defend themselves from environmental intrusions. To a few, the schools seem to be essentially fraudulent organizations; to others, they are classic examples of organizational ineptitude.

This is an astonishing picture of an organizational arrangement that by many important criteria has been spectacularly successful. Huge amounts of money are allocated in a very stable way from year to year to support the operation of schools. Personnel and programs are maintained stably. School organizations—in contrast to other types of organizations—fail infrequently. Further, surveys reveal that levels of participant and constituent satisfaction with schools are generally very high.[1]

Thus, the problem may not be with the organization of schools, but with the types of models social scientists apply to examine them. We proceed now to elaborate the institutional model, which appears to us to provide a better basis for understanding educational organizations (see also Meyer and Rowan, 1977, 1978).

The institutional model is built around two main ideas. First, school organizational structures reflect environmentally created institutional rules concerning education. Second, these organizational structures are decoupled from the technical work of education and many of its vagaries and problems. Organizational attention is directed toward maintaining conformity with the socially standardized categories of the educational system, while little effort is expended in the control and coordination of instructional activities. We will examine each of these features more closely.

EDUCATIONAL ORGANIZATION AS A
REFLECTION OF INSTITUTIONAL RULES

We first consider the ways educational organizations are structurally formed, not to coordinate their own technical work, but to conform to rules institutionalized in their environments. We also consider some of the consequences this has for educational organizations.

Structural homogeneity across schools and districts. Many observers have noted the surprising homogeneity of schools within the American school system. This feature is reflected in survey data we collected in 1975 from a sample of schools in the San Francisco Bay area.[2] Interview and questionnaire data were obtained from superintendents in 30 school districts, from principals in 103 elementary schools within these districts, and from 469 teachers in a subsample of 16 schools within these districts. The San Francisco Bay Area is not presumed to be representative in its educational systems of other parts of the country. However, the selection process, which entailed the random selection of school districts from four size strata, did yield a diverse set of schools. Organizationally, schools ranged from those containing self-contained classrooms with relatively isolated, independent teachers to those containing open-space facilities and highly interdependent teaching teams. Instructionally, schools varied from those in which entire classes were using identical materials to those in which students followed individually tailored learning programs. The environmental setting of sample schools ranged from urban locations with a high proportion of lower-income minority students, to suburban locations serving predominantly upper-income white students, to rural areas.

As part of this survey, superintendents, principals, and teachers were asked to what extent they perceived explicit school-wide policies in several areas. (We were interested in the existence of policies *not* in the extent to which they are implemented.) Table 6-1 presents the simple marginal tabulations of the responses for each category of respondent. Several features of these results deserve comment. First, there was quite substantial agreement among the superintendents, principals, and teachers concerning the presence of policies or formal rule structures. As we would expect, the perception of formal rules tended to relate to hierarchical position, with superintendents perceiving more explicit policies than principals, and principals more than teachers. But the amount of consensus among role groups is more compelling than are the differences: the parties substantially agreed on the kind of system they are in and on the extent of guidance provided by the formal rules. Second, the extent to which formal policies were perceived to exist varied substantially across substantive areas. We observe, for example, agreement among all respondent groups that there are explicit policies governing the reporting of grades, while there are not explicit policies governing instructional methods to be used by teachers. Such variations, showing consensus among role groups about differences between areas, add to our confidence that these data provide a fairly accurate picture of the formal norms within these schools.

The results in Table 6-1 suggest a system in which there is a great deal of overall agreement about the extent of formal policies and the areas to which they apply. What explains this high level of agreement? Two possibilities suggest them-

Table 6-1.

Superintendent, Principal, and Teacher Perceptions of the Presence of School-Wide Policies

Policies	Super-intendent (%)	Principal (%)	Teacher (%)
Type of curricular materials to be used			
Little or no policy	16	24	11
General guidelines only	47	65	75
Detailed explicit policy	33	11	13
Instructional methods or techniques teachers use			
Little or no policy	47	58	39
General guidelines only	49	41	52
Detailed explicit policy	0	1	8
Rules for student conduct on school grounds			
Little or no policy	11	2	3
General guidelines only	33	48	52
Detailed explicit policy	52	51	42
Written reports of student progress on grades			
Little or no policy	3	6	5
General guidelines only	14	22	44
Detailed explicit policy	79	72	50
Identifying students with learning disabilities			
Little or no policy	0	2	(not asked)
General guidelines only	17	26	
Detailed explicit policy	79	72	
Dealing with chronic student absence			
Little or no policy	6	14	19
General guidelines only	38	46	52
Detailed explicit policy	52	40	28
Ensuring that needy students have adequate food and clothing			
Little or no policy	18	31	24
General guidelines only	43	37	46
Detailed explicit policy	35	31	29

Table 6-1—Continued

Policies	Super-intendent (%)	Principal (%)	Teacher (%)
Criteria to be used in evaluating student learning			
Little or no policy	25	12	13
General guidelines only	33	48	61
Detailed explicit policy	37	41	25
Student conduct in classroom			
Little or no policy	25	18	17
General guidelines only	48	57	70
Detailed explicit policy	22	20	12
N	30	103	469

Question: To what extent are there explicit school-wide policies in each of the following areas? We are interested in the existence of policies, *not* in how they are implemented.

Note: All groups of responses do not add up to 100 percent because of non-responses to the specific item.

selves—two very different processes by which such consensus could arise. The first is organizational. Superintendents, principals, and teachers in the same districts or schools may create and perceive a common normative environment. Because of environmental and instructional differences between schools and districts, some variation occurs between schools or districts with consensus occurring within these systems. When responses of participants are aggregated across schools and districts, the average level of consensus is reasonably high because of the high level of consensus within the systems analyzed. The second process is institutional. According to this view, agreements on the nature of the school system and the norms governing it are worked out at quite general collective levels (through political processes, the development of common symbols, occupational agreements). Each school and district— and each teacher, principal, and district officer—acquires an understanding of the educational process and division of labor, not from relating to others within the same organizational unit, but from participating in the same institutional environment, from sharing the same educational "culture."

It is possible to determine which of these views is the more accurate one. While an organizational explanation would predict more agreement within than between schools and districts, an institutional explanation would predict high levels of agreement across all of the organizations, without higher consensus within schools and districts. Table 6-2 reports the results of correlation and analysis of variance procedures that allow us to determine which explanation is more consistent with the patterns of agreement observed in our sample of schools. For each of the policy areas already identified in Table 6-1, we show in Table 6-2 correlations between superintendent responses and the (aggregated) responses of the principals in that superintendent's district. Similarly, we show the correlations between the responses of principals and those of their (aggregated) teachers.[3] Finally, we report analyses of variance, which show the proportion of variance in principals' responses that is accounted for by the district they are in, and the proportion of variance in teachers' responses accounted for by the school they are in.

The findings are dramatic. Superintendents and principals in the same district showed no special inclination to agree on explicitness of policies; and principals showed no special agreement with teachers in their own schools in describing school policies. And the analyses of variance revealed that very low proportions of the variance in principals' responses are accounted for by their district. While a somewhat higher proportion of the variance in teachers' responses was associated with the school in which they are located (compared to that which would occur by chance), the amount of variance explained by school location was still quite small. The particular data reported in Tables 6-1 and 6-2 are representative of many similar analyses we have carried out to examine the patterning of agreement among participants in school systems (see Meyer et al., 1978). Somewhat similar results have also been reported by Gross and Herriott (1965). Findings such as these call into question a conventional organizational interpretation, which would have participants in the organizational units—whether

Table 6-2.

*Correlations and Proportions of Variance,
Perceptions of School-Wide Policies*

	Correlations*		Analyses of Variance†	
Policies	Principal–Super-intendent	Principal–Teachers	Principal Reports Eta-Squared‡	Teacher Reports Eta-Squared§
Curricular materials	.11	.29	.35	.27
Instructional methods	.12	− .06	.24	.28
Student conduct on school grounds	− .04	− .21	.27	.32
Reports of student progress	.23	.23	.38	.21
Identifying learning disabilities	− .16	(n.a.)	.22	(n.a.)
Dealing with chronic absence	.09	.24	.42	.30
Ensuring needy students have food	.01	− .24	.29	.27
Criteria for evaluating learning	− .05	.02	.23	.34
Student conduct in classroom	.09	.00	.28	.23
N	97	28		

Question: To what extent are there explicit school-wide policies in each of the following areas?

*Correlations between superintendents and principals, and between teachers and principals, in reporting the presence of school-wide policies.
†Proportions of variance accounted for in principal reports of the presence of policy by which district they are in. Proportions of variance accounted for in teacher reports of policy by which school they are in.
‡Percent of variance between districts. N = 106, 26 (chance value about .28).
§Percent of variance between schools. N = 469, 28 (chance value about .14).

schools or districts—working out and reporting on a common normative structure somewhat distinctive to a particular unit. Instead, these data suggest that participants share a common conception of general features of the educational system in which they participate that is little affected by their specific organizational context. The high level of agreement about this institutional system (as reflected in such data as those reported in Table 6-1) arises because these participants are describing a normative system that exists outside any particular educational organization. This institutional system permeates each school and district, reflecting its order. The participants within any given organizational unit, however, share only a limited set of rules or roles that are specific to that unit (as reflected in data such as those reported in Table 6-2). Most of their educational world, and most of their interpretations of that world, are institutionally constructed.

Of course, an alternative interpretation might be that schools and districts are rent with conflict—that the lack of consensus peculiar to each school and district shown in Table 6-2 indicates not institutional or system-wide consensus, but organizational conflict. Nothing in our data supports this view (see Table 6-3, panel B). Principals and teachers report low levels of conflict among teachers (70 percent of the former and 69 percent of the latter say there is little or none). Most (86 percent) of the principals and 64 percent of the teachers report little or no conflict between teachers and principal. And 79 percent of the superintendents and 68 percent of the principals report little or no conflict between school and district.

Structural conformity to institutional rules. To show more clearly how institutional rules influence organizational structure, we must elaborate on some obvious but often overlooked features of school organization. School organizations go to the greatest lengths, not to accomplish instructional ends, but to maintain their legitimate status as schools. They seek *accreditation*, which depends on structural conformity with a set of rules that are professionally specified and legally mandated, and react in panic when it is threatened. They hire teachers who are properly *credentialled*. Persons lacking such certification will not be employed regardless of their knowledge and instructional abilities. These teachers are assigned to carefully defined *students* who are classified in *grades* that are given standardized meanings throughout the country (although there is enormous educational heterogeneity in any given grade). The teachers apply to the students a *curriculum*, which is in turn organized into a large number of fairly standardized categories (reading, mathematics, social studies) that are given some specification at the district and school levels, but are rather homogeneous in their meaning and content across the country (though there is little organizational inspection to see that this curriculum is actually taught or learned). Instruction takes place in buildings and classrooms whose characteristics and contents must conform to state laws.

This apparatus is managed by *principals* and *superintendents*, whose roles are also defined (and sometimes credentialled) by the wider environment. Similarly, schools and districts have, in their organizational structure, functionaries mandated or funded by state and federal programs (not by the internal requirements of the organization). Thus, as the state creates and credentials reading specialists, and provides incentives for the discovery of handicapped readers, the schools elaborate these positions in their structures (see Rowan, 1977). (There is little evidence of effective implementation, since many parents might object to the segregation of their children from their peers, but the programs and administrators exist.) Schools even create counter-programs—as when radicals object to the official stigmatization of pupils created by one set of programs, and demand the installation of another set to make sure that the hypothetically segregated handicapped students are effectively "mainstreamed."

At the district level, many parts of the organizational structure are similarly mandated, or made advantageous, by features of the institutional environment. A great variety of special state and federal programs and fundings create the need for special functionaries.

The larger point here is that individual school organizations conform to institutional rules defining what a school is. As illustrated, some of these rules are generalized cultural beliefs (such as definitions of teacher roles, and such categories as reading and mathematics), some are requirements enforced by occupational associations (such as tenure rules), and some are mandated by state or federal legislation (such as certification and accreditation requirements). Schools conform to these rules because it is adaptive for them to do so: their survival and resources depend upon their conformity with institutional requirements. Schools whose legitimacy or accreditation status are in any way suspect suffer drastically lowered survival prospects, irrespective of any evidence of their instructional effectiveness.

Consider a hypothetical study, for instance, that compared two small samples of schools selected in 1950. Sample 1 is simply a random sample of the routinely organized and accredited elementary schools in the country. Sample 2 is made up of those structurally experimental elementary schools identified by sophisticated observers and researchers as being most effective in instruction or socialization. Now suppose we return in 1980. Which sample of schools will show the greatest survival rate? Obviously, the standard set, which goes on, unquestioned and supported, year after year. The experimental set will have experienced waves of conflict and questioning—and eventually many of its leaders will have left education or retreated to conduct research or create ideology as professors and critics of education.

Organizational responsiveness to environmental demands. An institutional model suggests that schools maintain high levels of interpenetration with their environments, not as a reflection of organizational weakness (as would be the case for a technical organization), but as a source of strength. While remaining stable and consistent in general structural features and broad institutional categories, schools are highly responsive to the demands of their local environments. They constantly create and renew the elements that link them with the surrounding community, attempting to retain high levels of legitimacy and support.

While it is common to decry the traditionalism of the American school system, it seems more appropriate to emphasize the extraordinary rate at which innovations of various kinds are incorporated into American schools (as well as the rapid rate with which they disappear). Our own survey revealed enormous numbers of then-fashionable innovative programs in the schools—team teaching, individualized instruction, and so on (Cohen et al., 1976). A set of organizations more constrained by the need to coordinate a core technology would be more restricted in its capacity to adopt and slough off innovations.

Participant and constituency satisfaction. Our argument suggests that schools succeed and fail according to their conformity to institutional rules, rather than by the effectiveness of their technical performance. A school succeeds if everyone agrees that it is a school; it fails if no one believes that it is a school, regardless of its success in instruction or socialization. This leads to the supposition that schools will be attentive to their general reputations and, as a component of this, will seek to satisfy their constituent and participant groups.

Both groups are important. Schools need to keep their environmental constituencies happy, and the evidence suggests that they have been able to do so. Any number of parent and community surveys (for example, Acland, 1975), show high levels of satisfaction with the schools—much higher than reported levels of satisfaction with most other public and private organizations. The schools also need to keep their own members happy. If there is no objective or "market" definition of success, the consensus of those most involved is obviously crucial. For this reason, school organizations are highly sensitive to dissidence and dissatisfaction, and attempt to moderate, coopt, and conceal it. By and large they succeed. Table 6-3 reports some data from our survey of the sample of Bay Area elementary schools, with information from teachers, principals, and superintendents. Panel A reports data on teachers', principals', and superintendents' satisfaction with their jobs, their colleagues, and their organizations. The data show—as do the results of many similar studies—rather high levels of satisfaction among participants in the system.

The same findings hold in studies of students. By and large they describe themselves as quite satisfied with their schools and their work. Many studies—commonly ignored—show these simple results. In our own survey, a sample of third-graders in a number of classrooms reported high satisfaction with schools (Cohen et al., 1976, chap. 8). Similar data at the high school level have been collected by Dornbusch and others at Stanford, and suggest that even students who are academic failures and frequently truant tend to define their schools as very satisfactory. The schools succeed in maintaining support even among those who they process into failure (Dornbusch et al., 1974).

Summary. An institutional theory of educational organization explains the system's structural conformity and overall

Table 6-3.

Answers to Questions on Job Satisfaction, Conflict, and Interaction and Evaluation

Questions	Super-intendent (%)	Principal (%)	Teacher (%)
A. Reported satisfaction			
very or extremely satisfied with job	80	86	88
very or extremely satisfied with school	—	76	79
very or extremely satisfied with teachers	85	81	—
very or extremely satisfied with principal(s)	94	—	66
reporting better-than-average teacher satisfaction	61	76	—
reporting above-average community satisfaction	62	70	—
reporting active community support	89	98	—
B. Reported conflict			
reporting little or no conflict among teachers	—	70	69
reporting little or no teacher-principal conflict	—	86	64
reporting little or no school-district conflict	79	68	—
C. Reported evaluation and work interaction reporting frequent reading teacher evaluation	—	49	20
reporting district evaluation of schools more than once a year	11	14	—
reporting principal is well-informed about teachers' instruction	—	—	36
reporting faculty meetings at least weekly	—	15	—
reporting frequent principal advice on teaching	—	29	2
N	30	103	469

homogeneity, and its overall focus on organizational responsiveness to internal and external constituents. The system maintains its coherence and legitimacy by conforming to an agreed-on set of institutional rules, by maintaining high levels of interpenetration with its environment, and by cultivating high levels of participant satisfaction.

EDUCATIONAL WORK AS DECOUPLED WITHIN SCHOOLS

We turn now to the second main aspect of an institutional theory of educational organization—the decoupling of educational work from the formal structure.

The organizational deemphasis on instruction. The data in Table 6-1 show a striking substantive result. Two of the areas in which respondents report the existence of the lowest levels of organizational policy are the "type of curricular materials to be used" and the "instructional methods or techniques teachers use." In other words, schools develop few policies in the areas of greatest significance for their central goals and purposes. These areas are delegated beyond the responsibility of the organization. Other studies have reported the same feature (for example, Bidwell, 1965; Lortie, 1973).

Some interpret this absence of policy control over instruction as reflecting the absence or perversion of instructional goals among educators ("goal displacement"), while others see it as a form of technological weakness to be repaired by soon-to-arrive reforms (that were also awaited by Horace Mann). It makes more sense to see instructional goals as central for school personnel. However, any attempt to develop actual direct controls over instruction would introduce enough arbitrariness and uncertainty into organizational life to cause all sorts of difficulties in enacting the standardized categories institutionally required of schools. These uncertainties can be stabilized by rendering them invisible—they can be delegated to the trusted care of particular teachers who operate backstage, behind closed doors.

The delegation of instructional matters to individual teachers is often justified by emphasizing teachers' professional characteristics. The creation of professional actors is a well-known device for dealing with technical uncertainty; but in the case of teachers, neither they nor the public seem able to accept this rhetoric at face value. Thus, Dornbusch and Scott (1975) report that elementary school teachers (in sharp contrast to nurses, for example) acknowledge that their training is of little value in helping them to perform effectively, and the support of colleagues and peer control systems seems to be virtually nonexistent.

The inactivity of the instruction-related control system. The nonuse of administrative evaluation and control of instruction and its outcomes have been extensively described elsewhere (for example, Dornbusch and Scott, 1975). Teachers are infrequently observed or evaluated; the same is true for principals (see Table 6-3, panel C). Although pupil achievement data are routinely collected for individual students and are used to monitor their progress and determine their opportunities, the same data are rarely aggregated so as to provide a basis for assessing the performance of individual teachers, schools, or districts.[4]

In most interpretations, this situation would be regarded as evidence for the structural weakness of school organizations. According to our argument, however, it demonstrates the institutional strength of the schools—their ability to lock themselves into place by adhering to institutional definitions that legitimate their activities so long as they are conducted according to agreed-upon rules. Efforts to actually inspect educational outputs, to coordinate the specifics of what is taught to individual students by particular teachers, would invariably increase conflicts with parents and students, cause dissatisfaction among teachers, and vastly increase the burdens of administrators. Whether or not these efforts would also lead to better education is uncertain. Conventional wisdom insists that improvement would result; we are less certain.

Loose coupling among structural units. In addition to the decoupling just described (in which formal control systems are infrequently used to inspect or coordinate instructional activities), units at the same level (such as classrooms) are permitted and even encouraged to pursue unrelated or contradictory programs. We have already mentioned the example of programs that isolate students for special educational purposes coexisting with programs that mainstream the same students. Loose coupling, which permits the simultaneous operation of inconsistent programs, permits schools to be responsive to contradictory environmental pressures, as Weick (1976) has noted.

Disimplementation. School organizations viewed over time incorporate and maintain a large number of new programs and services. As innovations arise and become legitimated in the environment, many are organizationally incorporated by schools and districts. An analysis by Rowan (1977) of a sample of public school districts in California reveals an interesting pattern in the survival of these innovations at the district level. Such innovations as school health and cafeteria services, which are relatively remote from core instructional activities, showed the most stable pattern of growth and development over time; such innovations as guidance and psychological services, which are moderately remote from instructional activities, showed an intermediate pattern of stability; but such programs as curriculum and instructional specialists—programs most directly relevant to the core technology of schools—were the least stable over time. Those innovations that were intended to organize and coordinate the instructional activities within the districts were themselves most likely to be disimplemented, either by being eliminated from the formal structure or by persisting but with little impact on actual instructional activities.

Shifting from the district level, there does appear to be a high level of innovation within individual classrooms. As already noted, new materials and methods are quite routinely introduced into classrooms, as individual teachers discover or invent instructional changes. However, little of this activity is systematically organized at the school or district level; rather, diffusion is random as new devices sweep through the educational world and die out only to be replaced by others. In our own research, we found a great deal of variation from classroom to classroom in materials and methods, but this was largely independent of the organizational features of the schools and districts. We concluded:

> In adopting new patterns of work or new instructional
> materials and techniques, the higher organizational
> levels do not control or coordinate the responses of the
> lower ones. Innovations do not appear to enter the
> school through formal organizational channels. On this
> basis, we are led to conclude that school organization is
> doubly segmented. Schools are segmentalized within
> the districts; classrooms are segmented within the
> schools. Each segment or level reacts to a highly in-
> novative educational climate, selecting from this en-
> vironment new and more complex organizational and
> instructional forms without a centralized center of
> coordination and control to make this selection a sys-
> tematic one. (Deal, Meyer, and Scott, 1975.)

In short, classrooms are sufficiently decoupled from school
and district structures that a good deal of innovation is possible, but by the same token, such innovations are unlikely to
persist in the absence of organizational supports.

Summary. Schools exist in environments that are highly
elaborated in their institutional structures but relatively poorly
developed in their technical systems. The absence of clearly
understood and efficacious technical processes for obtaining
desired outcomes has been frequently noted. This absence can
explain many of the current features of educational organizations—their sensitivity to environmental pressures, their inclination to avoid evaluation of instructional programs or outputs, and their failure to implement adopted programs. For in
many respects conformity to wider institutional rules is incompatible with detailed control over technical work activity. Such
control reveals inconsistencies and conflicts among institutional rules, raises questions about the effectiveness of the programs, exposes vague and vacuous goals and procedures, and
makes explicit the difficulties and problems of implementation. Under such circumstances, tight coupling of the organizational structure with the technical activities can only lower
the legitimacy and threaten the survival of the organization.

Some Unresolved Theoretical Problems

As presently stated, the institutional model of organizations provides a general set of images and ideas that can be applied to educational—as well as many other—organizations. It offers an account of some of the distinctive aspects of these organizations—an account that varies substantially from the conventional one—but it does so in terms that are often vague and ambiguous. In its present form, it offers more an interpretation of (selected aspects of) observed phenomena than precise directions for further empirical work. In order to facilitate the pursuit of these ideas, we have identified several theoretical issues that seem especially important to work through if we are to develop more precise predictions. Three general issues are discussed here.

RECONCEPTUALIZING THE DISTINCTION BETWEEN TECHNICAL AND INSTITUTIONAL ENVIRONMENTS

We have broadly distinguished two types of organizational environments, but our distinction immediately runs into difficulties. Most obviously, technical and institutional environments are not necessarily opposites: Technologies become institutionalized in their own right, and organizations come to be required to conform to them in actual work activity for institutional rather than technical reasons. Further, rationalized institutional arrangements in society often come to spell out and enforce technologies of action (whether objectively or socially defined as efficacious) in great detail. Hence, institutional environments may not always lead to a decoupling of organizational structure from technical activities. For example, many specific medical technologies become institutionalized, and enter into the environment of the hospital both as available technologies and as institutions to which conformity is demanded. Pressures to utilize them are both institutionally enforced (failure to give proper appearances may lead to loss of accreditation) and technically required to produce satisfactory outcomes. Our theory is very ambiguous here: Will the resultant organizational arrangements be tightly or loosely coupled? Are the two processes really at odds much of the time in organizational life? Are conflicts produced, or is the system simply very highly integrated?

Some of these issues arise in educational organizations too, but often at the margins of central instructional activity. Rules concerning student attendance, for instance, can affect the behavior of classroom teachers, who are expected to enforce them, as well as the administrators who keep the official records of the school. But these issues arise with greater force, perhaps, in other kinds of organizations. And we can understand both the issues and their implications by studying them comparatively, that is, in more than one type of organization.

We have identified five theoretical questions within this general area that require further work.

First, what is the degree and focus of environmental specification of the organization's work; in particular, what is the degree of environmental specification of organizational *structure* (work roles and organizational arrangements)? What is the degree of environmental specification of organizational technical work *processes*? And what is the degree of environmental specification of organization *outputs* (see Scott, 1977)? These questions can be answered rather clearly with respect to educational organizations. Environmental specification attaches to organizational structures (qualifications of teachers, categorization of pupils, size of classes, and so forth), but very little to technical work processes, and even less to outputs (aside from case-by-case parental inspections and nationwide disputations about the relation between "Johnny" and "reading"). But other kinds of organizations vary greatly along this dimension.

But, second, what is the organizational level at which the environment specifies organizational work? At which levels are proper structures, technical work processes, and outputs defined? For schools, at least three organizational levels may be usefully identified: classroom, individual school, and district organization (see Meyer et al., 1978). The identification of organizational levels makes it clear that our answers to the first question above were simplistic. In education, environments specify some aspects of structural arrangements down to the classroom level, but little within that level. Work process specifications are very weak, but vague definitions are made at several levels. Outputs, however, which are almost unassessed at the classroom level, are checked carefully at the level of the school and district, though in an odd way: Environments attend carefully to the numbers of students processed and graduates produced, but leave the question of who graduates up to the most vague structural definitions and organizational choices.

Third, the first two issues are interwoven with another question: What is the nature of the technology environmentally imposed on the organization? That is, what are the links between structures, work processes, and outputs? These links may be treated as objectified technical truths, as when it is entirely clear to everyone that certain professional skills or organizational arrangements uniformly produce certain specified work processes, which in turn uniformly produce certain specified outputs. Or these links may be social tautologies, as when certain arrangements of teachers and pupils (structures) are by definition understood to produce appropriate work processes (teaching) and certain outputs (such as credit and graduates).

Fourth, organizations are associated with many diverse environments that force on them institutional rules and technical specifications. Our theory is formulated as if environments were unitary. But educational organizations, for instance, produce different outputs under different controls, for varying categories of students, parents, community sectors, and state concerns. These varying environmental constituencies simultaneously impose different institutional constraints and technologies on educational organizations. Indeed, one can argue that, apart from the institutional considerations already discussed, American educational organizations are loosely coupled precisely because of the extreme pluralism of their environments (Meyer and Rowan, 1977). We need to consider both the fragmentation built into organizational environments as well as the way in which it is systematically reflected in organizational structures and processes. Many parents and students, for instance, inspect schools on processes and outcomes. State agencies inspect mainly structural arrangements. And one of the reasons schools decouple higher from lower organizational levels is to simultaneously satisfy the demands of both constituencies.

Fifth, two types of environments have been identified as influencing organizational structures, processes, and outcomes. Inasmuch as the environments identified are quite different in character, we should also expect the mechanisms by which they affect organizational arrangements to vary. Market mechanisms are presumed to be of primary importance in the case of the technical environments. This suggests that organizational conformity (whether in structure, processes, or outputs) is not compelled by formal rules or the threat of delegitimation but by a concern for profitability and survival in a competitive market. In addition, as Pfeffer, Miles, and Snow (1974) have suggested, there is no reason to expect a single structural form or set of organizational processes to be associated with effective adaptation; rather, a *range* of organizational arrangements may be equally adaptive for a given technical environment. By contrast, institutional environments are expected to produce their organizational effects by the use of such mechanisms as rules, regulations, and inspections. In these environments, organizational survival is dependent on conformity to institutional norms and procedures. In response to these differing mechanisms, we would expect to observe greater variability among organizational structures, processes, and outputs within technical environments than within institutional environments.

We need to specify such arguments and variables as these with much greater clarity, and to consider their impact on organizational arrangements and on the relation between these arrangements and ongoing work activity. And in order to make such a specification more general, we need to consider variations, not only among educational organizations, but for other types of organizations operating in different contexts.

THE MEANING OF BUFFERING

Our theory proposes that organizations maintain stability by buffering themselves from parts of their complex social and technical worlds that bring instability to their existence. Following Thompson (1967), we suppose that organizations in more technical environments buffer their core technical activities from environmental instabilities. And we argue that organizations in highly institutional environments organize around their core institutional elements, with managers buffering their technical core from close regulation or inspection, whether of technical activities or of work outputs.

These ideas are generally useful, but we need to explore a central problem in the formulation. The term *buffering* has meanings that vary greatly along a continuum running from *management* to *concealment*. Elements may be buffered from each other by arrangements for their explicit coordination, as when inventories are maintained, or planning undertaken, or stabilizing agreements formulated, These kinds of management devices tend to increase coordination, control, and the organizational division of labor. But at the other extreme, buffering can take the form of decoupling, or immunization, or insulation, as interdependence and coordination among units is decreased, along with (in all probability) the organizational division of labor. And, of course, there are all sorts of intermediate positions on this continuum. In the real world, it may not be entirely clear whether a given managerial arrangement is buffering by concealment or buffering by effective coordination. The manager often supposes the latter is happening, while others sometimes suppose the former. The two are not incompatible, and some of both is usually going on. Expanded accounting systems, for instance, both coordinate and conceal or insulate activities from each other.

It seems a great mistake to lump such disparate phenomena, with distinct organizational implications, together under the heading of buffering. In our theoretical formulation, we tend to evade this problem by implying that buffering the technical core in institutional environments always involves insulation and concealment, while buffering in technical environments always involves management and coordination. But this kind of cynical Populist assumption (validating the market and delegitimizing institutional arrangements) is clearly naive. It tends to ignore, for instance, the ways that technical organizations satisfy their environments with all sorts of commodities of abstract value that turn out to be concretely useless. And it misses the fact that much of the institutional responsiveness of schools leads, not only to concealment, but to the relatively effective management of organizational work processes. In response to the institutional pressures on them, for instance, schools manage with considerable precision very complex systems that transport large numbers of pupils from their homes to school, guide them through a complex set of differentiated organizational routines, and return them home again.

We need to rethink the meaning of buffering, to distinguish more specific variables under the general heading, and to consider the origins and consequences of each. Schools, our prototypical institutionalized organizations, certainly operate by insulation and concealment (loose coupling) in important respects. In other respects, however, they are highly coordinated both institutionally and organizationally. We need to define these different kinds of buffering more clearly, to understand the factors that produce various types of buffering, and to consider the disparate consequences of these various types.

SPECIFYING THE NATURE OF ORGANIZATIONAL SUCCESS

We have argued that organizations in technical environments succeed through efficient technical coordination, while more institutionalized organizations succeed through conformity with larger rules. We have defined success in very general terms to mean resource acquisition, long-run survival, and so on. These general terms can usefully be elaborated and specified.

Success can be broken down into a series of components. It seems very likely that the different types of organizations we distinguish end up with systematically different *mixes* of these components of success. Successful technically structured organizations, which often exist in exchange markets, acquire mixes of resources emphasizing financial value more and social prestige and guarantees less. Institutionally structured organizations, by contrast, are likely to acquire high levels of social support, legitimacy, and other fixed capital, and guaranteed viability, but may receive proportionately fewer financial resources for discretionary use. Obviously, as noted above, we need to distinguish more kinds of organizations and organizational environments. Equally obviously, we need to greatly elaborate our definitions of organizational success, and identify the equilibrium states of resource mixes involved in success for the various types of organizations.

This theoretical problem is relevant, not only to understanding educational organization, but also to the general analysis of post-industrial society. This kind of evolving society can be defined by the great expansion of institutionalized rules and organizational structures that define and produce services rather than market commodities. If we understand the distinctive resource mixes controlled by such institutionalized organizations, we can better understand the shifting value and stratification system of post-industrial society. This is an urgent problem in the study of national social development generally. It has widely been noticed that currently developing societies acquire the institutionalized services of post-industrial society very rapidly—not after industrialization, as in the history of the west. One may take very different views of this process. Conservatives call it socialism, liberals call it modernity, and radicals tend to refer to it as the "bloated tertiary sector." In any event, it is a rapidly occurring, world-wide phenomenon. And much of the distinctive structure and value involved in these social changes is built into what we have called institutionalized organizations.

Notes

1. We continue to believe these assertions even though at the current time there have been a sizable number of school closings and staff retrenchments associated with the shrinking population of school-age children. Indeed, we take it as an indication of the strength of these organizations that claims are made for their continuation even in the absence of a clientele to serve!

2. The survey data reported here were obtained in the second wave of a longitudinal survey. Details on the survey design and school sample are reported in Cohen et al., 1979.

3. Note that this approach over-estimates the extent of agreement within schools and districts by ignoring disagreements among principals in the same district and among teachers in the same school. This bias favors the organizational over the institutional explanation.

4. Some data of this kind are beginning to be made available for school and district evaluations in California, as well as in other states, but only under the pressure of the state legislature, not the administrative system.

References

Acland, Henry. "Parents Love Schools?" *Interchange* 6 (April 1975).

Baldridge, J. Victor, and Terrence E. Deal, eds. *Managing Change in Educational Organizations*. Berkeley, Cal.: McCutchan, 1975.

Bidwell, Charles. "The School as a Formal Organization." In James G. March, ed., *Handbook of Organizations*. Chicago: Rand McNally, 1965.

Cohen, Elizabeth G., Terrence E. Deal, John W. Meyer, and W. Richard Scott. *Organization and Instruction in Elementary Schools*. Technical Report No. 50. Stanford, Cal.: Stanford Center for Research and Development in Teaching, 1976.

———. "Technology and Teaming in the Elementary School." *Sociology of Education* 52 (Jan. 1979): 20–33.

Deal, Terrence E., John W. Meyer, and W. Richard Scott. "Organizational Influences on Educational Innovation." In J. V. Baldridge and T. E. Deal, eds., *Managing Change in Educational Organizations*. Berkeley, Cal.: McCutchan, 1975.

Dornbusch, Sanford M., et al. *Student Perception of the Link between School and Work*. Report to the Vocational Educational Research Section of the California State Department of Education, Nov. 1974.

Dornbusch, Sanford M., and W. Richard Scott. *Evaluation and the Exercise of Authority*. San Francisco: Jossey-Bass, 1975.

Galbraith, Jay. *Designing Complex Organizations*. Reading, Mass.: Addison-Wesley, 1973.

Gross, Neal, and Robert E. Herriott. *Staff Leadership in Public Schools: A Sociological Inquiry*. New York: Wiley, 1965.

Lortie, D. C. "Observations on Teaching as Work." In R. M. W. Travers, ed., *Second Handbook of Research on Teaching*. Chicago: Rand McNally, 1973.

March, James G., and Johann P. Olsen. *Ambiguity and Choice in Organizations*. Bergen, Norway: Universitetsforlaget, 1976.

Meyer, John W., and Brian Rowan. "Institutionalized Organizations: Formal Structure as Myth and Ceremony." *American Journal of Sociology* 83 (Sep. 1977): 440–63.

———. "Notes on the Structure of Educational Organizations." In M. Meyer, ed., *Environments and*

Organizations. San Francisco: Jossey-Bass, 1978.

Meyer, John W., W. Richard Scott, Sally Cole, and Jo-Ann K. Intilli. "Schools as Organizations: Instructional Dissensus and Institutional Consensus." In M. Meyer, ed., *Environments and Organizations.* San Francisco: Jossey-Bass, 1978.

Pfeffer, Jeffrey, Raymond Miles, and Charles Snow. "Organization and Environment: Concepts and Issues." *Industrial Relations,* Oct. 1974.

Rowan, Brian. "Bureaucratization in the Institutional Environment: The Case of California Public Schools, 1930–1970." In Margaret R. Davis, Terrence E. Deal, John W. Meyer, Brian Rowan,

W. Richard Scott, and E. Anne Stackhouse, *The Structure of Educational Systems: Explorations in the Theory of Loosely-Coupled Organizations.* Stanford, Cal.: Stanford Center for Research and Development in Teaching, June 1977.

Scott, W. Richard. "Effectiveness of Organizational Effectiveness Studies." In P. S. Goodman and J. S. Pennings, eds., *New Perspectives on Organizational Effectiveness.* San Francisco: Jossey-Bass, 1977.

Thompson, James D. *Organizations in Action.* New York: McGraw-Hill, 1967.

Weick, Karl E. "Educational Organizations as Loosely Coupled Systems." *Administrative Science Quarterly* 21 (March 1976): 1–19.

Chapter 7.

Use of Social Science Research

in Organizations:

The Constrained Repertoire Theory

Carol H. Weiss

Social scientists who do research on organizations tend to assume that they have a ready-made audience for their work. Particularly when the organization sponsors their research, they believe that its managers want to hear their conclusions and use them as a basis for decisionmaking. They take for granted that once research results are reported, the organization will ponder them, pursue their implications, and take the requisite steps to modify program and policy. Otherwise the organization would hardly have funded research in the first place. Even research done without organizational sponsorship, if relevant to the organization's mission and performance, is expected to be taken seriously.

Of course, horror stories come to light about organizations that have neglected research results or purposely swept them under the rug. But policy researchers tend to attribute such acts to failures in communication or stupidity of individuals. Their general expectation is that good research, well reported, is almost bound to gain a hearing and affects organizational action.

At the same time that these assumptions prevail, other social scientists have been conducting investigations of organizations' use of research. Their studies demonstrate that organizations are unlikely to put research results to direct use. Even when research is expressly commissioned to help solve organizational problems, it rarely has clear and measurable effects on the organization's decisions. For example, evaluation studies disclosing almost total failure to achieve program goals can leave an organization and its programs untouched. Organizations in a range of fields—education, criminal justice, manpower training, social services—continue operations virtually unscathed by evidence of major failures.

A recent study of twenty health program evaluations concluded that, while the evaluations had some effect, they served mainly to provide "additional pieces of information in the difficult puzzle of program action, thereby permitting some reduction in the uncertainty within which any federal decision-maker inevitably operates" (Patton et al., 1977, p. 145). That is, the major use of the evaluations was to reduce uncertainty about what the agency was probably going to do anyway. Other uses reported were equally marginal, such as "providing an impetus for finally getting things rolling" when the agency already knew that something had to be done and what it planned to do (Patton et al., 1977, p. 147). Yet the authors of this report indicated—rightly—that their conclusions were more positive than most previous analyses.

The expectant audience that most policy researchers envision for their work is usually not there. Agencies are not eagerly awaiting reports of the latest research to guide their decisions. Regardless of the fanfare with which studies are launched or how much money is spent on them, the agency's typical reaction to research reports is indifference. Research comes and goes, and agencies apparently give it only passing attention.

I'd like to explore two possible explanations for this phenomenon. The first starts with the phenomenon of bureaucratic decisionmaking. Drawing from organizational theory and organizational research, it offers a framework for understanding why the responses of bureaucratic agencies to evaluation research and other informational inputs are often so lethargic. The second explanation centers on the ambiguity of the process of "using research information." The argument here is that use of social science research encompasses a broad range of activities and that our attention has been directed to only a narrow segment of that range.

Organizational Decisionmaking under Conditions of Complexity

In order to understand why agencies apparently pay little attention to the results of research, we start with the nature of the decisionmaking process in organizations. Researchers like to start at the research end, consider the research in hand, and ask, Why isn't it being used? It seems to me that the answer has to come from an understanding of how decisions are routinely arrived at in the complex bureaucracies that are government agencies. There is a relevant literature that discusses large organizations with layered hierarchies and multiple component units and their processes of decisionmaking under conditions of complexity. The lessons offered by the work of Simon, Barnard, March, Lindblom, Allison, and others make mincemeat of the stereotypes of the "rational organization."

In the popular imagery, a bureaucratic organization proceeds in orderly and logical fashion. Periodically it takes stock of its performance. If achievement of goals is less than optimal, it analyzes its shortcomings and identifies the source of trouble. Then it searches out a series of alternative measures that would remedy the problem. Carefully it weighs the advantages and disadvantages of each of the alternatives and selects the option with the most beneficial consequences. This is the prototype of organizational decisionmaking, and all information that sheds light on performance, trouble spots, alternatives, costs, and benefits is grist for the mill.

But organizations observed in the light of day do not usually engage in the goal-maximizing behavior of this rational mode. Not even that quintessentially rational organization, the private business firm, makes decisions in this fashion, and such a sequence is even less likely in public organizations, where both goals and measures of goal achievement are more ambiguous. Rather they bumble alone, or in Lindblom's (1959) term, "muddle through," without ever surveying all possible alternatives for achieving superior performance.

Among the key concepts developed by Simon and his followers about organizational behavior are these:[1]

1. *Bounded rationality.* Organizations do not employ "comprehensive rationality" in making choices, since such a course would require generating all possible alternatives for the attainment of given ends, assessing the probable outcomes of all the possible alternatives, and evaluating each set of consequences for all relevant goals. These requirements exceed the cognitive capacities of individuals and the capabilities of organizations. Therefore, organizations limit the alternatives they generate, the information they process, and the evaluations they make. Their actions are characterized by bounded rationality.

2. *Satisficing.* Organizations do not seek to maximize their achievement of goals. Rather they find a course of action that is "good enough." Once they have found a course that satisfies enough objectives to be acceptable, the organization calls off its search for alternatives. It does not go on to look for the best of all possible actions.

3. *Search.* Because it stops searching as soon as an acceptable alternative is located, the order in which an organization conducts its search becomes crucial. Organizations generate alternatives in stable ways. The prevailing pattern is to begin the search in the near neighborhood of existing organizational practices. If a once-a-week counseling program for delinquents does not reduce deviant behavior, a likely next step is to increase the number of counseling sessions to two or three a week.

4. *Factored problems.* Only a limited number of aspects of a problem are attended to. Many important facets and possible consequences are never examined. The problem is factored into subcomponents, and these are assigned to different units of the organization to work on. Each unit considers its piece of the problem from the standpoint of its own interests.

5. *Unit subgoals and sequential attention.* The units within an organization each have their own subgoals. Subgoals are in partial conflict with each other and with the overall goals of the

organization. Thus, for example, the outreach unit of a job training organization wants to bring in sufficient numbers of people to fill the program, the training unit wants to teach the curriculum that it is skilled in teaching, the placement unit wants a good record of placing graduates in jobs. These goals are not fully compatible with each other or with the organization's overall goal of preparing chronically unemployed people for reasonably well-paying jobs. It might be expected that upper management reconciles the different and partly conflicting goals, but this is not, in fact, what occurs. The managers of an organization do not look at all issues simultaneously and make an overall determination. Rather, they pay attention to problems as they arise. They consider each problem independently and resolve it without reference to other problems and other units. Each unit has its own turn at management attention. Therefore, the organization continues to live with partly incompatible goals and only partially resolved internal conflicts.

6. *Incremental adjustment.* In complex situations organizations are reluctant to base actions on estimates of an uncertain future. They much prefer to take small steps and get rapid feedback, much as a thermostat registers temperature and takes prompt action to bring it back to the desired level. A federal education agency that is discontented with school district performance will tinker with guidelines and compliance procedures, rather than undertake drastic revisions in programming. The notion of making fundamental changes in policy at one swoop, without the possibility of early adjustment, is frightening and to be avoided.

7. *Uncertainty avoidance.* All organizations seek to avoid uncertainty. One means to accomplish this end is to solve immediate problems rather than to try to impose long range plans. Another technique is to stay within the vicinity of the known. All organizations have established routines for coping with the outside world. They know the consequences of these routines. Even when activities must be altered to deal with changed environments, the organization tends to cling to its routines in order to avoid the uncertainties of using new procedures.

8. *Repertoires.* Organizations build routines into stable programs of action. "Programs," in the sense of patterned sequences of actions like computer programs, constitute the available responses that an agency can make to events. The limited number of programs that an agency develops and practices constitutes its repertoire. The repertoire of available programs represents an organization's range of effective choice. An organization knows how to do only a limited range of things. Its staff has skills in these activities. It builds up expectations in individuals and other organizations that its practice will consist of the given pattern of activities. Therefore, its range of choices is constrained by the existing repertoire.

9. *Decisions.* Organizational persistence does not preclude change. In spite of limits on the capacity of organizational leaders to embark on radically new courses of action, they do in fact make changes in organizational behavior. However, the degree of shift is severely constrained by the range of existing organizational programs.

With these concepts as background, we can take a more sophisticated view of how organizations seek and use information in the decisionmaking process. That organizations collect information is unquestionable. They collect information in enormous quantities. Some of the data collection is ritualistic; it demonstrates that the organizations are progressive and forward-looking and taking their mission seriously. The ceremonies of evaluation and analysis are observed, but there is little intent to pay attention to the information that is generated. Some data are collected because they have always been collected, and the traditional procedures persist. The necessity for much data collection is foisted upon organizations from the outside; they have no self-generated interest in the information and simply comply with regulations. But organizations also purposefully and self-consciously seek out certain kinds of information with keen appetite. Since their primary imperative is survival, they must monitor events both inside the organization and in the external world that might threaten their life and growth. What they must have is advance warning of pending catastrophe. Therefore, they set up indicator systems, both formal and informal, that will provide signals of jeopardy.

Policy research, particularly evaluation research, clearly can fall within the rubric of early warning systems. It can provide signals that the organization is failing to meet its goals. In some cases, this will be important news to an organization intent on survival—*on the condition that* failure to attain explicit organizational goals will endanger its support and appropriations. However, the work of some students of organizations suggests that organizational goals are not serious statements of intention. Rather they are a set of lower boundary limits below which organizational performance must not be allowed to fall. So long as organizational performance is within the safe range of performance, the organization may be uninterested in its exact location on the range. Therefore, organizations may perceive evaluation research (and other kinds of policy research) not so much as a needle on a scale to tell them precisely how well they are doing, but as a set of idiot lights to indicate "safety" or "danger." Only when evaluation research discloses that the lower bounds have been exceeded and organizational performance is in the danger zone will the organization give full attention to the findings.

And even this is sometimes an optimistic statement. Organizations know that not all measures are equally important. Poor performance in some areas rarely calls forth retribution. Some purported goals can be neglected without danger of penalty. Unfortunately for the public, there are times when the central goals of a public agency can be violated without fear of outcry, budget cuts, or personnel changes. Thus poor pupil achievement is not usually likely to call forth massive shakeup of a school system; a research granting agency may not get into trouble because of low rates of submission of final research reports. More peripheral goals, on the other hand, may have serious consequences. Evidence of misuse of public funds can call down a cascade of fire and brimstone, and rapidly escalating costs may signal immediate and highly newsworthy review. Discourtesy to the staff of a powerful senator or proposals that irritate the leaders of an influential interest group can evoke even quicker retribution. Performance on these measures is monitored carefully and continuously by any canny agency chief.

To review, organizations collect a great deal of information. Given the cognitive limits of individuals and organizations, they cannot and do not process all of it. Constant review of multiple indicators would devour resources, time, and scarce skills. If the organization withheld its decisions until appropriate data were available or if it sought to ground all decisions in objective evidence, it would essentially be paralyzed, and even those few steps it managed to take might be no wiser for the extensive analytic endeavor. Under conditions of complexity, organizations monitor only a very few indicators of performance, those that they believe are likely to threaten organizational continuity. When organizational performance falls below the very wide band of "acceptability" on a measure that can be expected to have serious consequences for the organization's continuance, then agency heads are likely to listen.

Let us suppose that evaluation research signals disaster. The agency is falling below permissible levels of performance on one or more key indicators. What does the agency do then? The rational model would expect the agency to embark on a search for alternative strategies, to assess the likely consequences of each alternative for each of the organization's major goals, to compare the relative advantages and disadvantages, and to select the best option. Not so, say Simon and others. Organizations start with their existing repertoire of programs. They do not canvass for alternatives much beyond that range. They are restricted to the action sequences that they have built up out of past experience. They know how to conduct only a small number of organizational programs, and when problems come up, they rely on the same constrained repertoire.

Organizational routine and the momentum of standard operating procedures are such powerful constraints that even under compelling circumstances organizations find it difficult to change. Allison (1971) cites the case of Soviet installation of missiles in Cuba in 1962. In building the launch pads, the Russians used the same distinctive design that they used for missiles in Russia. The recognizable pattern enabled American intelligence to identify the sites from photographs before the missiles were in place. Obviously the Russians, who were intent on secrecy, should have changed the design of the launch pad, but so strong was organizational routine that it prevailed over the most potent contrary requirements.

The organization confronting negative data on performance thus has to overcome strong conservative biases. Its initial response is to make marginal adjustments in strategies currently in use. Only when such a move is patently unwise and will fail to extricate it from jeopardy is the organization likely to consider alternatives. One would expect that the organization, even if constrained by its existing repertoire, would select the strategy best calculated to lead to improved performance. But calculation is not always an organizational strong point, and the alternative that is selected is just as likely to be "the next item in the response repertory." Cyert and March give an example of this penchant: a firm that had had an industrial accident installed a piece of new equipment that it had been considering buying, even though the connection between the equipment and the actual cause of the accident was at best remote and probably nonexistent (1963, pp. 80 ff.).

In human service organizations, where the causes of problems are extremely difficult to fathom and the technologies for coping with problems are weak and inexact, selecting the appropriate response is no easy matter. Given the ambiguity of causal relationships, the organization places greater stock in doing *something*, however tenuously related to performance improvement, than in expending effort on analysis. Action of almost any kind symbolizes responsiveness to conditions, which both internal and external audiences are likely to applaud, whereas further research and analysis symbolize delay—and probably stand little chance of identifying more effective strategies of action (Meyer and Rowan, 1977).[2] The pessimistic message is that only when threatened with dire consequences are organizations likely to act, and then they are not apt to choose the course of action best suited to remedy the cause of failure.

But an organization can learn from its experiences. If it activates a program that does not succeed in restoring the critical variables to tolerable range, it will try another program.

If, on the second try, feedback shows that the critical variable is within the desired range, it will persist with this program until the next disruption. Learning of this type is not analytic, fore-thoughtful, or efficient. It depends on trial and error, a series of disasters with accompanying negative reinforcement, and the gradual elimination of unsuccessful strategies (Steinbruner, 1974, pp. 78–80). The whole process is dominated by established procedures of activity.

If this is how organizations function, then it is little wonder that they make scant use of policy research. Only a narrow band of messages is heeded, and only a narrow band of responses is available for implementation. And to compound the confusion, the responses are not necessarily geared to the messages. The world revealed by this school of organizational theory is hardly likely to gladden the hearts of applied social scientists.

A quotation from Franklin D. Roosevelt encapsulates the view. Although he was talking of the frustration of presidential power rather than of empirical evidence, he gives a vivid description of the inert organization:

> The Treasury is so large and far-flung and ingrained in its practices that I find it almost impossible to get the action and results I want. . . . But the Treasury is not to be compared with the State Department. You should go through the experience of trying to get any changes in the thinking, policy, and action of the career diplomats and then you'd know what a real problem was. But the Treasury and the State Department put together are nothing as compared with the Na-a-vy. . . . To change anything in the Na-a-vy is like punching a feather bed. You punch it with your right and you punch it with your left until you are finally exhausted, and then you find the damn bed just as it was before you started punching. (Eccles, 1951, p. 336.)

THE CONSTRAINED REPERTOIRE AS EXPLANATION

This view of organizations as bundles of standardized routines captures important features of organizational behavior. Anyone who has worked in a large organization encounters the description with a jolt of recognition. Yet I believe that the picture is overdrawn. No doubt some organizations act in such conservative ways all of the time, and most organizations act that way some of the time, but patterns of organizational behavior are much more diverse and variable than the analysis suggests. Even the Navy, Roosevelt's worst case, has since been moved and shaped by (among other things) the policy analysis procedures that Robert MacNamara introduced into the Defense Department. Many organizations pay serious attention to shortcomings in policy and program; many organizations continually scout for alternatives that promise improved performance; many are willing and able to implement courses of action that are at considerable variance with what they have previously done.

The history of public bureaucracies in the past two decades discloses major discontinuities in policy and many significant changes in program and procedures. Major new efforts have been initiated and important programs abandoned or drastically restructured. Although most of the changes have come about because of political rather than bureaucratic action, that is, the passage of new laws, they were usually stirred and shaped by recommendations from operating staff. Organizational staff members have been willing, sometimes eager, to redirect organizational activities at a pace and to a degree far beyond the predictions of the constrained repertoire theorists.

Proponents of the view have exaggerated their case in order to counteract the stereotypical picture of organizations as rational actors intent on maximizing the attainment of organizational goals. To overcome such naive expectations, they have overstated the strength of the forces that push toward cautious, anti-rational, risk-minimizing behavior. At the extreme, they question whether organizations have any substantive "goals" at all, and look upon decisionmaking as a "garbage can" process in which streams of actors, problems, opportunities, and solutions flow along until they coalesce at some arbitrary point (March and Olsen, 1976). Information of any sort is seen as peripheral to the game.

It is not necessary to accept the gloomiest view in order to recognize the validity of much of the organizational inertia analysis. The patterns that organizational theorists have highlighted, even if exaggerated, are pervasive and familiar enough to warrant serious attention. Above all, we must recognize the limitations that an organization's constrained repertoire imposes on its ability to use information.

Using Policy Research in Decisionmaking

Another interpretation of organizational response to policy research comes from social scientists who have investigated the effects of research studies on organizational decisionmaking. These students of research utilization have been concerned with the consequences either of particular studies (Boeckmann, 1976; Burt, Hatry, and Fisk, 1972; Research Triangle Institute, 1979; Rich, 1977; Patton et al., 1977; Weiss, 1970) or of a body of policy-relevant research (Caplan, Morrison, and Stambaugh, 1975; Caplan, 1977; Berg, Brudney, Fuller Michael, and Roth, 1978; Weiss, 1977; Knorr, 1977; Cohen and Weiss, 1977). Rather than starting with the processes by which decisions are routinely arrived at in bureaucratic organizations, they start with the relevant research in hand and ask how it affects organizational decisions.

It is from these investigations that we have learned that few direct effects are apparent. Neither evaluation studies, policy analyses, technology assessments, nor policy-related research studies have immediate impact upon specific decisions. Although study findings are not infrequently taken up, cited, and discussed in organizational deliberations, they rarely shift the course of organizational action from the path it would have taken had the research not been done.

The reasons appear to be threefold. First, few organizational decisions hinge mainly on information. Organizations have many ways to keep track of their internal and external environments (Kaufman 1973), and policy research often tells them little that they were not (at least unsystematically) aware of before. Most important decisions involve negotiations among interests rather than solutions to puzzles, and the contribution of new data is of peripheral significance. Second, even when vital "factual" questions are unresolved, research rarely answers them authoritatively. It is the unusual study that addresses *all* the variables that might be relevant and that provides conclusions of unchallengeable cogency. For example, even the Negative Income Tax experiments, whose findings of small withdrawals from the labor force by recipients of a guaranteed income were scientifically persuasive, did not yield information relevant to other objections to the incomes policy. Third, the organization is concerned with much besides the logically best solution. Decisions are weighed not only against standards of effective performance, but also against considerations of organizational survival, growth, convenience, and reputation. Even in the unusual case where research or analysis points to a clear-cut best decision, the organization has to balance interests, values, feasibilities, and resources. It has to take into account the repercussions that the decision will have on many aspects of the organizational system—staff morale, budget, interorganizational relationships, reactions of the Congress, attitudes of clients, and so on. Public organizations function within a political environment, and maintenance of credibility and support has high priority.

It takes a remarkable concatenation of circumstances for a particular research conclusion to be used instrumentally to reorder decisions—a clear-cut gap in information, competent and comprehensive research with unambiguous conclusions, implications for action that are feasible and that fall within the agency's authority and resources, reports that are on time for the decision and that fit the decision parameters, top officials who listen to the research, understand it, and are willing to fight for it, and pliable external conditions. Such an array of circumstances does not often fall handily into place. When it does, it is usually around minor, relatively low-level issues. On important matters, research is rarely so authoritative and the environment rarely so hospitable as to allow direct segue from data to decision.

But if students of research use have documented the rarity of specific effects on specific decisions, they have contributed the important insight that research nevertheless can have significant consequences. Previous observers did not find them because they were looking in the wrong place. They were concentrating on immediate decisional impact, whereas the major contribution of research is a diffuse accretion of understanding on issues of policy importance. The results of one study are not used as a basis for making particular decisions, but as evidence builds up over time, the generalizations from a range of social science studies come to the attention of attentive publics. The generalizations, the ideas, the concepts begin to alter the way that informed people think about public issues. In time they lead to shifts in how problems are perceived, which issues come onto the agenda, and how they are formulated for action. It is this uncatalogued, undirected process that constitutes the major "research utilization"—the percolation of social science findings and ideas into the consciousness of public actors. As the process goes on, research data become transmuted into generalizations, the generalizations into concepts, qualifications are pared away, the original sources are forgotten, some of the ideas get distorted, many are oversimplified, but a stratum of ideas is deposited. It is the progressive buildup of this stratum of new orientations, what I have called "knowledge creep," that leads to significant intellectual reorientation on major issues.

In a recent study of decisionmakers in federal, state, and local mental health agencies, I found evidence that many officials are aware of this kind of gradual assimilation. They stress that it is difficult, almost impossible, to name a specific study that influenced their actions or to point to a concrete decision that was changed because of the results of research. Rather, they explain that they are exposed to an ongoing stream of research and, as one respondent said, "I don't think there is a specific way I take a piece of research and apply it in a precise manner. You build up a sequence of related pieces of research, you take it in, evaluating, assimilating, and at a later point, you use it." The hallmark of this mode of research use is that users are rarely aware of which particular studies they are using—or even that they are using research at all.

Sometimes officials use social science research not only to contribute to their own thinking but also to convince others of the rightness of their views. There is an element of legitimation in this type of use, justifying decisions already made on other grounds. But often there is also a bona fide effort to apply the insights that social science research offers in the adoption of their initial position—and then backing it up with supporting research. Thus, one respondent said: "[I seek research] to clarify my own thinking. Before I take a position, I want to see what others have said on a topic and studied . . . . If I am going to prepare something, I want to be able to document it. I feel I am always subject to challenge, and I want to document . . . . When I'm trying to push a particular position, I am going to scurry around and find all the articles for it. The assumption is if you can cite somebody who has done a careful study, it carries more weight than just another study." Even this kind of research use, which moves from clarification to documentation to legitimation, seems to represent a conceptual contribution rather than the instrumental application of specific findings to specific problems.

Our inquiry showed that officials are receptive to social science research and value its insights. Its major value to them is the framework of ideas it provides. It gives them new frames of reference for making sense of events and understanding how events are connected. They rarely use one study or even a body of studies as a basis for specific action or discrete decisions. Rather they use the perspectives they gain from a congeries of studies to think about issues, raise questions, and consider alternatives. Research is a mode of enlightenment.

In many ways social science research serves as continuing education to keep officeholders up to date on issues in their field. It is a medium of news about needs, services, promising approaches, pitfalls and obstacles, and the most recent information about human behavior. It helps them maintain their currency and their professional expertise. It gives them assurance that they are in touch with the intellectual issues that are engaging social scientists and that they are sensitive to the challenges and the opportunities that may lie ahead.

At a more basic level, social science research provides a language of discourse. Increasingly public policy debates are being conducted in the language, and with the conceptual and empirical apparatus, of the social sciences. The research vocabulary has become an essential mode of communication and persuasion in the policymaking arena. Actors expect a case to be made in terms of data, statistics, evidence, and the organizing theories of social science. They look for documentation from objective scientific sources. In this sense, social science has pervaded the public debate. Participants in decisionmaking must learn to speak the language in order to make their positions visible and communicate across the boundaries of profession, agency, and philosophical viewpoint. The terminology of the social sciences has become a common language, and it has the special standing of "rationality" in the public forum. Even when people use the language only to decorate the positions that they would have taken in the absence of social science evidence—as is not infrequently the case—the mere adoption of the conceptual vocabulary exercises subtle pressures on the nature and direction of argument (Weiss, 1980).

Perhaps the most optimistic implication of research use as enlightenment is that it represents a receptivity even to ideas that are critical of current agency policy (Weiss and Bucuvalas, 1980). Research need not fit the parameters of feasible organizational action in order to be attended to; officials will often welcome it even when its conclusions are not presently practical. What it offers them is a new way of thinking about issues, new models for making sense of organizational activities and outcomes. Although they are not likely to implement research results in an immediate decision, over time their altered orientation can have important consequences for the facet of the issue they focus on and the range of alternatives they consider. In this sense, research can help to counteract the taken-for-granted assumptions, the musty *sameness*, that tends to infect every organization. It represents an opening to new constructions of social reality.

ENLIGHTENMENT AS EXPLANATION

Just as the constrained organizational repertoire is an over-drawn interpretation of organizations' limited use of information, so too the enlightenment interpretation contains elements of exaggeration. It seems to promise that, without special effort in designing, conducting, or communicating research, relevant results will almost inevitably seep into the consciousness of organizational actors and affect their perceptions of events. Obviously this is not the case. Even the conceptual sense in which enlightenment takes place, there is nothing inevitable about it. Which research comes to attention appears to be the result of haphazard events, determined perhaps more by current fads than by the cogency of the research. Many social science generalizations that officials absorb into their stock of knowledge are partial, biased, obsolete, or just plain wrong. No quality control mechanisms screen out the trendy, the shoddy, or the merely sensational. No mechanisms work to guarantee that the most valid, recent, relevant, comprehensive, or useful studies get a hearing.

Even when important understandings from social science research percolate through, the process is by no means efficient. A long time may elapse before appropriate decision-makers learn about them, and in the process, the original findings may become so oversimplified and distorted that the original authors would refuse to recognize them as legitimate. The process may constitute "endarkenment" as much as enlightenment.

A final limitation is that enlightenment does not ensure action. Even if organization members come to see events in different and more fruitful patterns, they may not rally the resources of the organization to put their insights to work. It takes more than understanding to move large organizations. Despite what the poets tell us, truth is not beauty and knowledge is not power. There are often telling reasons why organizations do not act upon the truths that they "know."

And yet, the enlightenment analysis is by no means unimportant. It lifts our sights from the narrow "decisionistic" frame of reference and directs attention to longer-term and possibly more pervasive influences. It gives us another perspective to use in understanding the intersection of policy research and organizational decisionmaking.

Toward a Theory of Organizational Use of Information

THREE FUNCTIONS OF INFORMATION

From the insights into organizational processes derived from organizational analysis and from the understandings derived from studies of the use of research, we can begin to construct a better model of the use of information. Juxtaposing these strands of investigation can produce a framework upon which theory can be built.

A first step is to recognize that information—including, but not limited to, research information—can serve three distinct functions for organizations. First, it provides *Warning*. It indicates that the organization is doing something, or failing to do something, that may incur penalties. Many forms of information can fulfill this function, from phone calls from disgruntled clients, staff grievances, or newspaper exposes to program statistics, audit reports, or public opinion polls. Evaluation research studies can be a social science warning, particularly when the studies disclose serious shortcomings on criteria that are central to organizational security.

As we noted earlier, the most critical measures may not involve the degree to which organizational goals are achieved. Sometimes other failings—high costs, fiscal impropriety, callous staff attitudes—are more important signals of trouble. Nevertheless, consistent failure to attain the mission of the organization is a serious warning when significant groups (such as Congress or interest groups) are monitoring organizational outcomes with some seriousness.

Infrequently are evaluation studies the first signal that organizations are falling short of expectations. Most staffs get enough feedback through informal channels to be at least impressionistically aware of performance problems. Nevertheless, the systematic and carefully documented evidence that evaluation studies provide can crystallize the warning. Studies can pinpoint the nature and dimensions of failure. They can make it visible to groups inside and outside the organization who have not been informed about shortcomings (including top management, whom lower-level staff may have shielded from unfavorable reports). High-echelon decisionmakers and/ or outside constituency groups may be more ready than line staff to take remedial action.

A second function of information, including social science information, is *Guidance*. It can give direction for improvement in agency activities. Again, most of the information that agencies use to adjust their activities comes from sources other than research and analysis, for example from the experience of practitioners. Nevertheless, research and analysis are also potential sources of guidance. Basic research, to the extent that it can clarify causal relationships and demonstrate the origins of social problems, can give effective policy direction. It can suggest which conditions must be attacked if change is to occur, and indicate the kinds of intervention that hold promise of success. Policy research can provide information on the relative effectiveness of alternative strategies of action. Analysis can marshal evidence on the costs and benefits of a range of strategies and help clarify the consequences of decisions.

Organizations' willingness to implement the guidance derived from research appears to be seriously constrained by their limited range of feasible options. An organization is skilled in performing only a modest set of activities, and its traditional procedures exercise a heavy drag on its flexibility to venture beyond accustomed patterns. Even if research should show that radically different strategies have a high probability of working better for both the organization and its clients, many organizations would be unprepared to make the fundamental alterations in staffing, structure, investment, and leadership that such change would require. Thus, research's major contribution is often negative: it demonstrates which activities in the organizational repertoire are ineffective and guides the organization in discarding them, reducing the resources committed to them, or perhaps restructuring them.

The proclivity of organizations to make piecemeal adjustments of this kind is reinforced by the nature of most research
evidence. Very rarely do research studies identify clear causes
of social problems or demonstrate the undisputed superiority
of new approaches for dealing with them. Much more commonly, the data show modest correlations between variables,
with a mixture of positive and negative effects, and often
several studies on the same subject reach contradictory conclusions. Research of this type hardly points to unequivocal "solutions." It is not illogical for organizations to use such research
warily, as suggestive rather than definitive, and to make incremental changes that can be tested further in actual practice.

As organizational analysts have suggested, the functions of
warning and guidance are different and distinct, and information that serves one function does not necessarily serve the
other. Research, particularly evaluation research, is useful to
signal warnings about achievement of performance objectives.
Although there are less expensive and faster ways to find out
about outcomes, competent evaluation studies can delineate
the location and scope of organizational failings and mobilize
attention outside as well as within the organization. But evaluations often provide little direction for remedying the situation.
Unless they have been explicitly designed to compare alternative strategies, and one strategy has patently better effects than
the others, they offer little in the way of prescription for the
future. The guidance function has to date been only modestly
fulfilled by social science research (Lindblom and Cohen,
1979). The ambivalence of research findings on many topics,
and organizations' reluctance to depart far from the known,
particularly when the evidence looks relatively flimsy, limit the
application of research as guidance. The continuing challenge
to social science research is to develop firmer, better-grounded
conclusions that will have greater cogency for organizational
decisionmaking.

But our excursion into enlightenment has alerted us to a
third function of social science: *Reorientation*. Research can
provide alternative perspectives for understanding and interpreting events. It can challenge the assumptions that underlie
organizational programs and offer new concepts, new ideas,

new ways of thinking about issues. For example, it can alter organization members' perceptions of what constitutes a warning to the stability of the organization, and it can create a shift in what is perceived as guidance. By offering new frames of reference, it can help an organization reinterpret what it has been doing and open new vistas for the future. Perhaps above all, it can provoke a willingness to think critically about the organization—its mission, its goals, its activities, its standards of success. The ideas from social science may be able to stimulate internal reexamination, which may often be the best route to organizational renewal.

TWO PURPOSES FOR INFORMATION USE

If the first step in reconceptualizing research use is to understand the three functions that information serves, the second step is to recognize that organizations use information for two analytically distinct purposes. So far I have concentrated on the achievement of organizational goals. This is the salient context for social science researchers and policy analysts whose work is concerned with mission performance. But as students of organizational behavior have emphasized, much of the time organizations are preoccupied with issues of survival and maintenance. Their attention is directed less toward achievement of programmatic aims than toward expansion of organizational programs, budget and influence.

Obviously they can use information in this cause as well. Merely sponsoring research and analysis can be a ritual protection by giving the organization the coloration of rationality and responsiveness. But they can also use the *information and ideas* that emerge from research to serve maintenance imperatives. In fact, because the issues are often simpler to analyze and appropriate responses are better defined, they may be more ready to put research to use for maintenance purposes. It is easier to survey and document the "unserved needs" that justify budget increases than to develop better means for serving those needs. It is easier to discover and coordinate overlapping services than to improve the effective content of the services provided.

Just as organizations use information as warning, guidance, and reorientation for the achievement of programmatic aims, they use information as Warning, Guidance, and Reorientation in the interest of organizational survival. Thus, we have a sixfold typology to serve as a taxonomic start toward a model of information use.[3] The next steps will be to understand the

Functions of information	Organizational Purposes	
	Goal achievement	Organizational maintenance
Warning	A	B
Guidance	C	D
Reorientation	E	F

circumstances under which organizations use information for these different purposes. A problem that has plagued the empirical study of research utilization has been the inexactness and ambiguity of what constitutes use of research (Weiss, 1979), and studies have adopted measures based on widely varying definitional premises. With better definition, we should be able to move ahead toward development of a cumulative body of knowledge on the subject.

Notes

1. This discussion focuses on only one strand in the large and diverse organizational literature. It attempts to give a broad-brush outline of the dominant themes of this tradition, bypassing the variations and differences among authors.

2. That information can be dysfunctional as well as beneficial for organizations should also be recognized. A persuasive case can be made that for human service organizations, whose technologies are weak and unpredictable, research and evaluation can disturb the "subtle networks of authority, communication, and confidence which allow organizations to deliver their services in a complex environment" (Knapp, 1979; also see Meyer and Rowan, 1977). By opening up new controversies, research information can jar the stability of organizations whose performance depends upon mutual good faith and continuity of relationships.

3. The uses of information as warning (cell B) and guidance (cell

D) for purposes of organizational survival and legitimation seem self-evident, but the use of information as reorientation is an inherently more diffuse phenomenon. Perhaps an illustration will clarify such use for organizational maintenance purposes (cell F). John Colombotos (1975) conducted a study of physicians' attitudes towards national health insurance and discovered that, despite the opposition of the American Medical Association at the time, most physicians accepted the program. Planners in federal health agencies could have used that information to discount the significance of the AMA as a spokesman for American medicine and to reorient their approach to bargaining with the AMA over program proposals. (In time, of course, the AMA put forward its own health insurance plan.) From the standpoint of the AMA's maintenance imperatives, the data could have served as warning.

References

Allison, Graham T. *Essence of Decision: Explaining the Cuban Missile Crisis*. Boston: Little, Brown, 1971.

Barnard, Chester I. *The Functions of the Executive*. Cambridge, Mass.: Harvard University Press, 1962. 1st ed. 1938.

Berg, Mark R., Jeffery L. Brudney, Theodore D. Fuller, Donald N. Michael, and Beverly K. Roth. *Factors Affecting Utilization of Technology Assessment Studies in Policy-Making*. Ann Arbor, Mich. Center for Research on Utilization of Scientific Knowledge, Institute for Social Research, University of Michigan, 1978.

Boeckmann, Margaret E. "Policy Impacts of the New Jersey Income Maintenance Experiment." *Policy Sciences* 7 (March 1976): 53–76.

Burt, Marvin R., Harry P. Hatry, and Donald M. Fisk. *Factors Affecting the Impact of Urban Policy Analysis: Ten Case Histories*. Washington, D.C.: Urban Institute, 1972.

Caplan, Nathan. "A Minimal Set of Conditions Necessary for the Utilization of Social Science Knowledge in Policy Formulation at the National Level." In C. H. Weiss, ed., *Using Social Research in Public Policy Making*, pp. 183–97. Lexington, Mass.: Lexington-Heath, 1977.

———, Andrea Morrison, and Russell J. Stambaugh. *The Use of Social Science Knowledge in Policy Decisions at the National Level: A Report to Respondents*. Ann Arbor, Mich.: Center for Research on Utilization of Scientific Knowledge, Institute for Social Research, University of Michigan, 1975.

Cohen, David K., and Janet A. Weiss. "Social Science and Social Policy: Schools and Race." In C. H. Weiss, ed., *Using Social Research in Public Policy Making*. Lexington, Mass.: Lexington-Heath, 1977.

Colombotos, John. "Physicians View National Health Insurance: A

National Study." *Medical Care* 13 (May 1975): 369–96.

Cyert, Richard M., and James C. March. *A Behavioral Theory of the Firm.* Englewood Cliffs, N.J.: Prentice-Hall, 1963.

Eccles, M. *Beckoning Frontiers.* New York, Knopf, 1951.

Kaufman, Herbert, with Michael Couzens. *Administrative Feedback.* Washington, D.C.: Brookings Institution, 1973.

Knapp, Michael S. "Tinkering with Open Systems: Organizational Theory Perspectives on Educational Program Evaluation." In Lois-Ellin Datta and Robert Perloff, eds., *Improving Evaluations.* Beverly Hills, Cal.: Sage, 1979.

Knorr, Karin D. "Policymakers' Use of Social Science Knowledge: Symbolic or Instrumental?" In C. H. Weiss, ed., *Using Social Research in Public Policy Making.* Lexington, Mass.: Lexington-Heath, 1977.

Lindblom, Charles E. "The Science of 'Muddling Through.'" *Public Administration Review* 19 (Spring 1959): 79–88.

———, and David K. Cohen. *Usable Knowledge: Social Science and Social Problem Solving.* New Haven, Conn.: Yale University Press, 1979.

March, James G., and Johan P. Olsen. *Ambiguity and Choice in Organizations.* Bergen, Norway: Universitetforlaget, 1976.

March, James G., and Herbert A. Simon. *Organizations.* New York: John Wiley and Sons, 1958.

Meyer, John W., and Brian Rowan. "Institutionalized Organizations: Formal Structure as Myth and Ceremony." In M. R. Davis, et al., *The Structure of Educational Systems: Explorations in the Theory of Loosely Coupled Organizations.* Stanford, Cal.: Center for Research and Development in Teaching, Stanford University, 1977.

Patton, Michael Q., et al. "In Search of Impact: An Analysis of the Utilization of Federal Health Evaluation Research." In C. H. Weiss, ed., *Using Social Research in Public Policy Making.* Lexington, Mass.: Lexington-Heath, 1977.

Research Triangle Institute. *Analysis of the Utility and Benefits of the National Crime Survey.* Research Triangle Park, N.C. : Research Triangle Institute, 1979.

Rich, Robert F. "Uses of Social Science Information by Federal Bureaucrats: Knowledge for Action versus Knowledge for Understanding." In C. H. Weiss, ed., *Using Social Research in Public Policy Making.* Lexington, Mass.: Lexington-Heath, 1977.

Simon, Herbert A. *Administrative Behavior.* 3rd ed. New York: Free Press, 1976.

Steinbruner, John D. *The Cybernetic Theory of Decision.* Princeton, N.J.: Princeton University Press, 1974.

Weiss, Carol H. *The Consequences of the Study of Federal Student Loan Programs: A Case Study in the Utilization of Social Research.* New York: Bureau of Applied Social Research, Columbia University, 1970.

———. "Research for Policy's Sake: The Enlightenment Function of Social Science Research." *Policy Analysis* 3, no. 4 (fall 1977): 521–45.

———. "The Many Meanings of Research Utilization." *Public*

Administration Review, Sept./Oct. 1979, pp. 426–31.

——, and Michael J. Bucuvalas. "Truth Tests and Utility Tests: Decision-Makers' Frames of Reference for Social Science Research." *American Sociological Review* 45 (April 1980): 302–13.

——, with Michael J. Bucuvalas. *Social Science Research and Decision-Making.* New York: Columbia University Press, 1980.

Chapter 8.

Management Control Systems in

Human Service Organizations

Regina E. Herzlinger

Definitions

Systems that control the pace and caliber of work are a normal aspect of American industry. They are essential to automated factories, large complex pieces of equipment such as satellites, and all servo-mechanistic machines. These control systems perform three functions. They *measure* some aspect of the work; *compare* the actual level to a desired level; and *adjust* the work in order to minimize the difference between the actual and desired level.

The systems that perform these functions in profit-seeking organizations are called management control systems. Their purpose is to motivate and evaluate the effectiveness and efficiency with which managerial plans are carried out. The systems consist of a *structure,* which measures both actual and expected performance, and a *process* for adjusting the differ-ence between the two.

This paper is in part a condensation of R. E. Herzlinger and N. M. Kane, *A Managerial Analysis of Federal Income Redistribution Mechanisms* (Cambridge, Mass.: Ballinger, 1979), chs. 1, 5.

Management Control Systems in Human Service Organizations

The control systems in human service organizations are most notable for their absence. Even the separate elements of such systems are usually missing: there is neither a control structure for measuring effectiveness and efficiency nor a control process for monitoring and evaluating performance.

I base this statement on my experiences as assistant secretary of the Office of Human Services in Massachusetts, and as a consultant to a large number and variety of human service organizations. Not one of more than one hundred large human service organizations with which I am familiar have man-

Table 8-1.

*Social Welfare Expenditures from Public Funds
in Relation to Total Government Expenditures*

Category of expenditure	1949–50	1969–70	1971–72	1972–73	1973–74
All public social welfare expenditures (\$ millions)*	22,741	140,074	184,502	206,591	230,110
Percent of total government expenditures	37.6	47.8	53.1	55.3	55.9
Federal social welfare expenditures (\$ millions)	10,541	77,074	106,002	122,291	137,310
Percent of total federal government expenditures	26.2	40.1	47.4	50.5	52.5
State and local social welfare expenditures (\$ millions)†	12,200	63,000	78,500	84,300	92,800
Percent of total state and local government expenditures	60.1	62.3	63.6	64.2	61.7

Source: Social Security Bulletin, *Annual Statistical Supplement 1974* (Washington, D.C.: GPC, 1974), table 2, p. 39.

*Expenditures from general revenues and from trust funds: excludes workmen's compensation and temporary disability insurance payments made through private carriers and self-insurers. Also excludes government contributions from general revenues to public employee retirement systems that are already reflected in social welfare expenditure data.
†From their own revenue sources. Excludes federal grants-in-aid.

agement control systems that are in any way comparable in quality to those in the private sector.[1]

The absence of good control systems is a major problem because, in the past thirty years, the percentage of governmental expenditures for human service programs has grown from 26.2 percent in 1950, which many believed overly frugal, into the single largest component of the budget (see Table 8-1). Included among these programs are federal dollars in support of welfare, Medicare and Medicaid, veterans' benefits, social services, higher vocational, elementary, and secondary educational programs, housing programs, manpower training, and a host of others. This astounding growth rate has alarmed even the staunchest supporters of human service programs, for many of the programs are ill-conceived and poorly executed. Welfare abuse, Medicaid fraud, student loan defaults, and profiteering in vocational education programs have all been front-page news so frequently that they can hardly be called news anymore. There is even substantial controversy about whether the programs have succeeded in redistributing income. So far, the government's attempts to police individual programs have accomplished little; many programs still fail to provide services to those who need them most, or provide them at a cost far higher than their market value.

THE CONTROL STRUCTURE PROBLEM

Most large human service organizations are out of control, both literally and figuratively. Why? In part, because it is difficult to measure either inputs or outputs in these organizations. Input measurement, or accounting, is complicated by the existence of three different audit guides for these organizations.[3] The guides do not dictate what the accounting statements should be, but they are a strong recommendation from the accounting profession to the human service field as to the form and content of the statements. The audit guides not only differ in the types of financial statements they recommend, but also in the way they recognize accounting events.

To rub salt in the wound, most human service organizations also need to comply with complex externally mandated cost-accounting system requirements. Hospitals, for example, are required by the major third-party payers to file a large matrix, which requires a multiple distribution of overhead expenses to the mission units. This form is the famous (or infamous) "stepdown," which usually requires computer assistance for its completion.

The external financial and cost-accounting requirements are so onerous that they drain managerial resources away from the development of internal management control systems. Further, because the accounting systems are based on external needs, they cannot be readily adopted for internal control purposes. For example, the hospital stepdown usually allocates large amounts of costs to the ancillary and outpatient departments, which are not as closely regulated as the inpatient departments and so can more readily absorb costs. These data are fine for maximizing reimbursement, but they are next to useless for internal control because they overstate or understate the costs of various departments. Similarly, the audit guide for voluntary health and welfare organizations and the United Way guidelines require cost data by programs; but control is usually exercised by organizational unit, not by program, and the external data aren't useful for internal purposes.

In some organizations, there is no accounting system at all. The state of West Virginia, for example, operates a single-entry accounting system, and a $100 million hospital just completed installation of a general ledger system! Both organizations suffer from an astronomical growth rate that distracted managers attention from the tedious job of installing a better system.

Difficulties in accounting for inputs, however, are dwarfed by the problems of output measurement. Most human service organizations produce a wide array of services that should be carefully measured. But in most organizations it is difficult to obtain even the simplest measures of output, such as volume of activity. Complex measures of quality, benefits, and recipient satisfaction are hardly ever found; and when they are present, they are the result of a special study or survey rather than of a routine measuring system. Some managers claim that it is difficult to measure output accurately ("How can you measure quality?"), and that the measurement process is untenable. The argument is attractive but pernicious; it implies that no measurement is better than mildly incorrect measurement.

THE CONTROL PROCESS PROBLEM

In the absence of relevant data, it is impossible to use a control process. Most human service organizations consequently do not use a routine system to motivate and evaluate their managers' and employees' performances; these functions are handled either by using data gathered for a particular occasion or by using no data at all.

However, even if the data were present, it is unclear that they would be used for control. Most human service organizations are managed by professionals—physicians, nurses, and social workers. Their professional training stressed peer respect, group interdependency, and professional competence. These norms are antithetical to the hierarchical, corporate version of the control process. Further, the motivational tools open to the private sector are frequently absent in human service organizations. Salaries may not be dramatically increased, firing is difficult, promotion is slow, and managerial slots are limited.

WHAT CAN BE DONE?

The problems exist because of the intrinsic difficulties of measurement, because of the exuberant growth in the activities of human service organizations, but also in large part because the managers of these organizations are both professionally and politically resistant to installing accurate output measurement systems. The professional resistance arises because most of the managers *are* professionals—complex and subtle people who resist the notion of encapsulating their work in ten easy numbers. The political resistance arises because all managers, indeed all people, don't enjoy having their performance measured. But in human service organizations there is no clear operational source of accountability, and managers can luxuriate in the privilege of not being subjected to measurement.

There are two solutions to the control problem of human service organizations. Control in these organizations is a very old function, dating back to the Roman Empire, which set up fund accounts for its cities. It is not lack of knowledge that inhibits the development of better control mechanisms, but rather the absence of an incentive to install such systems. There is no competition for survival, the clients are usually at the mercy of the organization, and the organization's services are frequently too complex and diffuse to be controlled by the legislature, the press, or the public.

A more promising avenue is to examine the nature of human service organizations to see if a change in their nature will lead to a change in the control process. My interest is not in the control process itself, but rather in investigating administrative mechanisms that would make human service organizations more responsive and efficient in their practices.

CHANGING THE NATURE OF HUMAN SERVICE ORGANIZATIONS

The government wears several hats to administer its human services programs. Sometimes, like a factory, it directly finances and produces human services. At other times, like an insurance company, it guarantees private sector loans to target consumers or private providers who purchase or produce specific services. It also acts like a commercial bank by making loans and equity capital grants to businesses. And finally, it sometimes acts like a savings bank by providing consumer loans or grants directly to the low-income consumer for specific human services.

Many of the agencies that administer human service programs wear all these hats simultaneously. A typical department of human services, for example, is a factory that helps to produce health care; an insurance firm that guarantees educational loans; a commercial bank that grants money to private developers of particular services; and a savings bank that provides welfare funds, Medicaid, and food stamps directly to recipients.

Each mechanism was developed for a reason. Running a factory guarantees a source of supply and ensures that the services needed will be produced. An insurance firm and a bank, both less costly mechanisms than the factory, considerably lever the government's investment. A bank, additionally, enables low-income consumers who cannot borrow money to receive direct infusions of capital.

While there are many reasons for having these separate administrative models, there is no reason to have all of them carrying out the same goal. Each mechanism emerged from a patchwork of legislation that responded to the crises of the moment by creating organizational testimonials to legislative concern. Their relative merits have never been carefully considered. As a general rule, policy concerns dominate managerial concerns in all aspects of the human services. The assumption is that the disappointing results of the programs to date are failures in policy, not in administration. But the assumption may be incorrect. Perhaps an examination of the effects of the various mechanisms will clarify their role in implementing human services. (Our labels—savings bank, insurance company, commercial bank, and factory—are meant as shorthand descriptions of each mechanism's characteristics. They are not designed to perfectly correspond with their private sector counterparts.)

The factory. Under this administrative mechanism, a unit of the federal, state, or local government manages production directly, and finances the capital and operating needs of the producer. Examples of the factory model are public housing programs, hospitals, neighborhood health centers, most manpower training programs, day care and social service programs, and mental health care facilities.

The insurance company. Under this administrative mechanism, the government insures the capital investment made by private sector providers of a target good or service. The mechanism is primarily used for low-income housing and education. The insurance company mechanism operates to correct the credit markets by providing governmental risk insurance. (Programs that insure consumers are classified under the savings bank model.)

The commercial bank. Under this administrative mechanism, the public sector gives capital or operating funds, either as grants or loans, to private providers of services in order to encourage the private sector to produce target goods or services. Most of the contracting out of human services is an example of the use of this mechanism. The educational performance contracting experiments conducted by the OEO are another example of the commercial bank model.

The savings bank. This model describes the cash transfer. It is the administrative mechanism in which the public sector finances the operating or capital needs of low-income consumers themselves, rather than financing the providers of goods and services targeted to low-income families. Under the savings bank model, the consumer is the focal point: the private (or public) provider of such services is held accountable to the consumer. Under the other models, the government is the focal point: whichever sector undertakes responsibility for the management and provision of the target goods or services is held accountable, primarily to an agency of the federal government.

In most public "savings bank" programs, the government, like a private savings bank, determines what goods or services its funds will be used to purchase—but based on social policy rather than on credit risk. Included under this mechanism are the Medicare and Medicaid health programs, which provide funds to the elderly and the poor to pay for certain kinds of health care; the food stamp program, which reduces the costs of food for participants; and all welfare programs. Among those savings bank programs in which consumers receive funds to purchase goods or services are the housing allowance, the Negative Income Tax, and the educational voucher experiment conducted in Alum Rock, California.

WHY FOUR MECHANISMS?

If the purpose of these programs is merely to transfer income from one part of the economy to another, the savings bank mechanism most clearly and efficiently accomplishes that goal. If their purpose is to affect the recipient's utility function, then an unrestricted cash transfer is the most effective medium, because cash is always preferred to the receipt of services. If desires other than those of the consumer are of concern as well, then a restricted cash transfer limits consumption to those goods and services that the donor chooses.

Why, then, do the other three mechanisms exist? As a class, they are used when the wish is not merely to redistribute income, but also to ensure production of particular goods or services.

The insurance company mechanism is used to induce production of credit to a particular target group whose credit risk is so high that the government needs to replace their risk with its own; for example, the insurance company mechanism can correct the underinvestment in human capital that might exist because the credit markets perceive investments in human beings to be riskier than investments in physical capital. The provision of insurance guarantees will correct this imperfection and facilitate accomplishment of the socially desirable goal of investments in both human and physical capital up to the point where both earn an equal additional return on an extra unit of investment. (Government intervention is necessary to ensure that the level of education will not be below a socially optimal level.)

The commercial bank mechanism is used when the supply of the desired good or service by the private sector would not be forthcoming without governmental support. It is socially desirable in industries with high fixed costs and rapidly declining average cost curves. Without governmental subsidy, the industry won't produce at its minimum cost level. The use of the commercial bank in this case would enable the quantity of production to reach the socially desired minimum cost level. It could be used, for example, to provide institutional financing for high-fixed-cost health care organizations to produce at an optimum level. It could also be used for those services where suppliers are unlikely to respond to the needs of the recipients without this financing for reasons of risk or taste; for example, private housing developers are unlikely to work in inner-city areas without federal subsidies.

The factory is a much more difficult administrative mechanism to rationalize. For pure public goods—such inexhaustible and indivisible items as a lighthouse or police services—a factory model is the only feasible one. The private sector wouldn't produce such a good because there is no effective way to bar anyone from using it, and hence no way to extract a price for its use. But services often found under the factory model, such as health care, education, and welfare, don't fit this public good definition. Why then are they produced by the public sector?

One school of thought argues that human service programs are public goods because each taxpayer receives benefits from such programs. When our neighbors become healthier we benefit because the possibility of our catching an infectious disease from them diminishes. If we didn't assist others by consuming these services, the level of consumption would be below the socially optimum one. Although this theory explains why a governmental unit should be involved when such external benefits exist, it does not explain why the factory mechanism should be used. The commercial bank, savings bank, or insurance company mechanisms could be used as well.

An alternative school of thought says that the factory model is created in those instances where special interest groups that desire the provision of a good or service are very powerful. These groups wish to have such programs in order to control society. They prefer to execute social control under the factory model because it is more readily controlled than the private-sector commercial bank model.

A related explanation is that the factory mechanism is needed in those sectors that are so imperfect that they would otherwise require intensive regulation. This theory is the most powerful and appealing of the three. For example, unlike the other explanations, it provides a sensible rationale for the elementary and secondary school, which produce services whose complexity and importance would, if left to private sector provision, require intensive regulation. Similarly, it explains the use of the factory model in the supply of inelastic health care, where the mere infusion of funds would cause a relatively greater inflation of prices than an increase in supply, and thus call for intensive regulation. The factory model, under which the government captures and controls the means of production, can help to overcome this tendency and avoid regulation.

A POLITICAL RATIONALE

If income redistribution is viewed from a broader perspective that encompasses its effects on the suppliers of the goods and services and the political structure, then the reasons for the existence of all four mechanisms become clearer and more persuasive.

All mechanisms except the savings bank benefit the supplier. To the extent that the supplier is an important factor in the choice, these mechanisms will be favored. In the arena of income redistribution programs, the power of the suppliers—physicians, educators, banks, and housing firms—is surely much greater than that of the recipients. If the motives for income redistribution are traced to political persuasions, the use of the factory, the commercial bank, and the insurance company provides ready organizational testimonials to political interest groups. Further, these mechanisms are political chameleons; they can be viewed simultaneously as politically conservative—because they attempt to transfer functions away from the federal government to private organizations or to state and local governments—and politically liberal—because they involve redistributive functions. Lastly, the existence of many different mechanisms makes it more difficult to readily alter the level of income redistribution.

ADMINISTRATIVE FEASIBILITY OF
THE FOUR MECHANISMS

An organization designed to provide human services, like any other organization, has three central administrative systems: a *marketing* system that ensures that the appropriate clients are advised of the availability of goods and services and that the channels for distributing them are readily available; a *production* system that carries out the program's activities; and a *control* system that audits the extent to which the organization's plans have been executed in an effective and efficient manner.

For all four mechanisms, the marketing function involves dissemination of information about the program to those who are potentially eligible for it. The skills involved in marketing are those of distinguishing the target group and reaching them with a clear and attractive message. A measure of marketing skill is the percentage of eligible individuals that becomes involved in the program. The marketing function is well performed under all four mechanisms because program managers tend to be both enthusiastic program advocates and knowledgeable about the substantive content of their programs.

The content of the production function differs under each of the four mechanisms. For the insurance company, it consists of providing insurance for loans and is a relatively small task; for the commercial bank, it consists of designing and executing a contract between the public and private sectors; for the factory, it consists of producing the desired goods and services; and for the savings bank, it consists of transferring funds. The insurance company and the savings bank require functional skills—the ability to handle and analyze massive amounts of data—that the professional manager is unlikely to have. The commercial bank requires expert negotiating skill, which again is unlikely to be mastered by the professional manager. Only the factory's production mechanism puts the professional's skills to their appropriate use.

The control function involves measuring the effectiveness and efficiency of output. It requires a record-keeping system, a mechanism for self-audit and for objective measurement of outcomes, a peer relationship when negotiating with the private sector, and the ability to correct abuses. This function requires immaculate records and the ability to manipulate those records in order to extricate the information required. The functional skills required are those of financial management, data processsing, and evaluation. It is unlikely that the professionals who manage these programs will have these skills.

Further, were it possible to exercise the control function, in many programs it would be undesirable to do so. Many human service programs arise from ambiguous motives. These motives would be clarified by effectively implementing the control function, and the fragile stability maintained between explicit and implicit goals would be disrupted. But there is no one demanding such clarification. On the contrary, most of those interested in the program would prefer that the clarification not occur. That is, the process of control may be antithetical to many of the program's sub rosa goals. Lacking a clear demand for accountability, the process is the most likely of the three functions to be poorly implemented.

THE RELATIVE DESIRABILITY OF
THE FOUR MECHANISMS

An insurance company sells protection against the risk of various catastrophic events. It earns a profit by charging premiums greater than the costs of these catastrophes. The more probable the catastrophe, the greater the premium. An insurance company minimizes its own risks by obtaining a volume of clients large enough that the impact of any event will be relatively small and by selecting risks with a lower chance of being catastrophic. Thus, most successful insurance firms are large, with assets in the billions of dollars, discriminate against high risks by refusing to offer coverage, and can raise premiums that will offset the expected present value of future losses. The administrative functions critical to an insurance company are marketing, in order to obtain volume, and control, to assess risks, price premiums properly, and audit claims.

In the public sector, the insurance company model should be used when the risk is so high that the private sector will either refuse to provide insurance or else provide insurance only at a very high premium. Unlike private sector firms, public mechanisms cannot discriminate against high risk situations, nor can they charge the high premiums necessary to break even. Thus the public insurance company has a large deficit and a high rate of catastrophic events. The important administrative function is marketing, to bring the program to the attention of the high-risk cases for which it was designed. Neither the control function nor the production function are central to the aims of the public insurance company and are understaffed.

As a result, the insurance company model has a high incidence of fraudulent claims. It also has the most favorable effect on volume: an insurance mechanism intrinsically requires large volume and, because its only costs are those of paying for defaults, it is much cheaper than the other mechanisms and thus will provide the greatest impact per dollar spent. Its quality effects varied with its intended use. If the insured loans were used to purchase services available to all consumers, it had no differential quality effect; but if it was used only for services produced for low-income consumers, its quality effects were indeterminate.

Under the commercial bank mechanism, the public sector contracts with the private sector to provide certain goods or services. In theory, this mechanism is used when the relatively unconstrained environment of the private sector enables it to achieve results impossible in the public sector. Additionally, because it uses existing suppliers, it ensures a rapid supply effect. Lastly, because it is done on a contractual basis, it is more flexible than the factory.

In practice, the commercial bank mechanism seems to be used to respond to the political demands of powerful private sector suppliers. For example, housing programs may well be designed more to accommodate the construction or banking lobby than to accommodate those who will be using the units. Similarly, many institutionally based higher education programs seem to be a response to the pressures of the education lobby, rather than to the (nonexistent) student or parent lobby. The pervasiveness of supplier influence is exemplified by the fact that the higher education policy debate is usually structured solely in terms of the roles of public versus private institutions. Thanks to their supplier orientation, commercial bank programs are well funded and thus have a large impact on supply. Their efficiency and quality effects depend on whether the goods or services are available to all—in which case they will have no effect—or are provided only to low-income consumers. If the latter, their effect is a function of the government's auditing capability.

The critical administrative function in the commercial bank mechanism is to structure an equitable contract between the public sector and its private sector provider and to audit and enforce adherence to that contract. This control function is never well executed. The functions of marketing and production are left to the private sector organizations. For these reasons, the commercial bank is not an attractive income redistributing device. It is aimed much more at the suppliers than the consumers. It is frequently the costliest mechanism, for it layers both private and public sector costs. It is also fraught with other hazards of low output or quality because of the weaknesses in the public sector's control abilities.

Both private and public sector organizations have the option of either producing or buying their products from an outside supplier or factory. This is referred to as the "make or buy" decision. The reasons for choosing to make rather than to buy are either economic or strategic in origin. In capital-intensive industries, internal production enables the firm to capture the benefits of economies of scale that would otherwise accrue to an outside supplier. Additionally, the firm may wish to control some characteristic such as quality through internal manufacture. Lastly, if the number of outside suppliers is small, the firm may wish to have its own manufacturing facilities so that its suppliers will not extract oligopolistic profits.

Public sector factories that produce human services have similar reasons for existence. They may help the public sector capture the benefits of economies of scale; however, because the services involved are labor-intensive rather than capital-intensive, it is doubtful that such benefits occur. More likely, they exist to ensure appropriate supply, price, quality, and so forth. For example, by running hospitals, the government ensures that health care services will be available for certain target groups, such as veterans. Further, governmental control of health care providers prevents them from extracting the large returns they might command in the private sector. Similarly, the provision of public housing ensures low-income citizens access to high-quality housing. The public sector factory also functions as a source of patronage power, which can strengthen the political base of its sponsors, and as a source of social control. There is no private sector analogue to these functions.

In practice, the precise reason for choosing to run a public sector factory is obscure. Most likely there is no one reason. Rather, the public factory is created for some combination of four motives: low cost, guaranteed provision of some desirable and otherwise unattainable characteristics, minimization of oligopolistic profits, and patronage powers.

Managers of private sector factories tend to have backgrounds in production rather than in marketing or control. They try to ensure that the intended aims of the factory are attained, be they low cost or high quality. In those cases where the factory has multiple goals imposed on it—for example, the attainment of low-cost production and an acceptable level of quality—the parent firm will include a number of control functions in the factory to assure that these aims are being attained. For example, many factories have an independent quality control unit and a cost control staff.

Public sector factories are also managed by people with a background in producing the particular good or service: hospitals are managed by physicians, schools by educators, and social service agencies by social workers. If there is a clear measure of performance for the factory, they will try to attain it; for example, a clear measure of performance for manpower programs is the number of placements, and the manpower specialists who manage such programs will do so with the end of maximizing job placements.

Most factory programs have multiple purposes, and it is unlikely that there will be one measure of performance. If the public sector has multiple control staffs to audit the attainment of each of these multiple outputs, the factory manager, as in the private sector, will try to attain them all. If such control capacity does not exist, the exact impact of the factory is unknown. It is likely that the professional managers will either revert to their professional norms for guidance or else will be "bureaucratic" in their managerial responses. Despite the vast literature on bureaucracies, it remains unclear what "being bureaucratic" involves: it may mean trying to raise expenses so as to maximize one's budget and patronage slots, or it may imply the formalization and routinization of work to promote efficiency.

Using each of these possible motivations, we find multiple-purpose factories producing very high-quality outputs (under the professional motivation school), or very expensive outputs (under the maximum budget theory), or very cost-effective outputs (under the bureaucratic model). The most frequent outcome is that the factory maximizes the most readily measurable and visible dimension of performance, volume of output.

Unlike the factory and commercial bank, the savings bank is oriented totally toward the consumer. It is even more directly linked to the consumer than the insurance company, which uses the capital markets as an intermediary. Because of its direct linkage to the consumer, the savings bank is generally the most efficient mechanism. First, it requires the lowest administrative costs of any of the four mechanisms, and second, it allows consumers to choose both the form and provider of goods and services that best meet their needs. The losses observed in the factory and commercial bank model for services whose quality is in excess of that desired by the consumers should occur to a relatively lower extent under the savings bank.

Second to the insurance company, the savings bank model has the greatest effect on supply per dollar spent. The savings bank mechanism permits the normal market mechanism to work, so that grossly inefficient providers should be driven out of business. Its quality effect, which can't be easily described, revolves around the motives for human service programs. If they are viewed as investments that cause social benefits, then the unrestricted savings bank mechanism may undermine those goals if low-income consumers prefer consumption patterns different from those that society as a whole would espouse. However, if the motives are charitable and non-paternalistic, intended for the benefit of the low-income consumer as he or she defines benefit, there need be little concern about quality levels.

The savings bank mechanism is the least biased in its distribution, because only those who have the desired attributes can qualify for it. It also has the lowest administrative and production costs attached to it, because it involves the simplest set of administrative functions. It may unleash great inflation, however, and it is greatly susceptible to provider and client fraud.

The Effects of the Mechanisms
in Different Sectors

The desirability of using a particular mechanism depends not only on its innate characteristics, but also on the sector in which it is to operate. In supply inelastic sectors whose production is closely controlled by the industry, the factory mechanism—in which the government controls the production process—seems to be the overall best mechanism. Relative to the others it achieves lower production costs, better distribution of services, and less inflation. Second only to the insurance company, it also achieves a high supply response. The effect on fraud and quality are uncertain; but many view factory quality as being the lowest among the four mechanisms.

Thus, for a human service program in a supply inelastic sector, such as portions of the health care industry, the factory model is surprisingly appealing. In supply elastic sectors, on the other hand, its appeal is considerably diminished. For those sectors, the unrestricted savings bank model is most capable of achieving the desired distribution, has the lowest production and administrative expenses, most clearly enables consumers to express their choice of quality levels, is the least susceptible to provider fraud and inflation, and, second to the insurance mechanism, has the greatest effect on supply. In those sectors where social benefits are important, the use of a restricted voucher is desirable—despite the welfare loss to the consumer involved.

In supply elastic sectors, both the commercial bank and the insurance company are poor administrative choices. Despite its potentially great economies, the insurance company has such poor distributional effects that it should not be used as the sole income redistribution mechanism. Because its administrators are forced to manage programs whose legislated objectives of self-sufficiency and income transfer are mutually exclusive, the programs tend to be poorly administered and their benefits poorly distributed. In practice, it becomes a savings bank; but the transfers are made to those who choose to default on their loans, rather than to those whom the programs were intended to benefit—a poor model for the purpose of income transfer. Conversely, the insurance company is an excellent vehicle for middle-class programs. Thus, if it were coupled with a program of substantial cash grants to low-income consumers, it could achieve the cost-effective results for which it is designed. Used in isolation, however, it is antithetical to the aims of human service programs.

The commercial bank mechanism is not as clearly undesirable as that of the insurance company. It is the most clearly supplier-oriented program, it tends to be well funded, and it generally produces positive supply effects—sometimes excessively so. Nevertheless, it is very susceptible to inflation and fraud, achieves poor distributional results, has high production and administrative costs, and severely strains the public sector's managerial capabilities. An even greater strain on those capabilities is imposed by the factory mechanism, and under supply elastic conditions there seems to be no compelling reason for its use. In both of these provider-oriented mechanisms, the impact on quality is indeterminate—but the range and diversity of choices available to the consumer are much more limited than under the savings bank or insurance company mechanisms.

In sectors that are supply elastic but nevertheless unlikely to service the designated target group, the use of a commercial bank or factory mechanism is necessary. For example, programs for recipients such as the mentally disabled or particular racial groups may not elicit a supply response, and thus necessitate a governmental factory or a contract with a private organization. These mechanisms should be used only under such stringent circumstances, because they exhibit otherwise undesirable characteristics.

Administrative Implications

Human service problems are frequently viewed as problems solely of economic policy. Thus the government has undertaken massive experiments varying the levels of support and taxation in order to hit upon the "right" negative income transfer policy. Once it is discovered, the assumption is that no problems will remain in the income redistribution area other than to fine-tune the levels of benefits and taxation.

But there is ample evidence from both the public and private sectors to indicate that the equation of policy with administration is incorrect, that conscious thought must be given to the delineation of the administrative mechanisms that will best execute a given strategy. This is especially true for income transfer programs, most of which have proved difficult to administer. To gain insight into appropriate administrative structures, it is useful to look at the private sector and to survey current structures in these programs.

A study of seventy major successful American firms found that "structure followed strategy": all the firms studied accompanied the successive delineation of new strategies with new administrative systems that could implement those strategies.[3] Another study found effective performance only in firms that had a good fit between the strategy of the organization and the administrative systems used to execute it.[4] The causal link between strategy and structure is not unidirectional. A study of a large firm's resource allocation process found that "structure shapes the manager's definition of . . . problems by directing, limiting, and coloring his focus and perceptions."[5] Sometimes the effects are pernicious, and structure prohibits strategy from being implemented in the intended manner. Numerous studies of traditional models of formalized, hierarchical, and rigid organizations have found them inappropriate for the complex interplays necessary to execute strategy effectively, leading to the pejorative implications currently attached to the word bureaucracy.

THE PRESENT ORGANIZATIONAL STRUCTURE

Given the evidence that attempting to solve policy problems while ignoring issues of structure is unwise, a review of the structure of existing human service programs is in order.

There are three basic forms of organizational structure: (1) A *programmatic* or divisionalized structure, whose component departments bear total responsibility for all phases of a program or product. (2) A *functional* structure, whose units are responsible for executing the functions critical to the organization, such as marketing, production, and control. (3) A *matrix* organization, in which one set of managers bears program responsibility while another set bears functional responsibility. Each cell within the matrix organization is thus under the joint management of a program and a functional supervisor.

Because human service programs are lodged in hundreds of federal agencies and executed by state and local governments as well as the private sector, it is not a simple task to identify organizational structure. Yet, despite the complexity, one characteristic does readily emerge from the multiplicity of agencies and levels: *all the activities are implemented by bureaus that carry programmatic titles and responsibilities.*

Why is this programmatic structure so pervasive? One answer is provided by the view that "the purpose of an organization in a political environment is to balance the competing interests within given programs so that none is immune to public control and capable of excluding less powerful segments of our society from effective participation in the system."[6] Because programmatic structuring is visible, it presumably enhances the ability of the "less powerful" to approach the organization. A different perspective is that (for social programs) ". . . ideology rarely rises above the level of symbol and sentiment; gestures and demonstrations of concern are all-important, impact and effectiveness are only the secondary concerns."[7] A programmatic organizational structure is an unambiguous gesture—clear evidence of Congressional concern for a particular group or problem.

The organization of American industry supports the wisdom of programmatic structuring. A recent study of major American firms found 75 percent of them to be organized on a divisionalized, product-centered basis.[8] Most of the firms had devised this structure consciously as an alternative to the functional structure that prevailed for American industry in the 1920s.

EVALUATION OF PROGRAMMATIC STRUCTURE

Programmatic structures are thus consistent with the pluralistic and democratic nature of American politics and with the motives of political representatives. Further, because they are so widely used in the private sector, they can be presumed to be efficient as well; the private sector, unlike the public one, is unconstrained by political motives and would likely select organizational structures, that are most efficient in executing strategy.

Yet there is reason for concern about the appropriateness of this organizational form for the delivery of human services. First, the empirical evidence discussed above indicates a widespread malaise in the administration of these programs. Where the problem is so severe, the causes are likely to be many; it is certainly worth considering structure as one possibility. Secondly, contingency theory, the most widely espoused theory of organization design, argues that while organizational structure is important to administration, there is no optimal method of organization and that the structure chosen should be contingent upon the environment and the tasks to be performed.

In *Organizations and Environment*, Paul Lawrence and Jay Lorsch persuasively illustrate the need to relate structure to the nature of tasks to be performed.[9] Under conditions of high uncertainty—technological change, changing characteristics of the environment, lack of information—the organization of tasks requires greater flexibility and independence than might otherwise be needed. Less specialization at lower levels of the organization can help to avoid organizational paralysis in the face of environmental changes: decisionmaking at a level too removed from the local environment would slow down critical response time. In such a case, a functional organization would behave less effectively than a programmatic organizational form.

Conversely, in a stable situation, a functional method of organization is advisable. It enables the organization to exploit the technical expertise of its functional managers and thus to be managed in the most efficient fashion. This line of reasoning is buttressed by findings that a "one-business" firm—where the supplier, product, and customer characteristics remain fairly stable and predictable—responded to growth by remaining functionally specialized with production, marketing, sales, and finance units. The functional design enabled the firm to become highly efficient by formalizing and standardizing each task. Further, because suppliers, customer characteristics, and the product did not vary in nature, only one "program" office was needed to integrate the functions and to ensure congruence of the programs with the goals set for the organization. When the nature of the business changes because of a change in market or product characteristics or diversification into other markets, functional firms develop "program" or "one-business" units of responsibility for each new business. These diversified, multibusiness firms are sometimes organized in a matrix of program and functional departments.

These results have been confirmed for multinational firms and in a number of other cultures.[10] They point unequivocally to the conclusion that organizational structure should be a function of the uncertainty and diversity of the tasks and environments of the organizational unit.

ENVIRONMENTAL AND TASK UNCERTAINTY
IN HUMAN SERVICE PROGRAMS

The size of human service programs has increased enormously over the past two decades—an increase spawned by a changing social and economic environment. The clients of the programs have also changed substantially; initially they were the aged, the infirm, and the handicapped, but by the late 1970s, every disadvantaged group was represented.

Despite these changes, the three tasks required to execute income transfer programs—marketing, production and control—have remained the same. In the marketing function, the clients are selected on unchanging criteria—for example, low-income transfers are intended for low-income people. The level of benefits may change, but the task of determining the appropriate amount of benefits is likely to remain the same. The production required for income transfer again may need volume adjustments, but few changes in technology or in uncertainty of information are likely. Finally, control functions—internal and external auditing, internal reporting, performance evaluation, and possibly regulation of provider industries—are unlikely to change. Although the tasks are stable in nature, they are specialized in content, requiring skills of an independent and technical nature. Thus the tasks required to implement income transfer are both specialized and standardized. On the basis of this analysis, a functional organizational structure seems highly desirable. The Internal Revenue Service reached the same conclusion and recommended a functional structure to execute their variant of the negative income tax.[11]

A functional organization is desirable no matter which income transfer mechanisms are used, since all four require efficient execution of the marketing, production, and control tasks in a stable environment; a functional organizational structure could provide the expertise needed to fulfill these tasks—an expertise that the current mechanisms so notably lack.

The personnel required to staff these units are for the most part presently employed by most government organizations. The employees for marketing-benefits determination should consist of policy analysts: economists, sociologists, program advocates, and specialists. Such people already work in the policy office of every agency. Merging them into one administrative unit would stimulate the design of a comprehensive income transfer program for the lower-income population. Local outreach and certification agency personnel are available in myriad public agencies—public housing agencies, welfare agencies, health insurance intermediaries, employment services—that are currently duplicating each other's efforts in every city of the country.

The production unit should be composed of personnel with experience in designing and implementing large fund transfer programs. Personnel from the tax bureau and large financial institutions would have the necessary background.

The third control task requires people skilled in financial and programmatic auditing. Personnel similar to GAO employees should be replicated in the executive branch for effective implementation of this task. Provider regulation is also needed. Staff from audit agencies, as well as existing state regulatory agencies, might begin to fill the personnel needs for this function.

CAN REORGANIZATION BE EFFECTED?

Almost every President from Theodore Roosevelt to Jimmy Carter has brought forth plans to reorganize the executive branch. Of late, they have rarely been successful. In general, it seems far easier to create a new organizational unit than to reorganize or consolidate an existing one. President Johnson, while initially successful in gaining Congressional approval of two new departments, failed in his plan to consolidate two existing departments. President Nixon's consolidation plans found a similar fate. Herbert Kaufman's study indicates that of the 175 federal government organizations that existed in 1923, 27 had died by 1973; but 246 were created in that same period.[12]

Kaufman attributes the "immortality" of organizations in the federal government to six factors: their statutory origins, which require Congressional action to be reversed; their support from friends in Congress; the gargantuan size of the federal budget and the tendency to review it only for changes from the previous year; the "independent" nature of some agencies, such as the Postal Service, which shelters them from review; their active development of friends and allies among their clients; and their strong ties with the dominant occupational group connected with that agency.[13]

All of these factors are likely to cause lively opposition to the functional reorganization of human service programs. Congressional protection of the existing structure is strong. Few Representatives are likely to be so altruistic as to vote for the repeal of the in-kind housing, educational, and manpower programs that so greatly enrich their districts. Further, the use of a functional structure would cause them to lose the simple public manifestation of their concerns that a programmatic structure affords. Even if they were so inclined, the suppliers, as well as the direct clients of these services, would be most concerned about the disappearance of "their" programs. It is difficult to persuade such intensely involved program advocates of the virtues of good management, particularly when its benefits are likely to appear not in the form of lower costs, but rather in more cost-effective behavior.

INCREMENTAL REORGANIZATIONS

Short of complete integration and functional reorganization of income maintenance programs, the most critical administrative need is for greater accountability and control. Not one of the programs studied had a reasonable degree of control over its expenditures and outputs, nor the kind of control system that a private firm of equal size would have. Improved measuring systems and auditing staffs are desperately needed.

The second most pressing administrative problem in the current income transfer system is the lack of integration among the numerous agencies involved in the process. This lack leads to the curious overlaps and omissions of the present programs. A poignant manifestation of this problem is the mentally disabled who, because of jurisdictional disputes among federal agencies and the absence of an integrated federal plan, are being discharged from state mental health hospitals into inadequate community facilities or custodial nursing homes. For them, as for many others, greater coordination among agencies is imperative.

It is, however, unlikely that either of these piecemeal reforms will be undertaken. The poor auditing capability of the government has long been of concern, and although "new" data systems are announced with tedious regularity, there is no evidence of progress. The reasons are two. Given the ambiguity of the motives underlying most income transfer programs, there is both an unwillingness and an inability to measure their results: unwillingness because the measuring effort would require clearer articulation of the goals against which to measure performance, and inability because it is difficult to imagine the process through which the articulation of goals would take place.

Similarly, although integration of human services has been supported by most state and local governments—which have created departments of human services—and by most academics and practitioners in the social welfare field, little progress has been made in truly integrating these services.

THE FUTURE

The vast array of congressionally mandated programs in housing, education, health, and social welfare involving income transfer are probably here to stay. The task for the future is to define and implement administrative mechanisms so that these programs can achieve their objectives efficiently. We have proposed a framework through which each program can be analyzed, and have discussed the applicability of the framework to each sector.

The factory model seems to be effective in cases where consumer judgment of products or services is difficult and where the supply is imperfect, as in health care. In such cases, a factory model, like the V.A. hospitals, is preferable in many ways to the other mechanisms.

Many programs involve a product or service that is subject to consumer preference, and for which numerous private suppliers exist, such as education, housing, and welfare services. In such cases, the savings bank mechanism enables the programs to reach the low-income consumer for whom they were intended and to have the most cost-effective impact on supply. Although wider use of the savings bank mechanism seems to be warranted, it will require a change in orientation from supplier-oriented programs.

In cases where high risk is not involved and where the target population is not totally without means, the insurance company mechanism can have the effect of a true insurance program; for example, the FHA has greatly broadened the credit markets for middle-income residential housing. In these cases, the insurance mechanism provides effective means of leveraging expenditures and achieving wide impact. Many so-called insurance programs do not have these characteristics and are similar to savings banks, but without the consumer choice explicit in the savings bank implementation.

The correct fit of mechanism to industry is only part of the solution, however. Each of these mechanisms requires proper execution of the control, marketing and production function. Organizational restructuring—by function rather than by program—will facilitate effective implementation of income redistribution programs. Without increased attention to these administrative issues, the human service task will be doomed to perpetuating past failures of control and execution.

Notes

1. The only exceptions to this generalization are very small organizations, such as those of the Visiting Nurses. However, because of their small size, they do not require formal control systems—control can be readily executed through personal observation. The larger versions of these organizations, such as the urban Visiting Nurses groups, suffer from the same control problems as the other large human service organizations.

2. The relevant audit guides are those for hospitals, voluntary health and welfare organizations, and state and local governments.

3. Alfred C. Chandler, *Strategy and Structure* (New York: Doubleday, 1961).

4. Lawrence E. Fouraker and John M. Stopford, "Organizational Structure and the Multinational Strategy," *Administrative Science Quarterly,* June 1968, pp. 46–64.

5. Joseph L. Bower, *Managing the Resource Allocation Process* (Boston: Division of Research, Harvard Business School, 1970), p. 71.

6. Harold Seidman, *Politics, Position and Power* (New York: Oxford University Press, 1975), p. 15.

7. David A. Stockman, "The Social Pork Barrel," *The Public Interest,* no. 39 (spring 1975), pp. 3–31.

8. Richard F. Vancil, *Decentralization: Managerial Ambiguity by Design* (New York: Financial Executives Research Foundation, 1979).

9. Paul R. Lawrence and Jay W. Lorsch, *Organization and Environment* (Boston: Division of Research, Harvard Business School, 1971).

10. See, for example, Fouraker and Stopford, "Organizational Structure"; Jerald Hage and Michael Aiken, "Routine Technology, Social Structure, and Organizational Goals," *Administrative Science Quarterly* 14 (1969): 366–77; Richard H. Hall, "Intraorganizational Structure Variation," *Administrative Science Quarterly,* Dec. 1962, pp. 295–308.

11. Internal Revenue Service, *Income Maintenance Program Task Force Report* (internal document, U.S. Office of the Treasury, April 24, 1974).

12. Herbert Kaufman, *Are Government Organizations Immortal?* (Washington, D.C.: Brookings Institution, 1976), p. 35.

13. Ibid., pp. 5–15.

Chapter 9.

The Role of Transfer Prices in

Purchase of Service Systems

in the Human Services

David W. Young

The use of transfer pricing is widespread in the corporate sector. Although transfer prices can exist in a variety of situations, they generally are defined as the unit price at which one division of a multidivisional corporation purchases goods or services from another. Since a free market mechanism does not exist for such purchases, the "price" must be set by corporate headquarters.

The absence of a free market mechanism poses several special considerations that might best be viewed by considering the following example:

> Delco and Chevrolet are two divisions of General Motors. Chevrolet, in manufacturing automobiles, requires batteries, which are produced by Delco. The price that the Chevrolet Division pays to the Delco Division for these batteries is the transfer price. What is the appropriate level for this price?

The answer is by no means intuitively obvious. Indeed, since several possible prices exist, the issue is highly debatable. The transfer price chosen can range from the incremental cost to Delco of producing one more battery (most likely the variable cost) to Delco's full market price, with several intermediate possibilities: direct cost, full cost, dealer price, and market price less an allowance are the most obvious. As a consequence, the appropriate transfer price is at best subjective, at worst highly ambiguous. Consider the following possible scenarios:

> Delco is operating at capacity, and selling 25 percent of its output to Chevrolet. Its market price includes selling expense plus an allowance for bad debts. If it were to sell its entire output to the outside (that is, not to other divisions of General Motors), it would most likely incur additional selling expenses and bad debt writeoffs. Should Delco charge Chevrolet its market price, or its market price less an allowance for selling expenses and bad debts?
>
> Regardless of the decision made above, the Chevrolet Division receives an offer from another company to sell its batteries of a comparable quality to Delco's at 10 percent less Delco's price. Should the Chevrolet Division be allowed to purchase the batteries from the other supplier, or should it be required to purchase its batteries from Delco?
>
> If Chevrolet is required to purchase its batteries from Delco, who should bear responsibility (and suffer the consequences) for the resulting decline in Chevrolet's profits?
>
> If Chevrolet is allowed to purchase its batteries from the outside, who should be held responsible for Delco's reduced profits resulting from higher selling expenses and bad debt writeoffs?

Although a variety of other situations and corresponding dilemmas could be presented, the above illustrations indicate the principal point: establishing appropriate transfer prices is a highly complex matter, having both technical accounting considerations and behavioral ramifications. The most appropriate transfer price becomes highly situational, contingent on a wide range of organizationally specific factors.[1]

Applicability to the Human Services

Beyond Chevrolet, Delco, and other multidivisional corporations, transfer pricing theory finds its way into the nonprofit sector as well. Here too the free market system is frequently curtailed in favor of some regulatory system whereby the public sector (federal, state, or local government) purchases service contracting entailing the purchase of goods or services from private agencies at something other than a "market" price. Such a situation is an integral part of the health care system, for example, where third parties such as Blue Cross, Medicare, and Medicaid purchase health care services from private hospitals at some price other than the standard hospital charge. This price is generally the full cost of the service as determined in accordance with cost accounting guidelines established by the third-party payers. Similar situations also exist when public sector agencies purchase various forms of human services from private agencies. A good example is the New York City Child Care System, where the city purchases foster home care, group home care, institutional care, adoption, and other child care services from some eighty voluntary child care agencies.[2]

Although a variety of issues are important to public sector managers involved in purchase of service contracting situations, the transfer price question clearly is an important one.[3] Indeed, under purchase of service contracting systems, the application of transfer pricing theory would appear to be of great significance for both public sector and private agency managers interested in the effective delivery of human services.

In the human service context, as in the corporate one, a key issue is that of incentives, since a transfer price is one mechanism for the public sector to signal to the private agencies its objectives and desired behavioral modalities. In fact, many of the problems frequently discussed in human service purchase of service settings can be directly tied to the use of inappropriate transfer prices. For example:

In many health care settings, the transfer price is set as either an all-inclusive per diem payment or a per diem payment designed to cover the routine care component of the patient's stay. In either instance, this per diem payment includes both the variable costs associated with the patient's stay and a portion of the hospital's fixed costs associated with its "readiness to serve." Under these circumstances, the hospital is highly motivated to maintain its patient days at or above budgeted levels in order to fully recover the fixed cost component of the per diem rate. As such, the transfer price, by design or default, signals the hospital that the third-party payers wish it to maintain its patient days at or above budgeted levels, rather than to reduce them whenever and wherever appropriate.

In the New York City Child Care System, a similar situation exists with the per diem rate. However, in addition to the incentives discussed above, the per diem rate is juxtaposed with a one-time payment for returning children to their natural families or placing them in adoptive homes. Because payments for these one-time activities have historically been quite low in comparison to the per diem rate, agencies have been penalized financially for moving a child from foster home care into a more permanent arrangement.[4] Here the relationship between two transfer prices (the one-time price and the ongoing price) sends a signal to the contracting agencies: ongoing foster home care is preferred to returns home or adoption.

Given these sorts of problems, and transfer pricing's key role in purchase of service settings, an exploration of transfer pricing theory and its applicability to purchase of service settings in the human services seems quite appropriate. The discussion will focus on one of the most prevalent purchases found in the human services: that of the public sector contracting with private agencies to deliver services to clients. The next section outlines some of the important transfer pricing considerations inherent in these situations.

Transfer Pricing Considerations

Although it is beyond the scope of this analysis to examine the historical development of purchase of service systems in the human services, there is, nevertheless, some evidence to suggest that many such systems have not given adequate consideration to what I have elsewhere termed "financial-programmatic congruence" (Young, 1979). Many purchase of service systems in health care, for instance, evolved out of an attempt to control costs without first considering desired programmatic effects. As increased lengths of stay came about, separate control mechanisms were developed instead of modifying the transfer pricing system.[5] One result is that utilization review procedures are now used in many states in an attempt to curtail unnecessarily long hospital stays.[6] Although modifications to the transfer pricing system have taken place in some instances, the changes have not fully eliminated the incentive to increase length of stay.[7]

Similar results have occurred in the New York City Child Care System. Minimal attempts by the contracting agencies to return children to their natural families or place them in adoptive homes resulted in the establishment of a separate control mechanism to mitigate the practice of maintaining children in foster care. Legislation now mandates a periodic review of each child in care, and agencies are required to present their plans to a judicial review. Justification for a decision to maintain a child in foster care can be made only on a quality of care basis.[8]

Analysis of these and similar situations leads to two important conclusions. First, many of the difficulties encountered by the public sector in achieving desired programmatic effects, such as the timely discharge of a patient or the placement of a child in a permanent living situation, have resulted from a transfer pricing system that sent inappropriate signals to the contracting agencies. Second, if the action taken by the public sector to correct agency behavior does not result in changes to the transfer pricing structure, but instead in increased regulatory activity, the result is both a higher cost to the taxpayer (to cover the increased regulation) and financial difficulties for the contracting agencies. Specifically, if an agency's budget is subjected to a review process, as frequently is the case, there is a possibility that the regulatory activity will reduce volume (for example, patient or client days) below budgeted levels. To the extent that the resulting reductions in payments cannot be matched by corresponding reductions in costs, the consequence is a larger than anticipated operating deficit.

The above analysis suggests three activities necessary for public sector managers who wish to improve upon the transfer pricing element in their purchase of service systems: first, to clearly delineate desired programmatic results; second, to obtain a clear understanding of the way in which contracting agencies can be expected to incur costs if they are to provide the desired results; and third, to design the transfer pricing system so that it fits both desired programmatic results and agencies' cost structures. Taken together, these activities constitute what might best be called the design process.

The Design Process

Although purchase of service systems has a variety of programmatic objectives, those that most frequently are tied to payments can be classified into three categories: (1) an ongoing service, such as a day of care; (2) a one-time service provided in conjunction with an ongoing service, such as a psychological test or a laboratory exam; and (3) a one-time service designed to eliminate the need for the ongoing service, such as adoption. In most instances the service in category 1 is not intended to continue indefinitely; indeed, from the perspective of the public sector manager concerned with both financial and programmatic objectives, it should continue only until the client is able to reach or return to a state of self-sufficiency. In some instances self-sufficiency is the result of an activity in category 3 (such as adoption); in others it is not. Finally, in most instances, some services from category 2 will be necessary either to prepare the client for self-sufficiency and the consequent elimination of the category 1 activity, or to prepare him or her for a category 3 activity and concomitant self-sufficiency.

In light of these three categories, some important public policy considerations emerge. First, although a category 1 activity should not be discontinued prematurely, it also should not extend any longer than necessary for the client to reach self-sufficiency. Second, category 2 services should be delivered only as necessary and appropriate in conjunction with a client's needs. Third, category 3 activities may involve complex cost-benefit considerations, depending on the cost of the one-time effort compared to the ongoing cost in category 1 and the resulting benefits derived by the client. However, as I have argued earlier (Young and Allen, 1977), the financial analysis can be viewed in terms of a traditional capital investment decision. It is only when the one time payment (or investment) is not financially feasible that non-financial benefits must be considered.

Juxtaposed with these policy considerations is the question of agencies' cost structures. In those purchase of service settings where the price for the product or service has been established through competitive bidding, public sector managers need not have an understanding of agencies' costs, since the bidding process requires an agency to set a price compatible with its cost structure. However, in those situations where the price is cost based and the public sector is attempting to maintain some control over the contracting agencies' cost levels, a clear understanding of the nature of an agency's costs and the way in which they are incurred while providing services to clients is essential.

The need for an understanding of agencies' cost structures is given further credence when one compares cost-based purchase of service arrangements in the public sector with the variety of interdivisional arrangements identified by Solomons in his lengthy analysis of interdivisional activities (1965, ch. 6). The comparable arrangement appears to be where "there is no outside competitive market for the transferred products, transfers constitute a predominant part of the supplying division's business, and it can meet all probable requirements." Under those circumstances, "the supplying division should operate as a service center, and transfers to consuming divisions should take place at standard variable cost." (p. 201).

Solomons's finding raises several important points. First, since standard (or budgeted) variable cost is used as the price, volume-related concerns are obviated. Specifically, an agency's tendency to extend length of stay would be eliminated if the per diem reimbursement were set equal to the standard variable cost of a unit of service (for example, a client day). Second, efficiency is rewarded, since an agency that is successful in keeping its actual variable cost below the standard could be allowed to retain the resulting savings. Finally, fixed costs, that is, those costs not related to volume but to what Feldstein (1968) has called a "readiness to serve," are reimbursed in Solomons's system on a period (monthly, for example) basis.[9] Once again efficiency can be rewarded (and inefficiency penalized) by reimbursing agencies at the standard amount negotiated prospectively as part of the budgetary process.

Additional Considerations

Solomons's transfer pricing framework appears extremely applicable to purchase of service settings in which reimbursement is cost-based and an agency's unit volume is uncertain. Since an agency's budgeted fixed costs are reimbursed on a period basis and its variable costs on a per unit basis, the system eliminates the financial incentive to extend a client's length of stay unnecessarily or to admit clients inappropriately. In transferring the framework from its corporate setting to a public sector one, however, some important considerations emerge.

First is the distinction between fixed and variable costs, and, perhaps more importantly, the question of semi-variable costs. Although semi-variable costs can be reimbursed on a combination of a period and a volume basis through the use of step function relationships, the cutting edge among these three types of costs is not a particularly clean one.[10] It is principally for this reason that public sector managers must have a clear understanding of agencies' cost structures. To negotiate budgets without such an understanding is a disservice to both taxpayers and the agencies themselves.

A second consideration is that of quality of care. Although the question of quality is implicit in Solomons's description of interdivisional relationships, it is not discussed explicitly, principally, one would guess, because consuming divisions would demand that certain quality standards be met. Measurement of quality in the corporate setting lies outside the financial control system, and can be expected to do so in a human service setting as well. Although quality measurement systems per se lie outside the scope of this chapter, it clearly is important to recognize their role and the need to structure them in such a way that they do not contain incentives inconsistent with the reimbursement process.

A third consideration is that of service differentiation. Just as separate standard variable costs would be established for each product supplied by a supplying division, so must they be established for each service provided in a purchase of service setting. Thus, the category 1 service would have one rate per unit, the various services in category 2 would each have a rate, and the one-time service in category 3 would have a rate.

A final consideration, and perhaps the most difficult one to address, is that of client characteristics. In a corporate setting the manufacture of a product generally can be performed within a fairly narrow range of variable costs. In the human services, the variable costs associated with the delivery of a given service frequently can extend over a much wider range. Care of a patient with acute myocardial infarction, for example, is far more costly than the care of a routine appendectomy, even when only the routine care costs are considered. Care of an adolescent with fire-setting or homicidal tendencies is more costly than care of one with truancy problems. Treatment of a schizophrenic costs more than treatment of a patient with anxiety neurosis. And so on.

Attempts to deal with difficulties such as these have been made in the human services with some success. In the health field, reimbursement in some states is based on diagnosis or procedure.[11] In the child care field, group homes and institutional facilities are being developed in some localities to serve clients with very clearly defined characteristics. Efforts such as these can assist in mitigating the uncertainty of the service to be delivered, and hence make the standard variable cost figure more meaningful.

Summary and Conclusions

Although some differences exist between transfer pricing in a corporate setting and in a human service one, some important similarities exist as well. In particular, the separation of fixed and variable costs for reimbursement purposes provides the potential to eliminate the incentive for agencies to increase volume inappropriately in an effort to recover budgeted fixed costs. Additionally, by reimbursing both fixed costs and variable costs per unit at budgeted (or standard) levels, the public sector can create incentives for efficiency. In order for such a system to work effectively, however, it will be necessary for public sector managers to have a thorough understanding of the way in which costs are incurred in the agencies with which they enter into purchase of service agreements. Under these circumstances, budgetary negotiations and standard-setting procedures can take place that both motivate agencies to operate effectively and efficiently, and that provide public sector managers with the information necessary to make meaningful inter-agency comparisons.

Notes

1. One of the most thorough treatments of transfer pricing issues is contained in Solomons (1965). He outlines a typology of transfer pricing situations and, in each instance, the resulting implications for establishing the most appropriate price. Some of the most thorough and complete analyses of the theoretical issues can be found in Hirshleifer (1956 and 1957). For additional theoretical details, see Gould (1964).

2. The situation is described in detail in Young (1979b), ch. 3.

3. Some of these issues are described in detail in Young (1977), which was presented at a conference of city managers in 1977, during which many city managers expressed a great concern over the dilemma of establishing appropriate prices when contracting out with private agencies.

4. This situation is discussed in detail in Young and Allen (1977).

5. See Berry (1976) for a discussion of this phenomenon in New York State.

6. It should be stressed that there may have been other factors contributing to the establishment of utilization review procedures. It seems logical to conclude, however, that the transfer pricing system, by providing financial encouragement to extend length of stay, was a primary force leading to the need for utilization review.

7. A system has been developed in some states that pays only a portion of the full per diem amount (typically 40 percent) for patient days that exceed the budgeted level. Depending on its incremental costs for these additional days, however, a hospital may or may not be motivated financially to curtail length of stay.

8. See Young (1979b), ch. 3, for further discussion of this legislation and its effects.

9. This is based on the standard accounting distinction between *product* costs and *period* costs. Product costs are those that can be easily traced to a product or service. Period costs are not traceable in this manner, and are more closely associated with the passage of (a period of) time. Although they may be allocated to products or services in a full cost-accounting system, they will fluctuate very little if at all as long as changes in the volume of production remain within the "relevant range."

10. For a good discussion of all three types of costs, in addition to a description of step function relationships, see Anthony and Welsch (1977).

11. The Diagnostic Related Group (DRG) experiment in New Jersey and the procedure-based reimbursement being used at the Massachusetts Eye and Ear Infirmary are two examples. For details see Reiss (1977) and Young (1979a).

References

Anthony, Robert N., and Glenn A. Welsch. *Fundamentals of Management Accounting*. Homewood, Ill.: Richard D. Irwin, 1977.

Berry, Ralph E. "Prospective Rate Reimbursement and Cost Containment: Formula Reimbursement in New York." *Inquiry*, Sept. 1976.

Feldstein, Paul J. "An Analysis of Reimbursement Plans." In U.S. Department of Health, Education, and Welfare, *Reimbursement Incentives for Hospital and Medical Care: Objectives and Alternatives*. Washington, D.C.: GPO, 1968.

Gould, J. R. "Internal Pricing in Firms When There Are Costs of Using an Outside Market." *Journal of Business*, Jan. 1964.

Hirshleifer, Jack. "On the Economics of Transfer Pricing." *Journal of Business*, July 1956.

———. "Economics of the Divisionalized Firm." *Journal of Business*, Apr. 1957.

Reiss, John B. *Proposed Case-Mix Rate Reimbursement*. Trenton,

N.J.: New Jersey Department of Health, 1977.

Solomons, David. *Divisional Performance: Measurement and Control.* Homewood, Ill.: Richard D. Irwin, 1965.

Young, David W. "Purchase of Service Contracting: A Researcher's Perspective." In Michael J. Murphy and Thomas Glynn, eds., *Human Services Management: Perspectives for Research.* Washington, D.C.: International City Management Association, 1977.

———. (1979a). Massachusetts Eye and Ear Infirmary (A), Boston Intercollegiate Case Clearing House, Harvard Business School, #9-179-505.

———. *The Managerial Process in Human Service Agencies.* New York: Praeger, 1979b.

———, and Brandt Allen. "Benefit Cost Analysis in the Social Services: The Example of Adoption Reimbursement." *Social Service Review,* June 1977.

Conference Participants

David M. Austin
Professor of Social Work and Administrator, Center for Social Work Research, University of Texas at Austin. Formerly Associate Professor, Graduate School for Advanced Studies in Social Welfare, Brandeis University. Author of "The Politics and Organization of Services: Consolidation and Integration," and numerous other papers. Formerly Chairman of the Public Welfare Advisory Board, State of Massachusetts, and Planning Director, Greater Cleveland Youth Services Planning Commission.

Harold W. Demone, Jr.
Dean, Graduate School of Social Work, Rutgers University. Formerly Executive Vice President, United Community Planning Corporation, Boston, and Executive Director, Medical Foundation, Boston. Coauthor of *Administrative and Planning Techniques in Human Service Organizations: A Handbook of Human Service Organizations*, and numerous articles.

Victor R. Fuchs
Fellow, Center for Advanced Studies in the Behavioral Sciences, 1978–79. Professor in the Economics Department and Medical School, Stanford University. Formerly Professor of Community Medicine, Mt. Sinai Medical School, New York City, and Director, National Bureau of Economic Research–West. Author of *Who Shall Live? Health, Economics and Social Choice*, and numerous research publications on the economics of health and medical care and of the service economy.

Regina E. Herzlinger
Associate Professor, Harvard Business School, where she developed the first course in "Management Control in Nonprofit Organizations." Consultant to the Massachusetts General Hospital and Director of courses for managers of public broadcasting stations. Formerly economist for the Federal Power

245

Commission, Vice-President of Urban Systems Research and Engineering, and Assistant Secretary for Planning and Program Analysis of the Massachusetts Office of Human Services. Coauthor of *Management Control in Nonprofit Organizations*, numerous publications and case studies, and several books in progress on management of nonprofit organizations.

John W. Meyer
Associate Professor of Sociology, Stanford University. Formerly with Bureau of Applied Social Research, Columbia University, and with Laboratory for Social Research at Stanford; in survey, organizational, and comparative research at Boys Town Center for Youth Development at Stanford. Currently engaged in studies of the organizational structure and effects of educational institutions, and studies of national development. Numerous published papers and chapters in anthologies.

Thomas M. Parham
At time of meeting, Deputy Assistant Secretary for Human Development Services, Department of Health, Education and Welfare. Currently, he is Professor of Social Work, School of Social Work, University of Georgia. Formerly Commissioner of the Georgia Department of Human Resources, and has held faculty positions at universities of Tennessee, Emory, and Georgia. Earlier experience included probation work and social service agency administration.

Gerald R. Salancik
Director of Graduate Studies and Professor, Department of Business Administration, University of Illinois at Urbana-Champaign. Author or coauthor of *The External Control of Organizations: A Resource Dependence Perspective, New Direction in Organizational Behavior*, a book of poetry, and numerous other publications.

W. Richard Scott
Professor of Sociology, Stanford University, and Professor, by courtesy, in Schools of Medicine, Education, and Business. Coauthor of *Formal Organization: A Comparative Approach, Evolution and the Exercise of Authority*, and research monographs

in the fields of education and medical care. Numerous published papers and chapters in organizational theory, methodology, and studies of organizational effectiveness.

John G. Simon

Augustus Lines Professor of Law, Yale University, and Director of Program on Nonprofit Organizations, at the Institution for Social and Policy Studies. Private law practice and service in Judge Advocate General's Corps and Assistant to the General Counsel, Office of the Secretary of the Army. President, Taconic Foundation. Coauthor of *The Ethical Investor* and articles on foundations and philanthropy.

Herman D. Stein

Fellow, Center for Advanced Study in the Behavioral Sciences, 1974–75 and 1978–79. University Professor and John Reynolds Harkness Professor of Social Administration, Case Western Reserve University, where formerly University Vice President, Provost of Social and Behavioral Sciences, and Dean of School of Applied Social Sciences. At Columbia University was Professor of Social Work and Director, Research Center. Senior Advisor to the Executive Director, UN Children's Fund. Author, editor, or coeditor of *The Crisis in Welfare in Cleveland, Planning for Children in Developing Countries, Social Perspectives on Behavior*, and other books and numerous articles.

Myra H. Strober

Assistant Professor of Economics, Graduate School of Business, Stanford University. Formerly lecturer, Department of Economics, University of California, Berkeley. Coeditor of *Bringing Women into Management*. Research publications on economics of child care, women in the economy, and on women economists.

Karl E. Weick

Nicholas H. Noyes Professor of Organizational Behavior and Professor of Psychology, Cornell University. Formerly Professor of Psychology at University of Minnesota, and Director, Laboratory for Research in Social Relations. Editor, *Administrative Science Quarterly*. Author of *The Social Psychology of Organizing*, coauthor of *Managerial Behavior, Performance, and Effec-*

tiveness, and numerous other publications in organizational research and theory.

Carol H. Weiss
School of Education, Harvard University; currently doing research on the usefulness of social science research for government decisionmakers. Author of *Evaluation Research: Methods of Assessing Program Effectiveness, Evaluating Action Programs: Readings in Social Action and Education, Using Social Research in Public Policy Making, Social Science Research and Decision Making*. Formerly at Columbia University, Bureau of Applied Social Research and Center for the Social Sciences.

David W. Young
Assistant Professor of Management, Harvard University, School of Public Health. Formerly Teaching Fellow in Economics, Harvard University. Author of *The Managerial Process in Human Service Agencies* and a number of journal articles on management information systems and cost-benefit analysis in the social services.

Mayer N. Zald
Professor of Sociology and Social Work, University of Michigan. Member of Sociology Advisory Panel, National Science Foundation. Editor of *Social Welfare Institutions* and *Power in Organizations*; coauthor of *The Political Economy of Public Organizations*, and numerous monographs and essays on organizational theory, research methodology, social movement, and social welfare organization.

Index

Accountability, 6, 103, 137, 209, 217, 230

Administrative mechanisms (systems), 210, 215, 224, 231. *See also* Centralization of administrative control; Decentralization of administrative control

Administrative theory, 84–85. *See also* Organizational theory

Administrators, 112, 115, 131–132, 135–136. *See also* Managers in public sector

Advocacy groups, 21, 77, 93, 101. *See also* Advocacy, politics of; Constituencies of human service organizations

Advocacy, politics of, 95, 102, 104

AFDC (Aid for Dependent Children), 52, 54, 56, 75, 89, 96

Alcoholism programs, 144

Alexander, Chauncey, 28

Allison, Graham T., 182

AMA (American Medical Association), 202 n.3

Artificial selection in organizations, 106, 117–118, 120. *See also* Organizational evolution

Assessment, 23, 95, 146. *See also* Evaluation

Auditing, internal and external, 227, 230. *See also* Control systems

Barnard, Chester I., 182

Black power movement, 70

Blau, Peter M., 33

Blue Cross, 235

Boulding, Kenneth, 59

Boundaries. *See* Organizational environment

Bounded rationality, 118, 183

Bridenbaugh, W. Duane, 28

Buffers (buffering), 8, 58–59, 152–155, 174–176. *See also* Decoupling; Loose coupling; Organizational structure

Bureaucracies, 99, 182, 190, 220, 224; decisionmaking in, 221. *See also* Bureaucratic model; Bureaucratic theory; Decisionmaking

Bureaucratic model, 221

Bureaucratic theory, 3

Burnout, 85

Campbell, Donald T., 107

Capital investment decision, 239

Cash grants, 223

Cash transfer, 212, 213

Carter, Jimmy, 229

Cause map, 109–110, 113, 118, 124–126. *See also* Enacted environments

Centralization of administrative control, 16, 17, 82. *See also* Administrative mechanisms (systems); Control process; Control systems; Decentralization of administrative control

CETA (Comprehensive Employment Training Act), 52–53

Charity organizations, 64. *See also* Philanthropic organizations

Chicano movement, 70

Citizen's Advisory Committee in San Francisco, 129–131

Child, John, 119

Commercial bank model of human services administration, 210, 212–218, 221–223

"Community control," 69

Compliance readiness, 19, 91, 93, 94, 102

361
St 819

114 289

DATE DUE